IMAGES
of America

CANONSBURG

On the cover: The Memorial Day parade of 1917 at the Oak Spring Cemetery served not only to honor the memories of departed Civil War veterans but to celebrate the forthcoming involvement of younger soldiers into the European conflicts in World War I. Students from the Pennsylvania Training School at Morganza joined in with the band. (Jefferson College Historical Society.)

IMAGES
of America

CANONSBURG

Jerry Grefenstette

ARCADIA
PUBLISHING

ISBN 978-0-7385-6533-0

Published by Arcadia Publishing
Charleston, South Carolina

Printed in the United States of America

Library of Congress Control Number: 2008940546

For all general information contact Arcadia Publishing at:
Telephone 843-853-2070
Fax 843-853-0044
E-mail sales@arcadiapublishing.com
For customer service and orders:
Toll-Free 1-888-313-2665

Visit us on the Internet at www.arcadiapublishing.com

For Anita, whose enthusiasm and endless fight was an inspiration to every life she touched

Contents

ACKNOWLEDGMENTS

My immediate thanks go to James T. Herron and Gina Nestor at the Jefferson College Historical Society for their assistance and materials used in this collection, including the book *Canonsburg Reflections 1802–2002*.

I also quickly learned that many belated thanks need also go out to decades of dedicated past Canonsburg photographers and photograph collectors. Their work provided historians with a strong visual representation of the people and events that made Canonsburg what it is today. Some of the them are featured themselves in this book, but thanks again must be given to James T. Herron Sr., Joseph Solobay, Frank Mirisciotti and the Mirisciotti Studio, Ern Weller, Martin Estep, Allen "Ducky" Swan, the photographers of the *Notes* and *Canon*, and countless others who made sure that a camera was there to capture these images.

Unless otherwise noted, all images are from the collection of the Jefferson College Historical Society.

I must also thank Sandy Henry, who introduced me to Arcadia Publishing when I assisted on her outstanding *Carnegie* book, also in the Images of America series.

And grateful thanks must also go out to editor Erin Vosgien, who made my first Arcadia publication a smooth and painless process.

—Jerry Grefenstette, January 2009

INTRODUCTION

Canonsburg is a small western Pennsylvania town that arose during the early 1770s, when Col. John Canon, who had served in the Washington County militia, became its first settler and proprietor. Around 1780, Canon purchased 1,200 acres of land from the state of Virginia, which had claimed the land from Pennsylvania in a dispute over ownership. A year or so later, Canon built a flour mill and sawmill on Chartiers Creek, the first such mill in the county. Canon's original mill business would continue to exist through changes in ownership into 1996.

In 1787, Canon began laying out the map of the town, selling plots to new settlers. By 1800, the town was taking shape, with property owners serving as carpenters, butchers, brewers, tavern owners, weavers, merchants, and masons. The town adopted Canonsburg as its name.

Canon died in debt, though, and not considered a success in business. His assets were sold off in a sheriff's auction, and by the 1820s, there were no remaining Canon family members even residing in the town that bore his name.

In July 1794, Canonsburg played a role in the Whiskey Rebellion, an organized protest against federal taxes on whiskey sales that was unfairly slanted against smaller whiskey producers, many of whom resided in Washington County. Rebels were believed to have met in the town's Black Horse Tavern, although it was never proven that any Canonsburg residents were involved in the violent attacks against Pennsylvanian officials and tax collectors.

On February 22, 1802, Canonsburg became the first town to be incorporated in Washington County. An election of officials soon followed, with Samuel Murdoch being named as the first burgess (mayor).

The town served initially as a postal stop between the larger municipalities of Pittsburgh and Washington. It thrived during the time as a market town, offering customers shops and taverns and providing such goods as grain (from city founder Canon's mill) and whiskey.

In the mid-1800s, Canonsburg became one of the leading college towns in Pennsylvania, as Jefferson College rose to prominence from Presbyterian preacher John McMillan's original one-room log house. The log house has served as such a major symbol to the town's history that it has survived several moves to new locations due to renovations in the town.

After expansion to a larger campus, Jefferson College flourished to become the largest college in the state and one of the largest in the country of its time. Specialties offered were varied, including classes in nursing and medicine. The college served as the central source for the town economy.

By the 1860s, however, the toll of the Civil War diminished the student base as southern students returned home. A failed scholarship plan also strained the college's financial resources, forcing its students to move to the campus of the school's sister college in nearby Washington, Pennsylvania. By the end of the decade, the Canonsburg campus was closed, although the combined Washington and Jefferson College continues to this day.

A newer academy aimed at younger students attempted to fill the economic gap created by the college's absence, but it was never successful. The void of the college forced town leaders to take the town in a new direction.

By the dawn of the 19th century, Canonsburg found its niche in manufacturing and mining, although neither thrived until the arrival and expansion of the railroad. One of the town's most celebrated visits came in 1921, when Marie Curie, discoverer of radium, toured the Standard Chemical plant where more radium was being produced than all other radium plants in the world combined.

The town's steel and tin businesses flourished for decades, even allowing the town to survive the Great Depression with little impact. The ever-present need for bridges and steel kept the operations active at the Standard Tin Plate and the Fort Pitt Bridge Works, and canning requirements also allowed the Continental Can Company to remain a viable business through the economic crisis.

In the 1940s, steelmakers were able to successfully transplant their factories in the early years of World War II, producing girders and bridges. Alcoa took over the former Standard Tin Plate factory to produce aircraft parts. Other factories were transformed to handle the production of shells for the navy. The former Standard Chemical plant was now involved as Vitro Chemical Works in secret uranium work for the Manhattan Project and the development of the atomic bomb.

Like all growing towns, natural disasters have occasionally created damage in the community. A destructive fire in November 1898 destroyed much of the business district. Flooding from Chartiers Creek has frequently been an issue, with notable examples coming in 1888, 1912, and 1956. A redevelopment plan that resulted in the widening and relocation of Chartiers Creek in the early 1970s finally proved to be a successful effort in limiting future flooding.

Canonsburg has suffered through its share of personal tragedies as well. A single, misspoken shout of panic led to a 1911 opera house stampede leaving 26 victims dead in the stairwell of the popular Morgan Building.

Among its more famous citizens are Dr. Jonathan Letterman, a Civil War–era physician who improved the efficiency and timeliness of battlefield treatment and led to the later Mobile Army Surgical Hospital (MASH) units that became prevalent in the Korean War; renowned singer and television entertainer Perry Como; polka singer Bobby Vinton; and the 1950s vocal group the Four Coins. In 1999, the town erected a life-size statue in honor of Como for his accomplishments.

Today Canonsburg is home to the thriving Sarris Candies, which began its candy-making operations in 1963. Sarris Candies has become one of the most respected names in the chocolate business and is available nationwide through the Hallmark greeting card chain, as well as its original Canonsburg location.

Canonsburg has always been a town proud of its heritage, with huge parades and celebrations honoring its anniversary milestones, dating back as far as a lavish Centennial Day celebration in 1902. Even today the town boasts having one of the largest annual Fourth of July parades in Pennsylvania.

One

Rise of a College Town

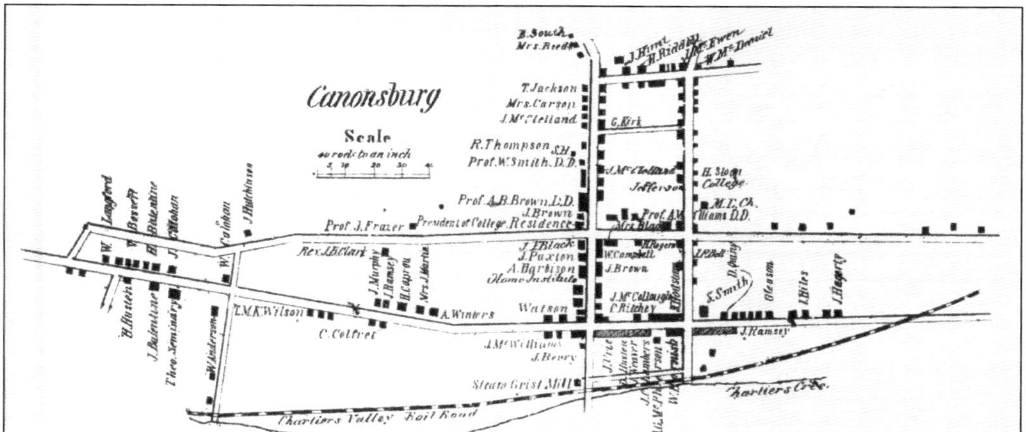

John Canon is credited with being the town's first settler in the 1770s. Canon purchased 1,200 acres of land from Virginia that had been under ownership dispute between the state and Pennsylvania. Canon began selling lots, and by the end of the 1780s, the early shape of the town's layout was formed. This image of the Barker's map of Washington County shows the ownership layout in 1856. (Barker's map of Washington County.)

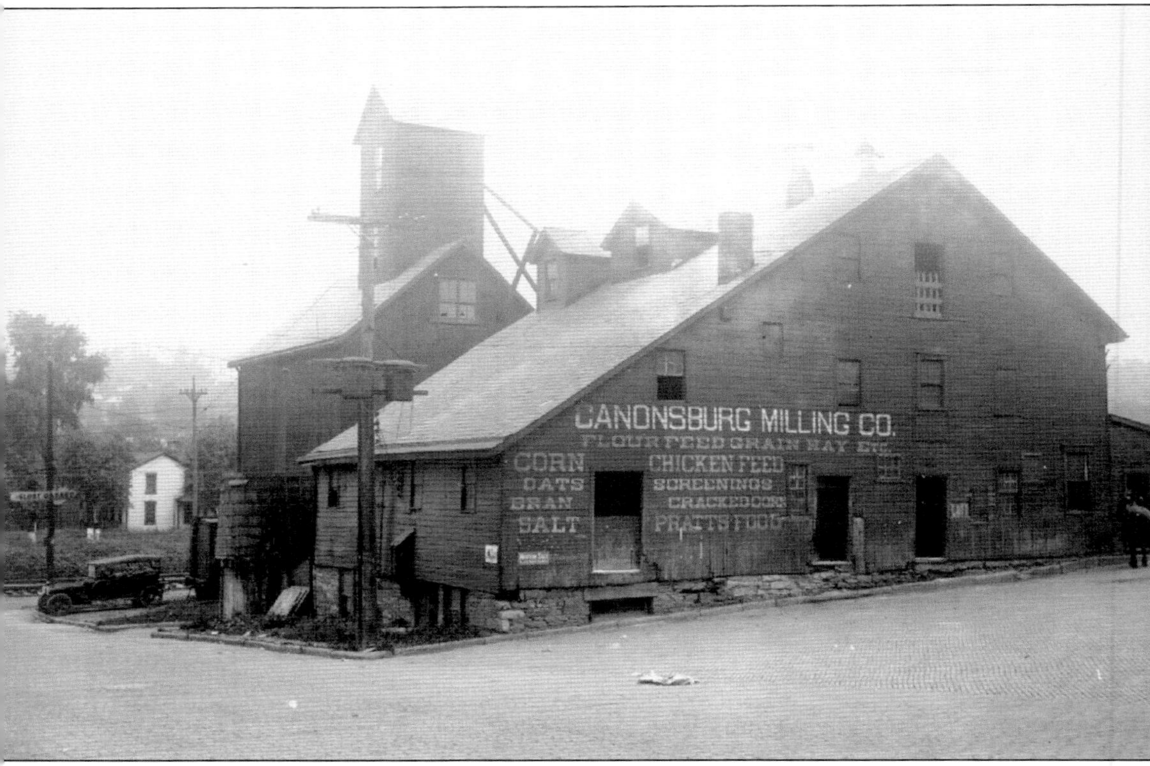

Despite his major role in the origins of the town that would eventually bear his name, little is known about John Canon's background. It is known he served as a justice in the Virginia courts, in an area that is now Pittsburgh. He later became a commander of Virginia militia, earning the nickname of "Colonel." After the land purchase from Virginia, Canon erected his grist- and sawmill on Chartiers Creek around 1780 or 1781 and was likely the earliest example of manufacturing in the town. During the Revolutionary War, Canon contracted to produce flour for the militia of Washington County. By the end of his life, however, Canon was a failure at business, leaving behind much unpaid debt at his death in 1798. Canon's remaining real estate holdings were auctioned off by the courts in 1800. This photograph represents the look of the mill in the early 1900s, after it was incorporated as the Canonsburg Milling Company. (Ern Weller.)

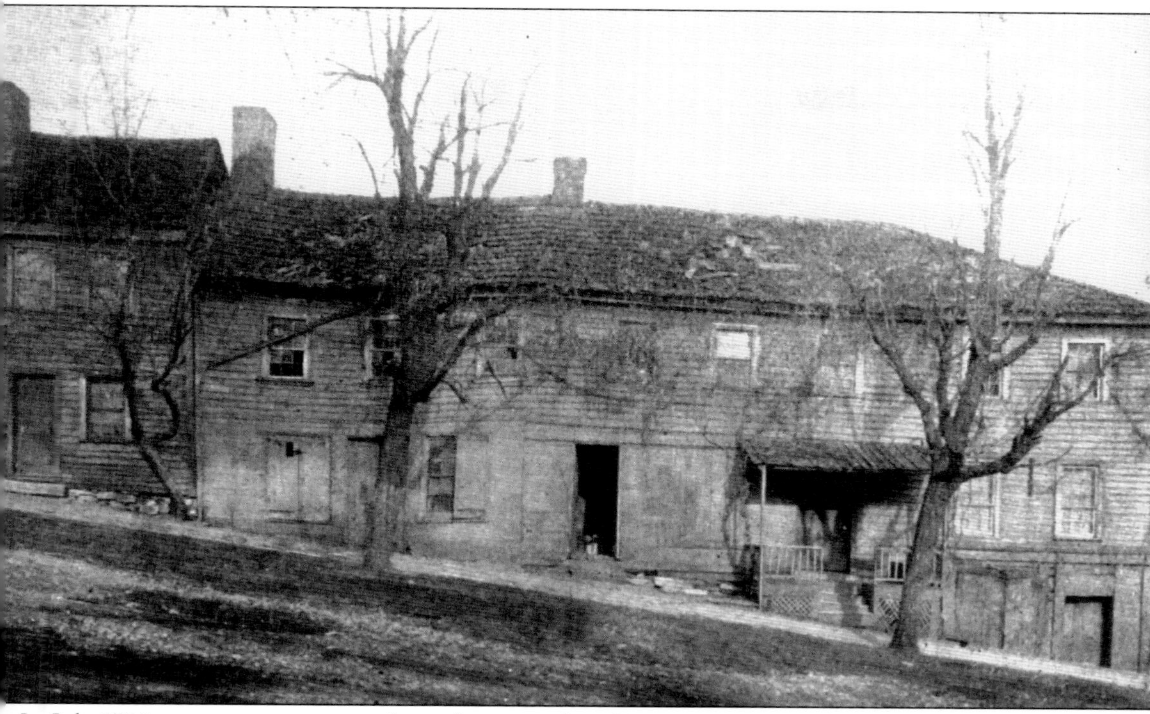

In July 1794, a protest movement formed against the 1791 excise tax on whiskey, which taxed smaller whiskey makers more than larger ones. The tax was seen as the first test of taxation by the new government. It also adversely affected Washington County producers, who operated more than 10 percent of the nation's distilleries. Members of the Whiskey Rebellion secretly met at this Canonsburg location, the Black Horse Tavern, to organize attack plans. The group of rebels, known at the time as either Whiskey Boys or Tom the Tinker's Men, began striking back against government officials and tax collectors, including physical attacks, theft, and vandalism. Military forces of nearly 13,000 soldiers were eventually called in from the East Coast to minimize further resistance in Pennsylvania. A truce was eventually signed, with amnesty offered to most of the minor offenders. The whiskey tax was eventually repealed in 1803. (Force C. Dunlevy.)

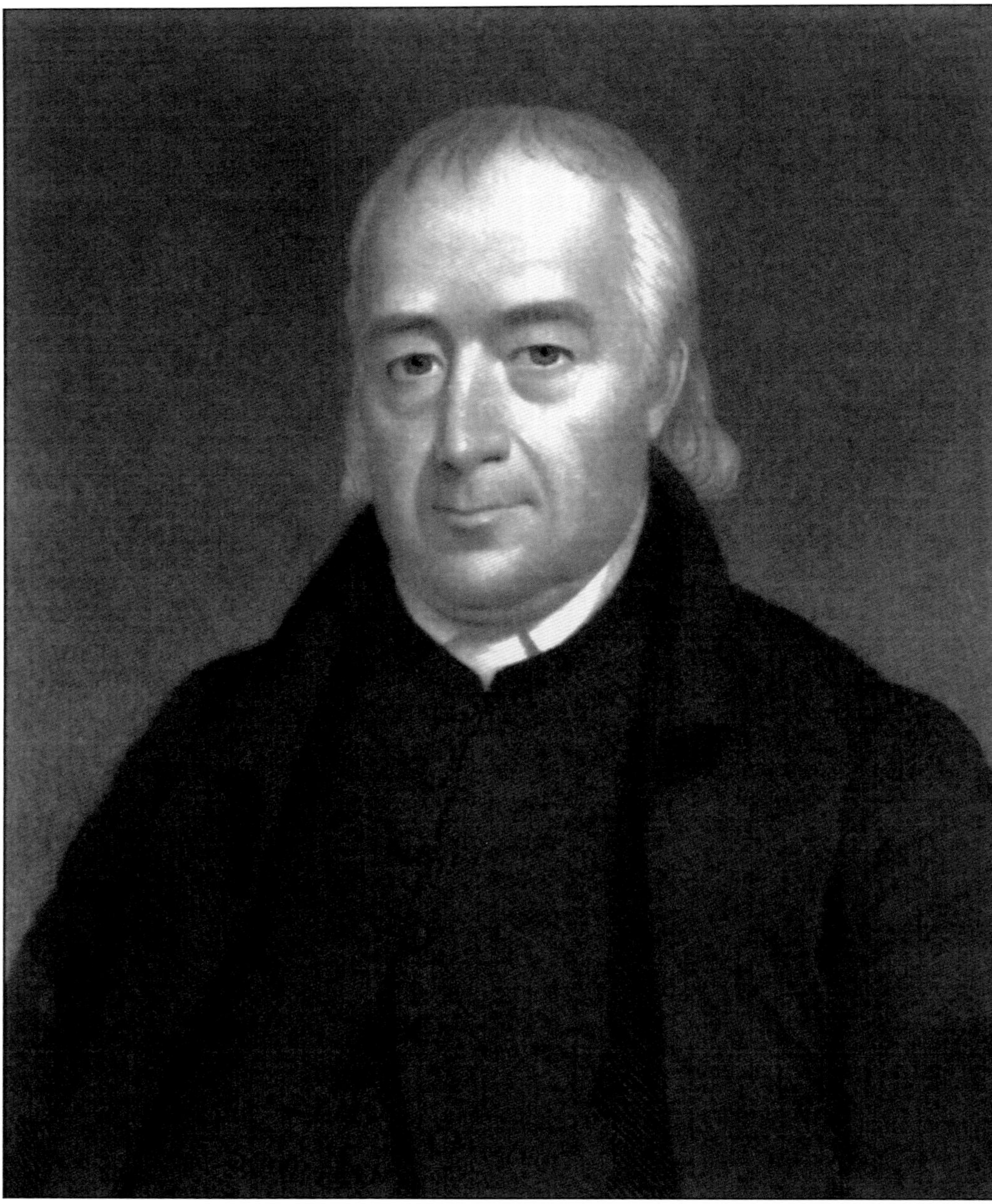

John McMillan (1752–1833) was a Presbyterian minister who dedicated his life to bringing education to the frontier regions. A graduate of Princeton, McMillan began a course of classical studies in a one-room log cabin around 1780. By 1787, McMillan and several other ministers opened larger academies in Pittsburgh and Washington. After the courthouse housing the Washington Academy burned in 1791, McMillan pushed to keep the academy open. City founder John Canon offered a building for the academy to use. Classes resumed, and in 1794, a charter was given to the school as the Canonsburg Academy and Library Company. In 1802, the name was changed to Jefferson College in honor of Pres. Thomas Jefferson. McMillan held the title of professor of divinity at the school and later served as the college's second president, after the death of John Watson, McMillan's son-in-law.

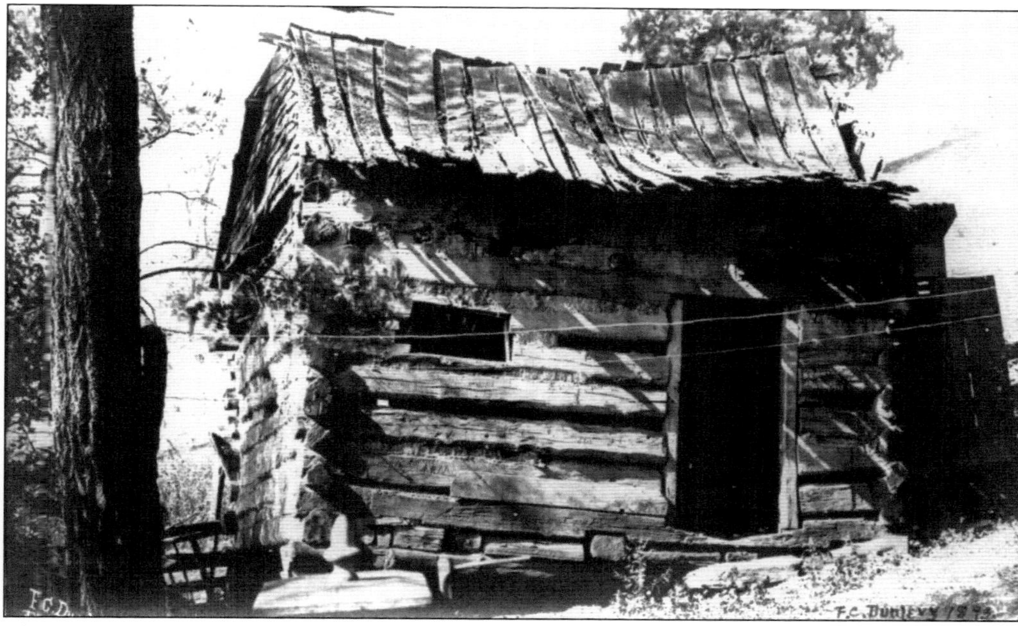

The lineage of what would become Jefferson College can be traced back to John McMillan's original one-room log school, likely built in the late 1770s. Located adjacent to McMillan's home, it served as the original schoolhouse for McMillan's academy, where students learned Greek and Latin languages, mathematics, and other classical subjects. (Force C. Dunlevy.)

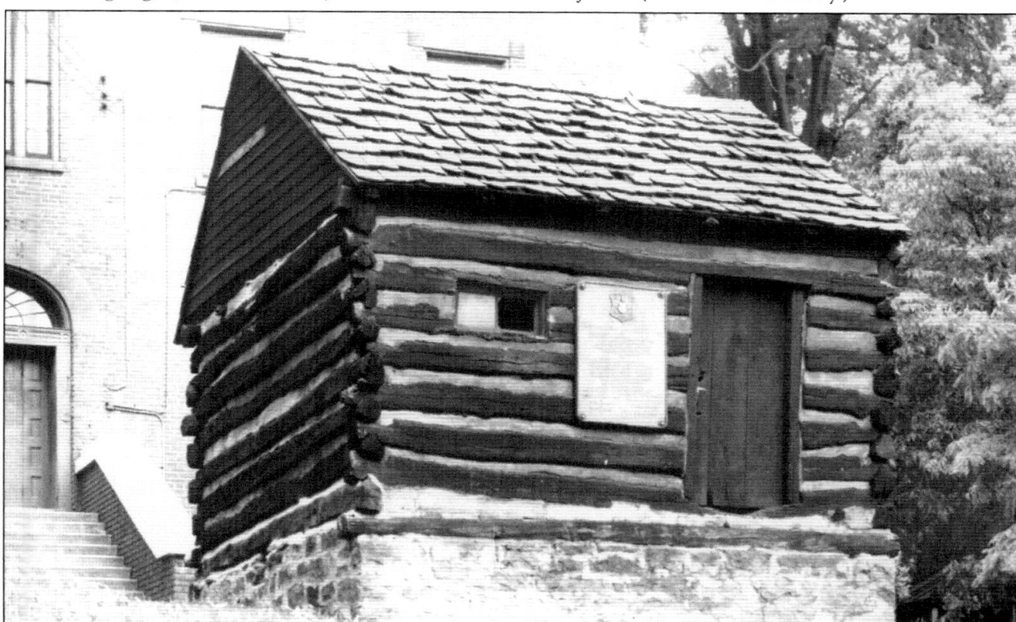

McMillan's log house was rebuilt in 1895 when it was moved to the rear of the Jefferson Academy. The cabin was again moved in 1912 on rollers to its present location on land that now houses the Canonsburg Middle School campus. A restoration of the cabin took place in 2004, with repairs to the foundation and walls. (Ducky Swan.)

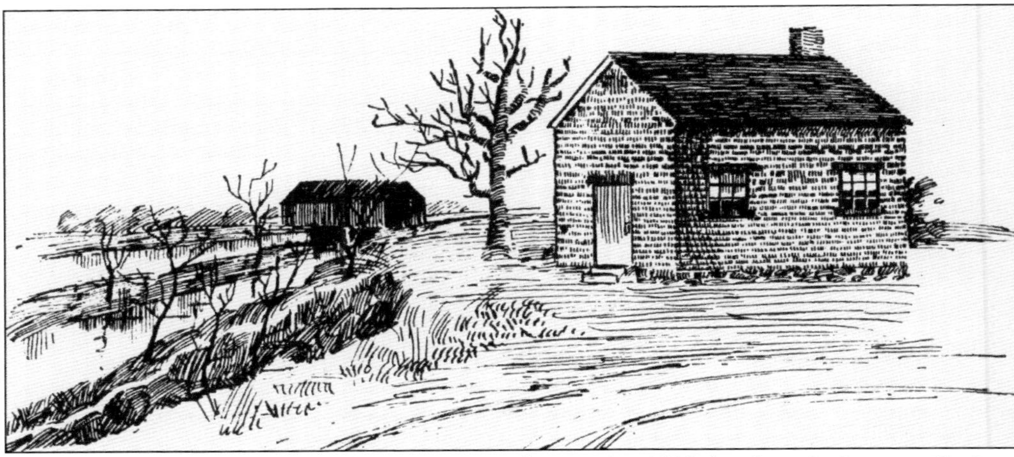

An early example of a school building in Canonsburg is this 1899 sketching by Jeanette Dickson of a small brick building, built in 1816, on Water Street. It replaced an earlier log cabin school that had been in use since 1791. The brick replacement was eventually destroyed by fire in 1893. (Daily Notes.)

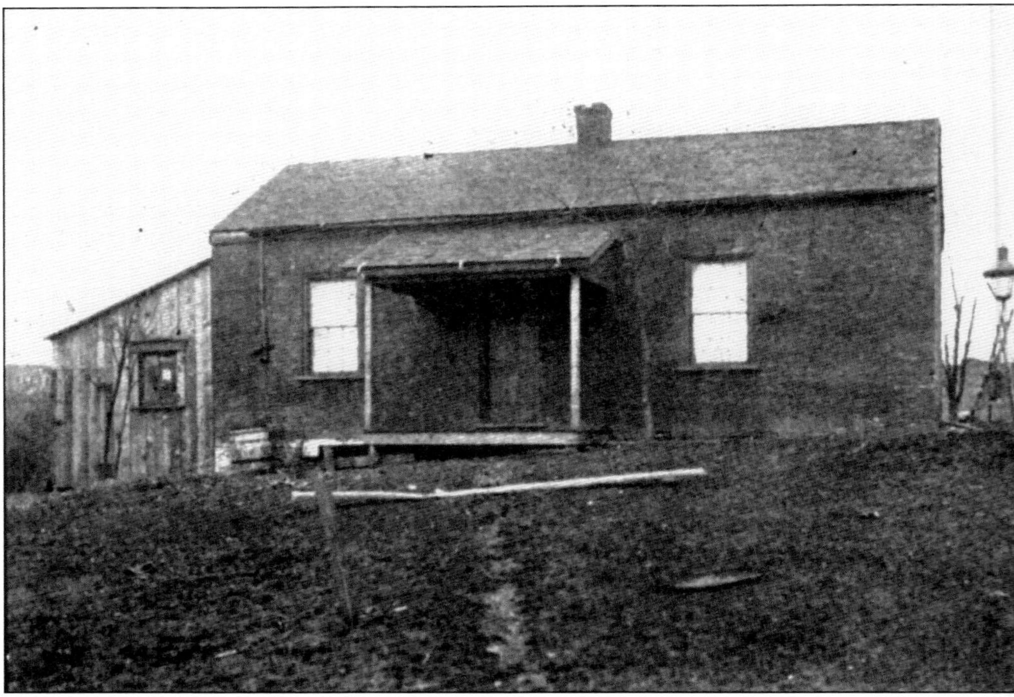

The Payne School, also known as the African School or the West End School, provided separate education for "Negro or mullato children," as quoted by state law requirements. The school opened for minority children in 1863. A protest demanding its closure was printed in local papers in 1880, and the school was closed in 1881 when a new law demanded segregated schools. (Daily Notes.)

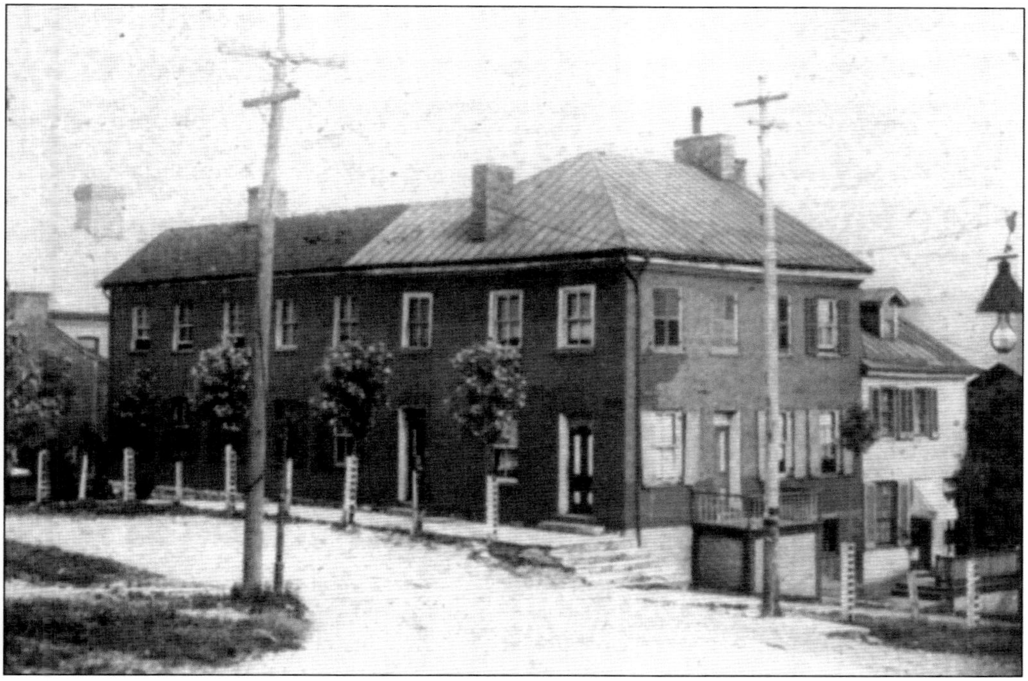

McFadden's Hotel was operated by Hector McFadden on the corner of Central Avenue and East College Street from 1822 until 1835. It was a popular meeting place for students from the college to socialize. The building later found use as dormitory rooms for college students after it was purchased by the school in 1850. (Force C. Dunlevy.)

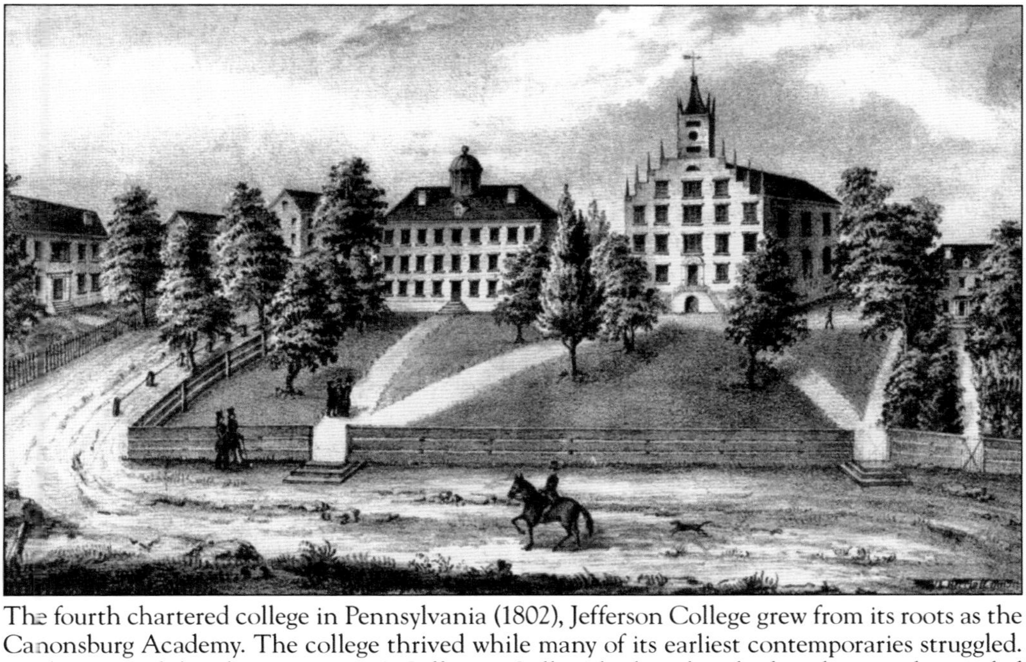

The fourth chartered college in Pennsylvania (1802), Jefferson College grew from its roots as the Canonsburg Academy. The college thrived while many of its earliest contemporaries struggled. By the time of this drawing in 1847, Jefferson College had student bodies that nearly equaled those of the five largest colleges in the country.

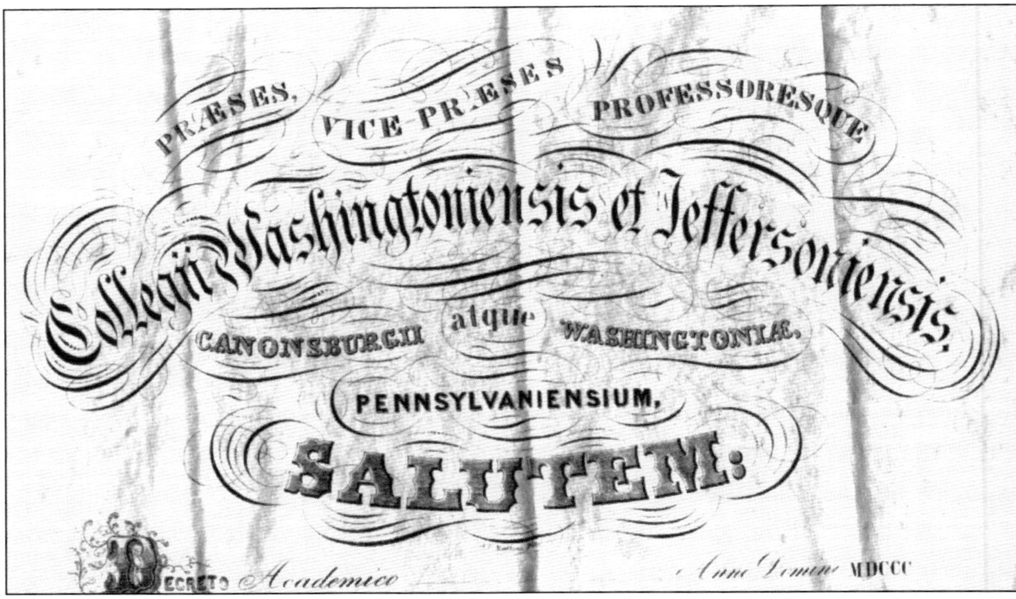

PRÆSES, VICE PRÆSES PROFESSORESQUE

Collegii Washingtoniensis et Jeffersoniensis

CANONSBURGII atque WASHINGTONIÆ,

PENNSYLVANIENSIUM,

SALUTEM:

Decreto Academico Anno Domini MDCCC

By the mid-1860s, the administration of Jefferson College was faced with a dwindling student base as southern students withdrew from the college as the Civil War approached. A failed scholarship plan also left the college in financial troubles. Washington College, the school's sister institution, was in equal difficulties. The schools were left with no option but to merge, with classes being conducted on both campuses. The first combined Washington and Jefferson College diplomas, as seen with this sample, were awarded to graduates beginning in 1864–1865.

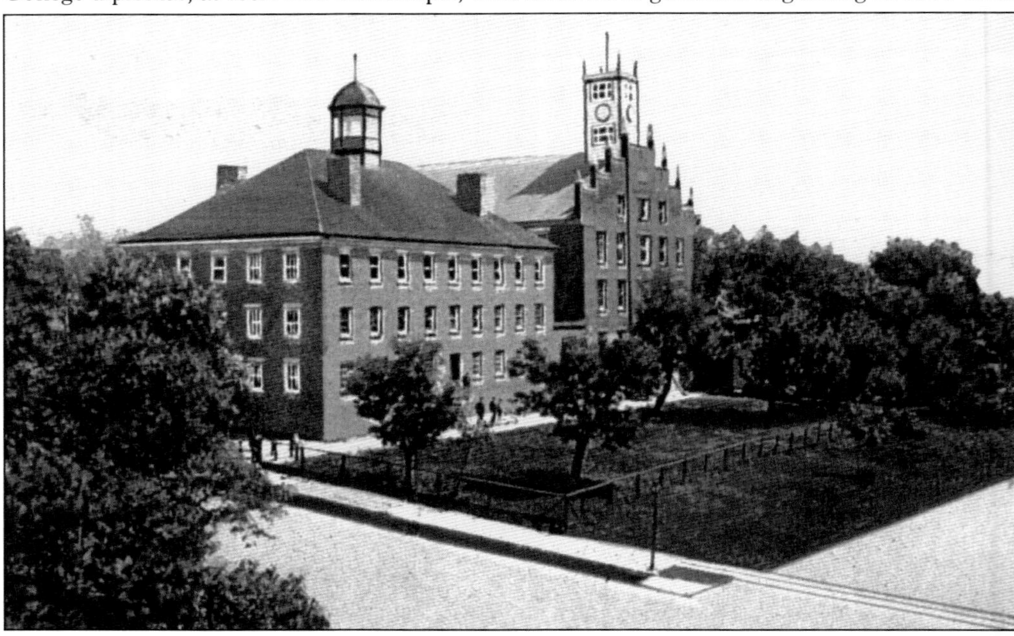

By 1869, classes were moved entirely to the Washington campus. Lawsuits followed in an effort to keep the Canonsburg campus in operation, but an 1871 decision against the arguments resulted in a final decision to close the campus. By that time, though, the campus found use as classrooms for the preparatory Jefferson Academy.

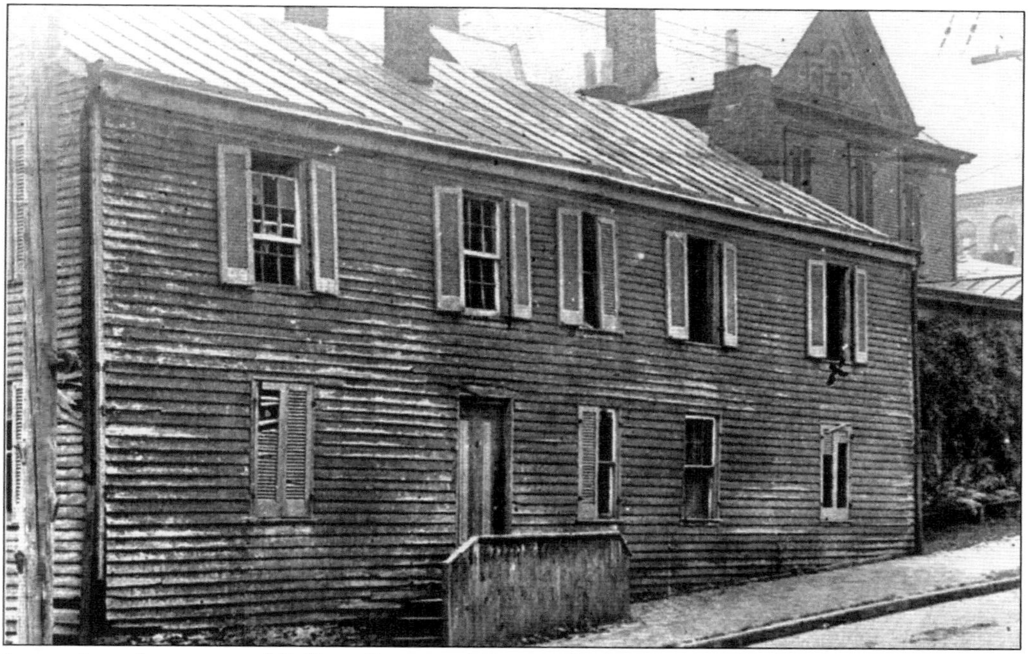

Located on the corner of College Street and Greenside Avenue was the building known as Fort Armstrong. The house served as a boarding home for students during the active days of the college. The Phi Gamma Delta fraternity chapter of Jefferson College was founded in the far right room of the second floor in 1848. The structure was razed in 1916.

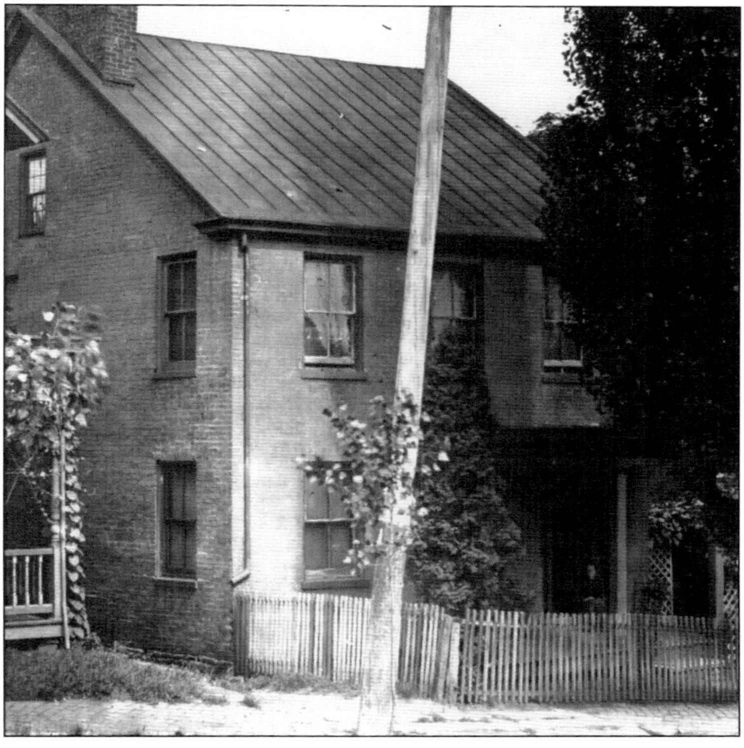

The Jefferson College chapter of Phi Kappa Psi fraternity was founded in 1852 in the attic of this house that was owned by noted physician Dr. Jonathan Letterman. The home was destroyed by a blaze in the 1960s. In all, there were 10 fraternities that had chapters at Jefferson College, 9 of which still exist.

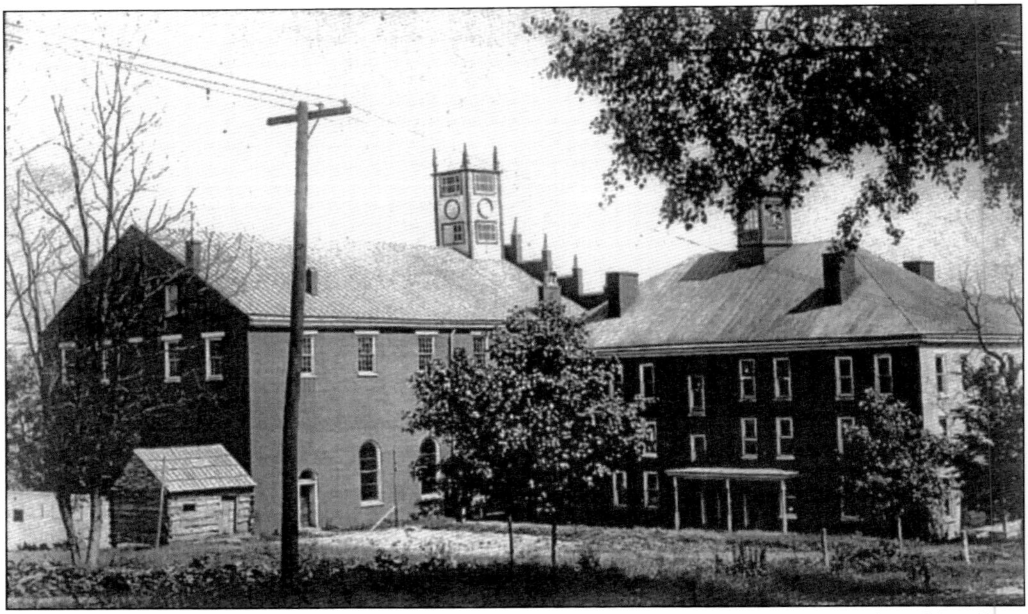

This photograph gives a rarely seen rear view of the campus buildings in 1897. The old college building, right, had been converted into a dormitory in 1892. Also evident in this photograph is the old McMillan log house, which had been moved from its original location and rebuilt in 1895. (Force C. Dunlevy.)

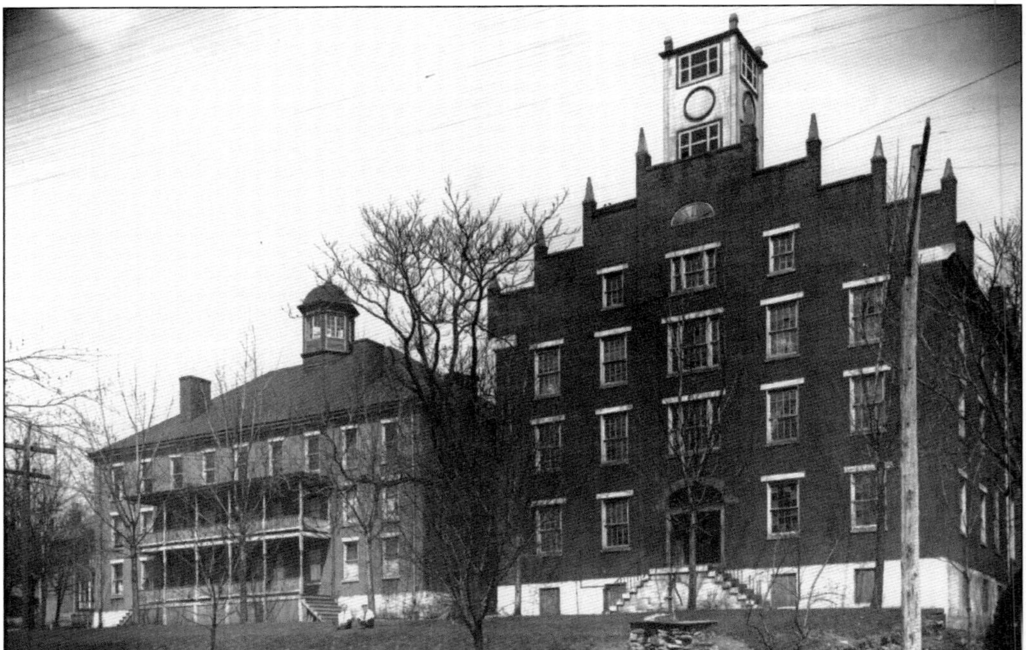

The Jefferson Academy closed in 1910 following years of dwindling enrollment, due in part to the opening of the Canonsburg High School. The circles on the tower may have been designed to hold clocks, but they were only decorative. The old college building, seen on the left, was demolished in 1912.

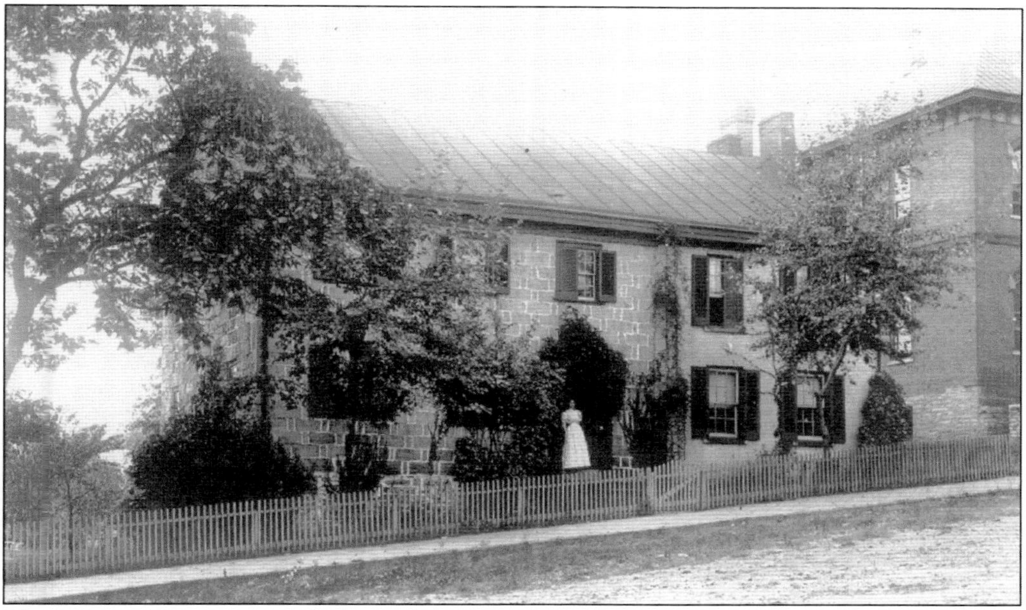

The Roberts House is named after early owner John Roberts, despite the fact that Roberts only owned the home for a few years. It might better be known as the residence of John Watson, first president of Jefferson College. The land for the home, which was built in many sections over the years, was purchased by Watson's father-in-law, John McMillan, in 1796. (Force C. Dunlevy.)

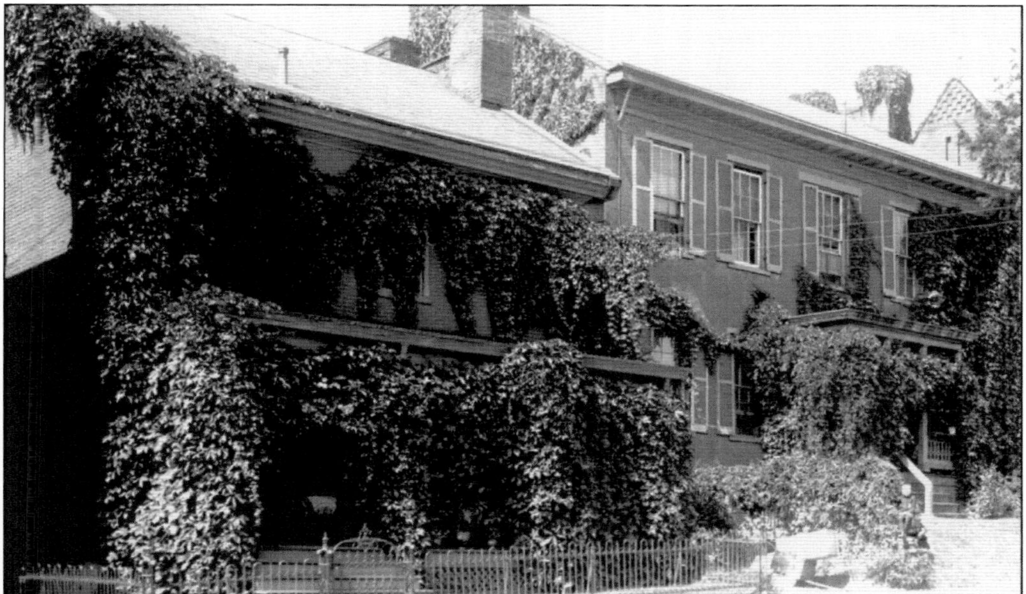

The Olome Institute for Young Ladies, seen in the two buildings on the left, was presided over by Olivia J. French. The unaccredited school operated on land donated by John Canon for the former Canonsburg Academy. Designed to help young women prepare for careers as teachers, the school closed in 1862 due to financial issues. A later attempt by French to reopen the academy proved to be unsuccessful. (Martin Estep.)

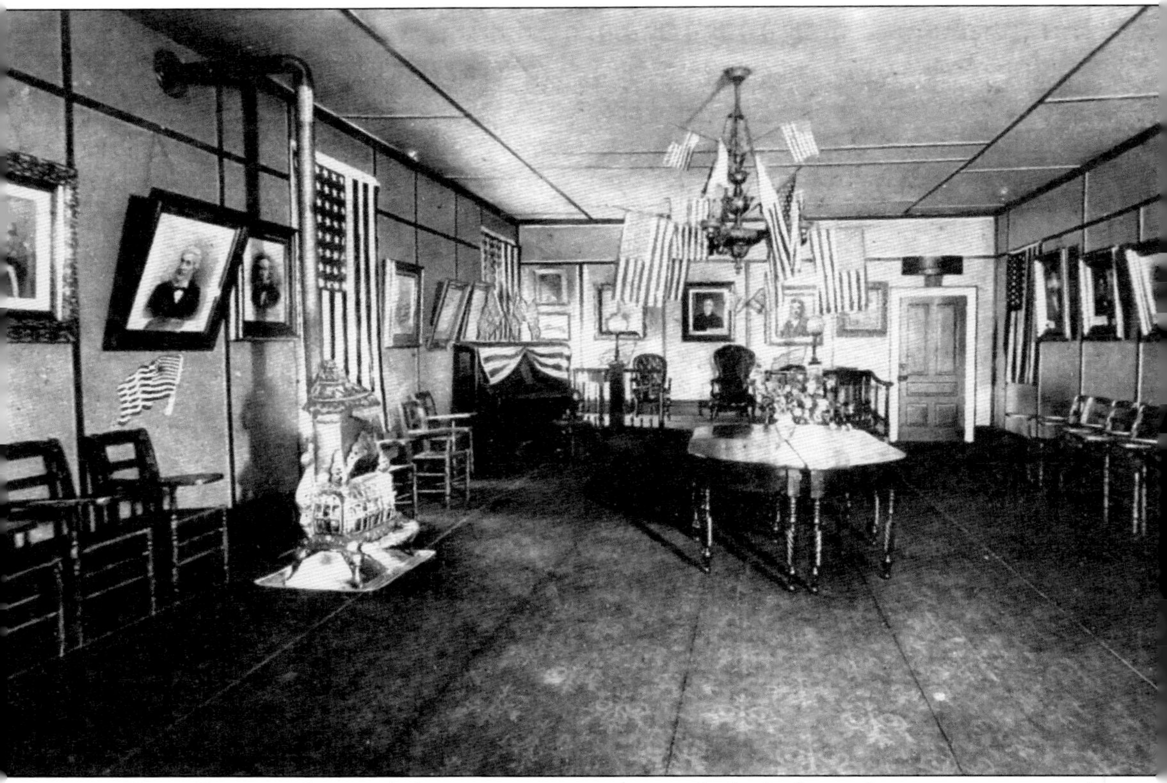

This collection of original chairs, portraits, and a speaker's platform adorns a re-creation of one of the college's meeting rooms. The college originally had two sets of suites above the chapel. The suites consisted of an atrium, an impressive library collection, and a hall used for the weekly meetings of the Philo and Franklin Literary Societies, founded in 1797. The rooms were connected by Goat Hall, a passageway that also served as a place for students to store their coats as well as the carpet slippers that were required by the societies. Students in these societies would engage in essay discussion and debates. At the conclusion of the school year, members of each society would engage in debating contests. The Philo suite and Goat Hall were later renovated into a basketball court by the Jefferson Academy in 1903. The Franklin suite was converted into Memorial Hall, which housed the relics seen here.

Two

POSTCOLLEGE DEVELOPMENT

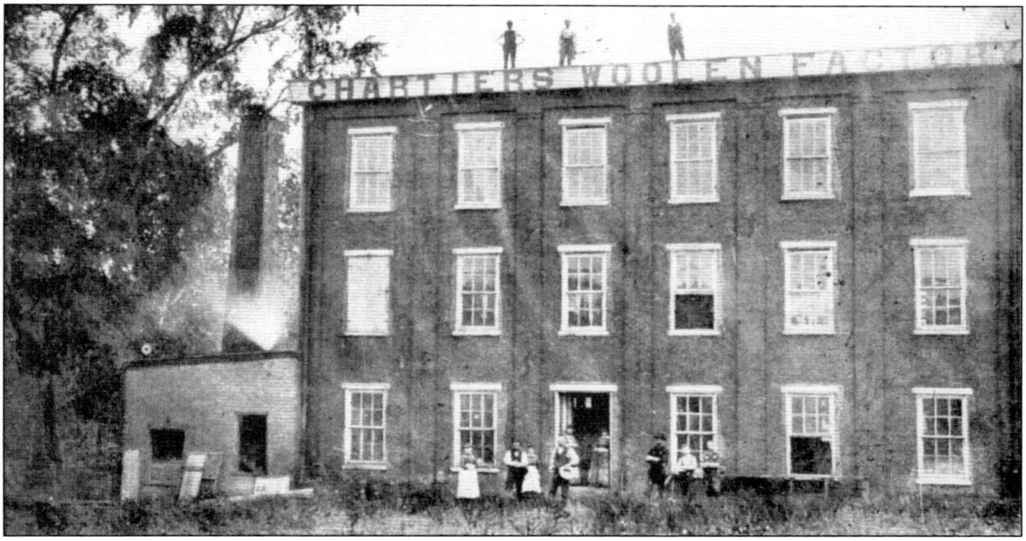

During the 1860s, the Chartiers Woolen Factory was one of the leading manufacturers of wool products in the country, operating out of this three-story brick factory on Pike Street. The business closed following a fire that destroyed the property on February 28, 1887. The land where the factory sat later was split into separate lots on West Pike Street and Strabane Avenue.

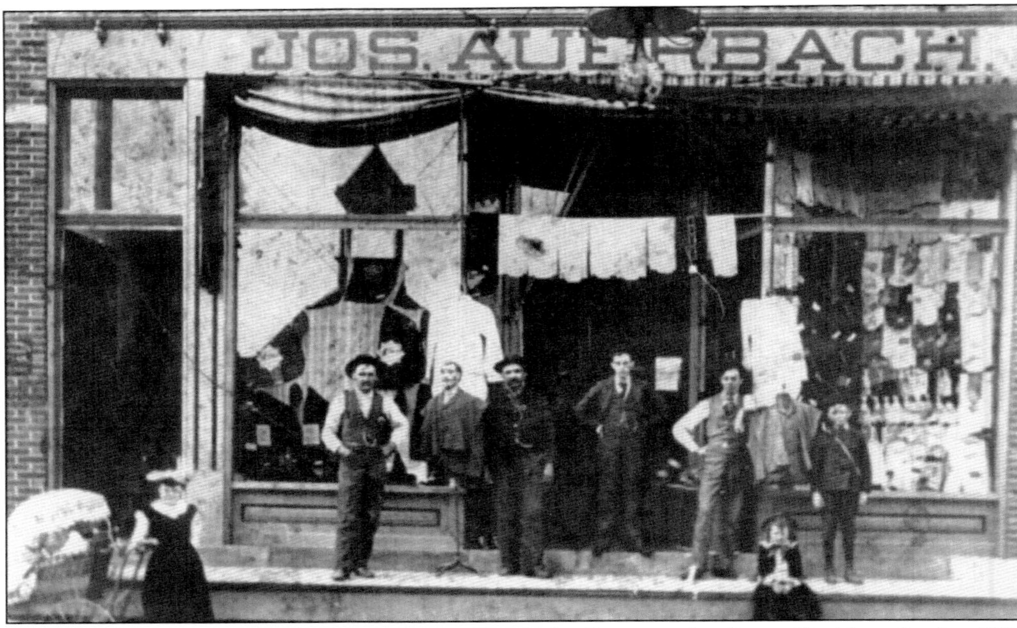

Joseph Auerbach owned a clothing store on West Pike Street in the Carter Building. In this 1894 photograph are, from left to right, Susie Auerbach (in buggy), Sarah Hartley, ? Espy, unidentified, Joseph Auerbach, ? Denny, Robert Gowern (sitting), and an unidentified boy. (Joseph A. Solobay collection.)

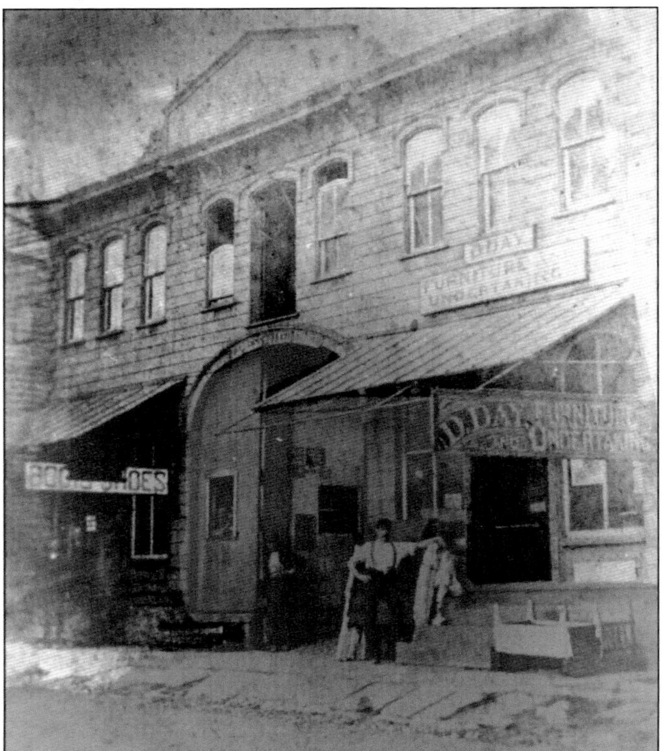

Many early undertakers of the 18th century also doubled as furniture makers and cabinetmakers. Daniel Day, a Civil War veteran, was typical of the occupation and is seen here in the 1880s outside his combined business on Pike Street. Day operated the business from 1883 until 1894, when it was sold to Alex Speer.

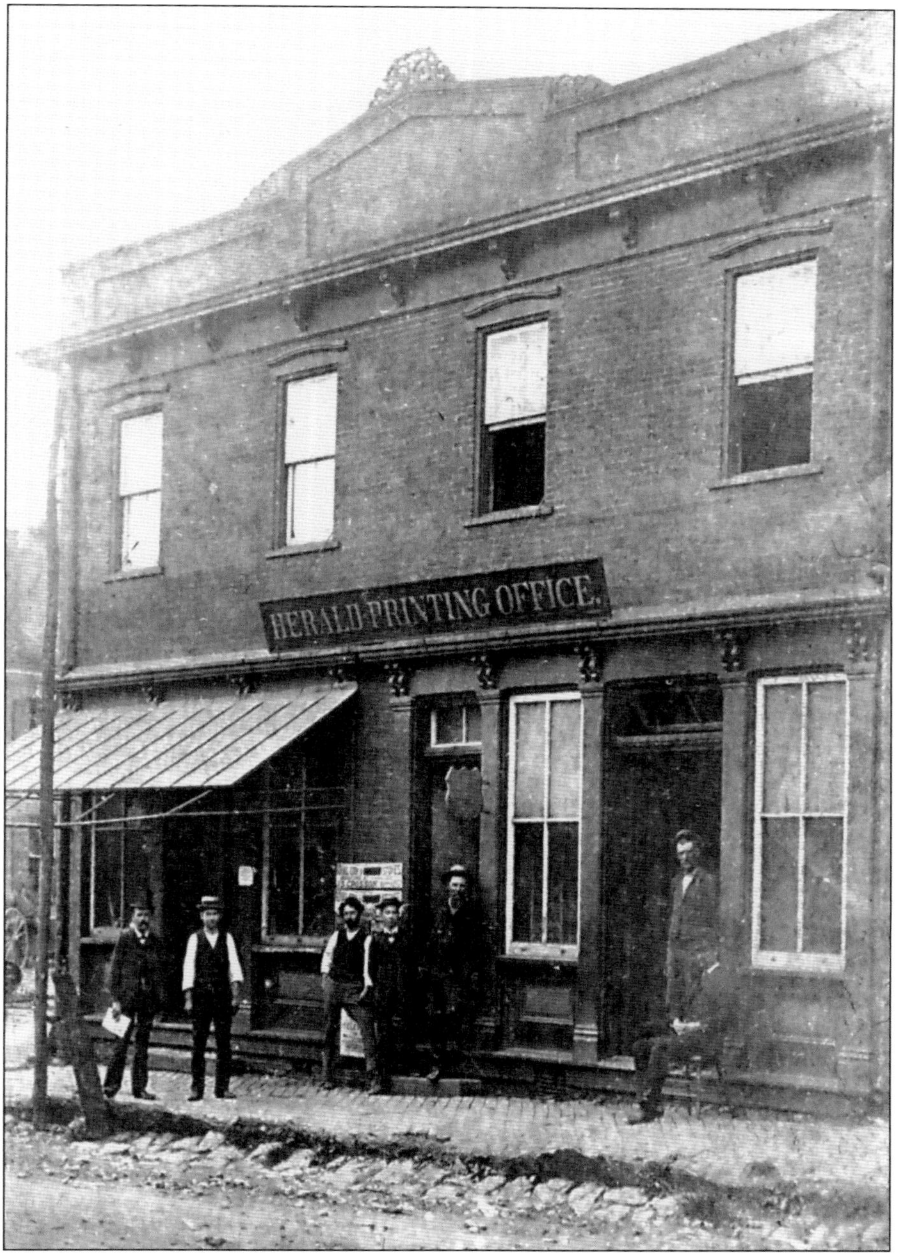

One of Canonsburg's first successful newspapers was the *Herald*, published originally by Thomas Maxwell Potts from 1872 to 1888. Potts, a former teacher, banked on the prospects of the growing railroad industry as a source of potential success and built a hardware store on Pike Street. Potts later installed a printing press on the second floor of his hardware store and began the four-page weekly newspaper the *Herald* in 1872. Potts was later named as justice of the peace and eventually sold the paper to Joseph G. Charlton, who had been publishing the *Canonsburg Local* since 1886. Charlton initially combined the two papers, first as the *Local-Herald*, and then simply as the daily issued *Herald* until it ended in 1906. This photograph offers an 1884 glimpse of Potts, standing in the center doorway under the shield.

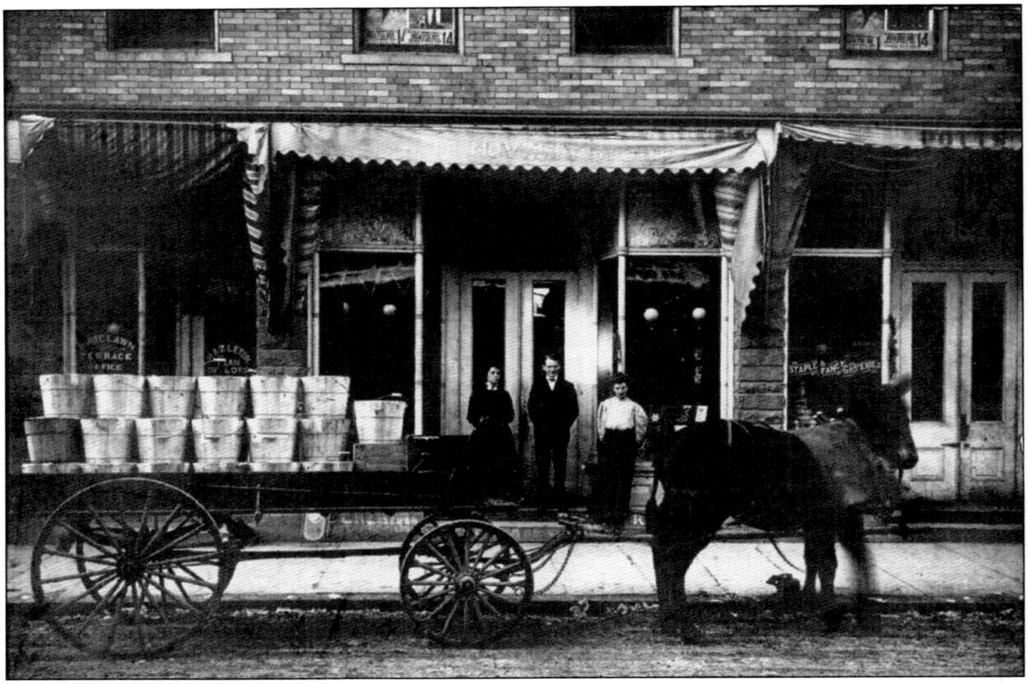

Ice cream, soda, candy, and other confectionaries were sold at this novelty shop by Ed Kerr on Pike Street, next to the Potts Brothers store.

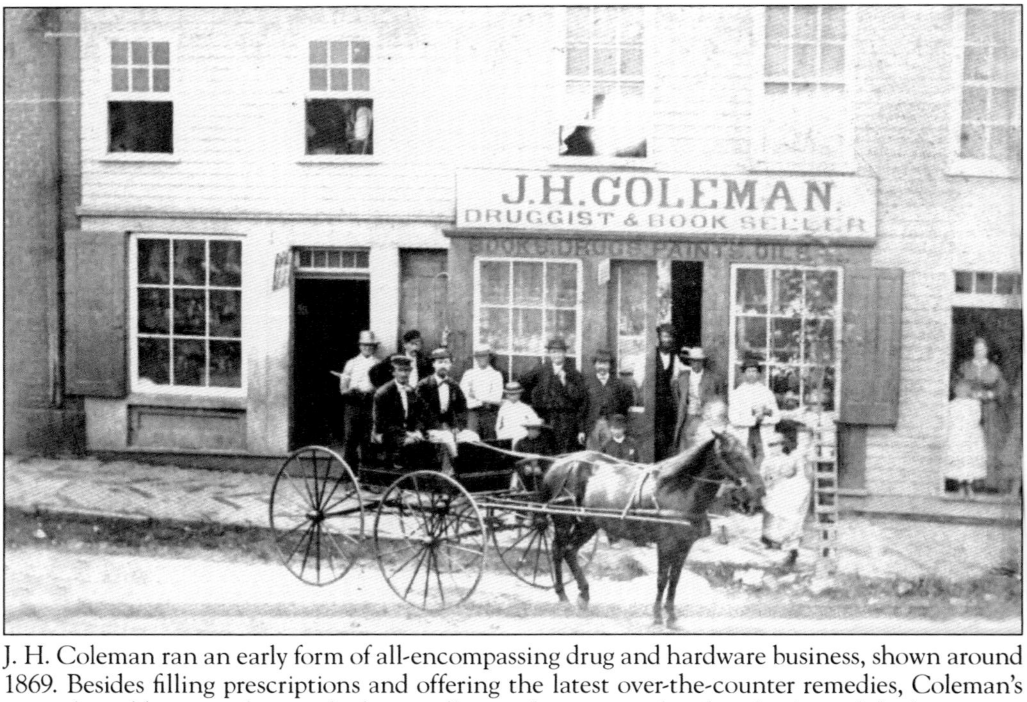

J. H. Coleman ran an early form of all-encompassing drug and hardware business, shown around 1869. Besides filling prescriptions and offering the latest over-the-counter remedies, Coleman's store also sold paints, glass, and oils, as well as reading material such as books and the latest copy of the *Daily Notes*.

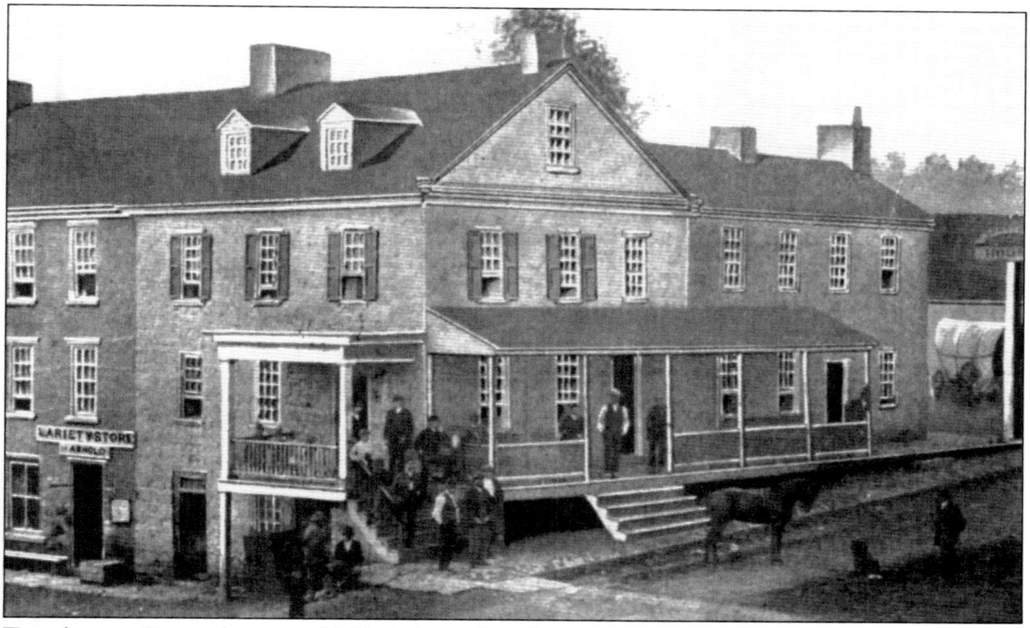

Travelers to Canonsburg would likely have found rooms to rent at the Briceland Tavern. The hotel was run by John Briceland, son of one of the town's earliest residents, Thomas Briceland. The hotel is believed to have opened around the 1840s and continued in later years as Sherman House and Central Hotel. It was razed in 1903 to allow for the construction of the Citizens' Trust Building. (Canonsburg centennial booklet.)

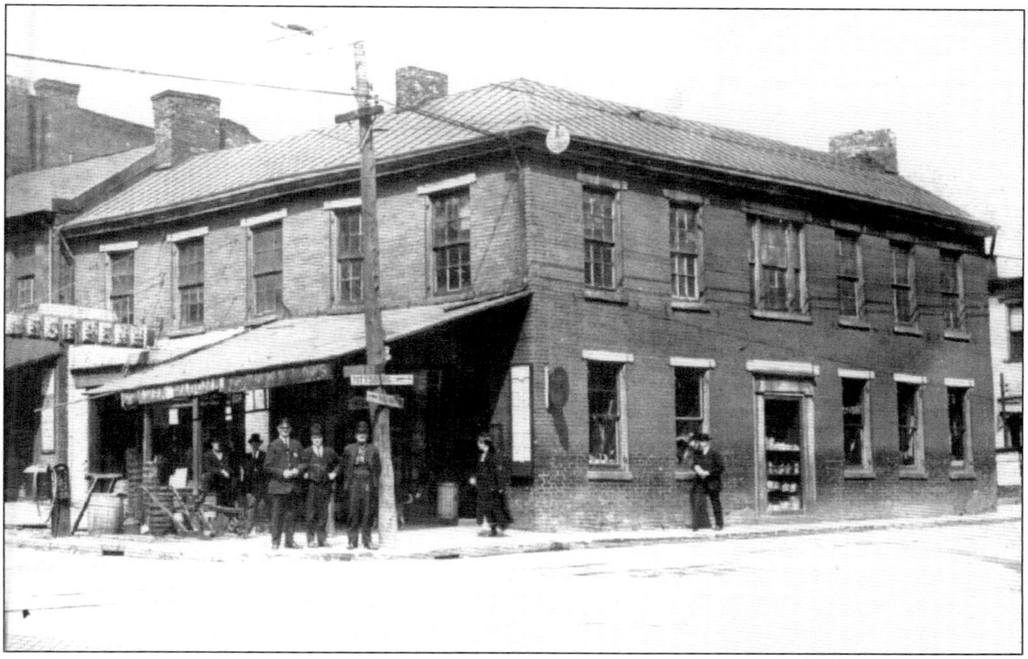

The Old Emery Tavern, seen here in 1923, was a popular stagecoach stop on the Washington–Pittsburgh turnpike. Joshua Emery built the tavern around 1820 on the corner of Pike Street and Central Avenue, located where the Citizens Bank now resides. (Force C. Dunlevy.)

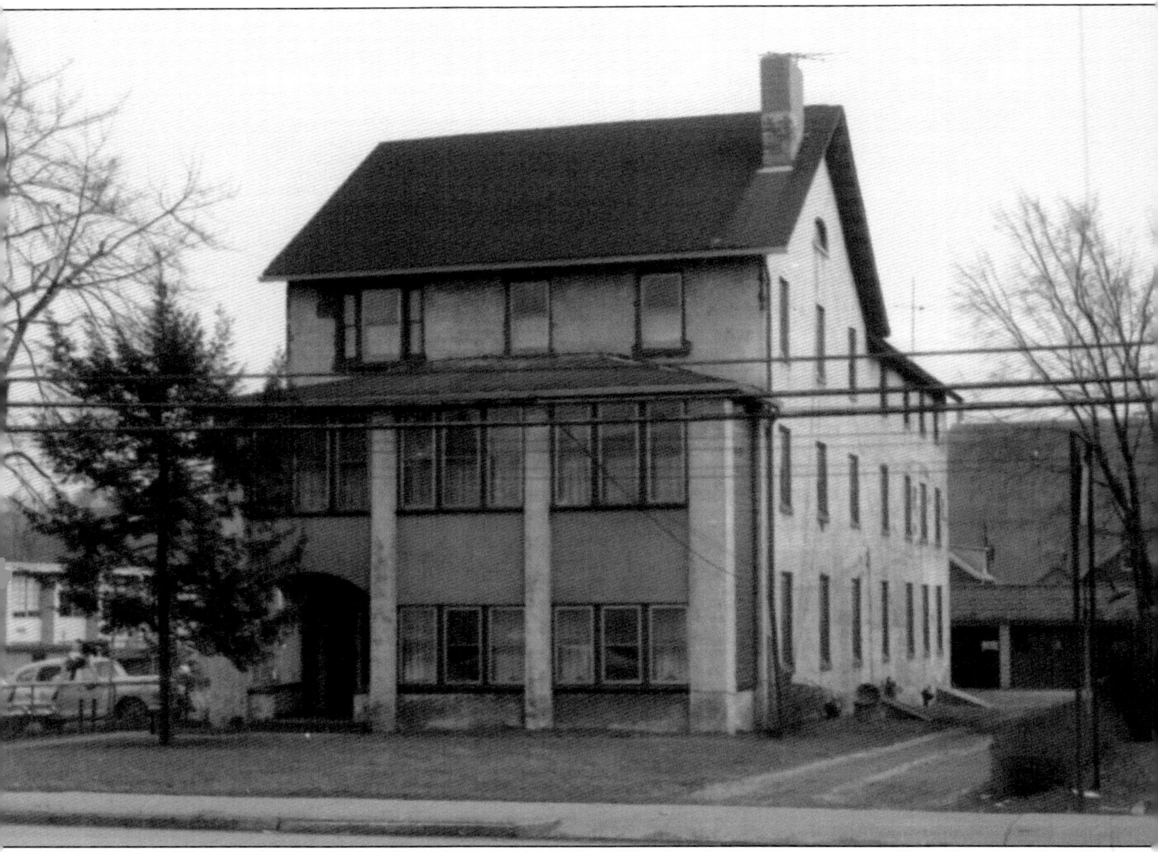

The Associate Presbyterian Church, founded in 1794, moved its theological seminary from Service to Canonsburg in 1821. Early enrollment numbers were small, allowing instruction to be made at the home of Rev. James Ramsey. Beginning in 1829, two rooms were used on the campus of Jefferson College. Construction of this three-story brick structure on the corner of West Pike Street and Payne Place was completed in 1832. It provided a chapel, lecture halls, and dormitory facilities for 30 students. When enrollment increased beyond the building's capacity in 1855, the school was moved to Ohio. In the decades that followed, it housed students from Jefferson College, when it earned the nickname of "Fort Jerusalem." From 1899 to 1902, children from the Children's Home at Arden roomed at the house. It was eventually razed in 1967 when St. Patrick Church purchased the building from the Podrasky family to serve as land for an expanded parking lot.

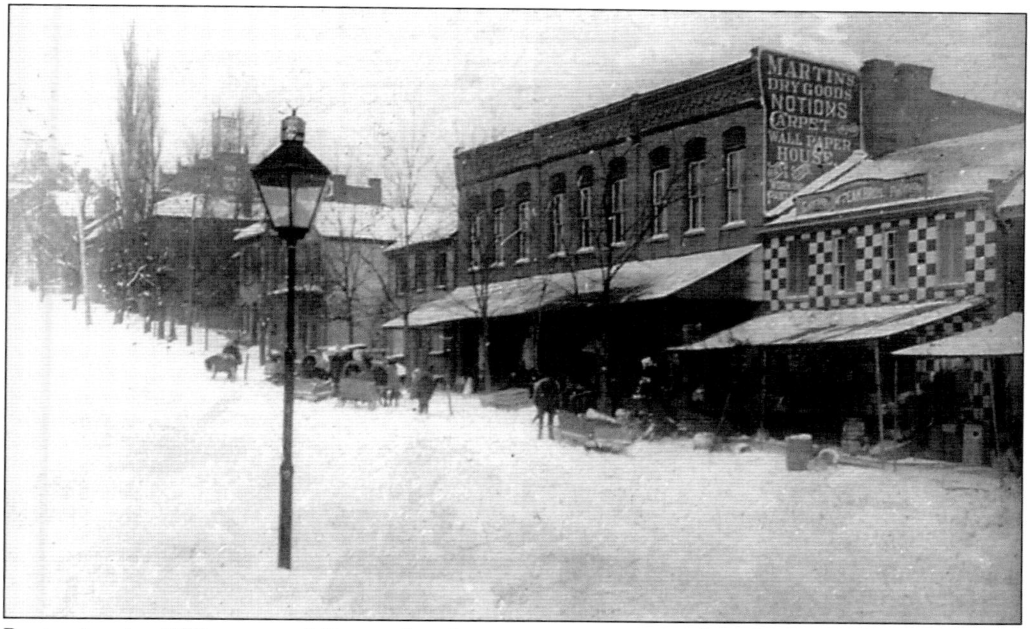

Beginning in 1887, many of Canonsburg's streets were equipped with new gaslit streetlamps, replacing kerosene-based lamps. Electric lights followed in 1894 after the formation of the Canonsburg Electric Light, Heat and Power Company. This early lamp at the intersection of Pike Street and Central Avenue aided customers of Martin's, the largest dry goods store at the time.

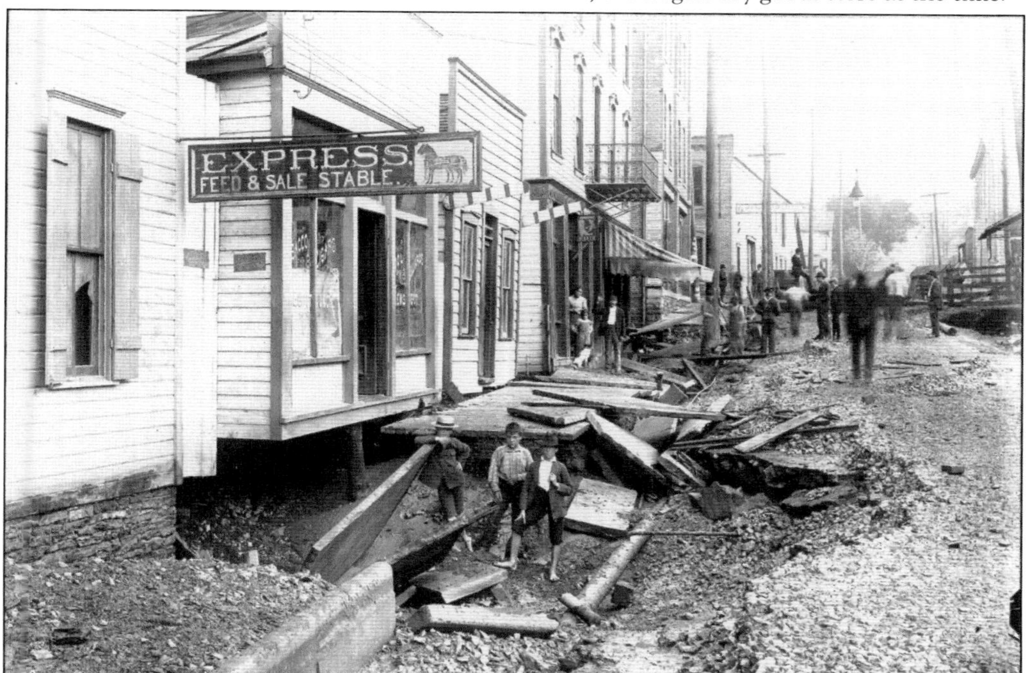

Owners assess the aftermath of the major flood of 1896, which caused catastrophic damage to a number of the building foundations of businesses and homes on Jefferson Avenue, as well as to the sidewalks and streets. (Force C. Dunlevy.)

FEDERAL TELEPHONE COMPANY.

[INDEPENDENT.]

DIRECTORY.

Please ask for numbers instead of names
Ring off when through talking.

A

16 Alexander, Dr. W. H. .... Office

C

2 Canonsburg Pharmacy............ Pay Station
11 Canonsburg Herald.............................. Office
20 Canonsburg DAILY NOTES................. Office
25 Canonsburg Coal Co.............................. Office
27 Cockins & McEwen,. Furniture, Undertaking

D

37 Donaldson, Dr. J. B........................... Office

E

18 Enlow, W. R.................................. Residence

F

2 Foote. Mrs. J. A.......................... Drug Store
15 Foote, Mrs. J. A.............................. Residence
24 Freight Office.................. P. C. C. St. L. R. R.
47 Fee, W. H. .... Residence
50 Fee, D. H....................................... Residence

G

30 Gilber [illegible] .... Bakery

H

25 Hitchman, E. T...................................... Office
38 Hitchman, E. T................................ Residence
19 Heagen, M. J.. Grocer

L

49 Little J. D..................................... Residence

M

6-2 McClelland, Jas.......................... Stock Farm
6-3 McClelland, E. B......................... Stock Farm
7 McClelland, Jno. L........... Real Estate Office
46 McClelland. Jno. L......................... Residence
9 Marple, B.............................. Market Gardener
43 Marple, Jno.................................... Residence
16 McBurney, A. F., Dentist......................... Office
22 McDowell & Dickson................. Planing Mill
23 Manufacturers' Gas Co............................ Office
48 Moore, Chas R................................ Residence

P

10 Potts Bros....................... Grocers, Chinaware
26 Potts, T. M.................................... Residence
5 Penn'a Reform School.............................. Office

S

42 Straub, T. A.................................... Residence

V

12 VanEman, J. J. & Son.................. Hardware
45 VanEman, J. J................................ Residence

W

14 Wilson, J. R.. Grocer
36 Wilson, J. R..................................... Residence
38 Young, D. Frank............................. Residence

Telephone service in Canonsburg began in 1885 with the arrival of the Bell Telephone Company. By the early 1900s, Bell was joined in competition by the Federal Telephone Company (represented by this 1900 directory) and the State Mutual Telephone Company. By 1916, though, Bell was the only one remaining after it purchased State Mutual and Federal ceased operations in 1907. (Daily Notes.)

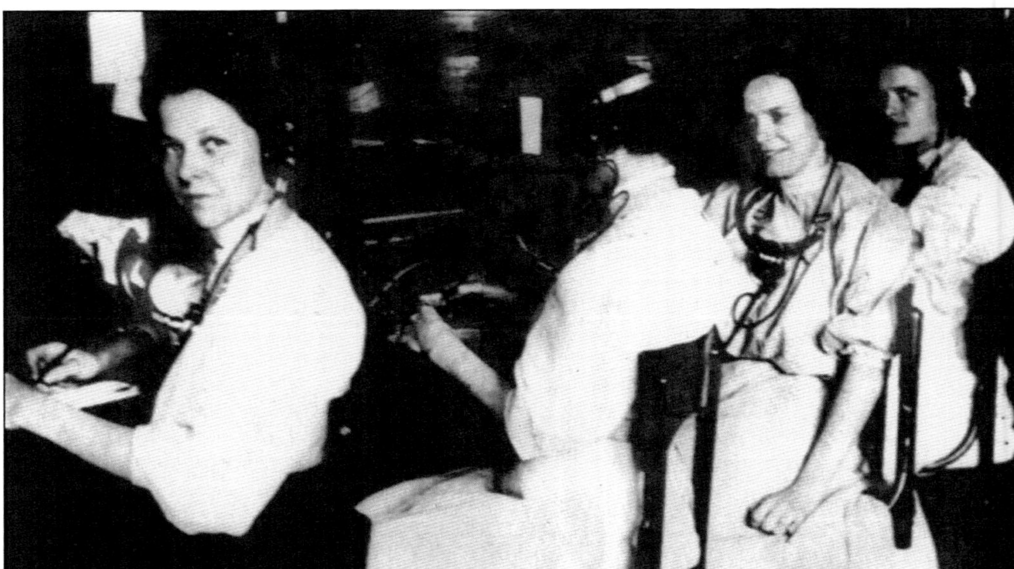

Early Canonsburg telephone operators assist customers from their stations at one of Canonsburg's three telephone companies, known at the time as "Hello Companies." While the battle for customers among the companies helped to keep rates low, customers were only allowed to call other residents from within their same company. Only after Federal folded and Bell purchased State Mutual were customers able to call any other telephone without restrictions. (Joseph A. Solobay collection.)

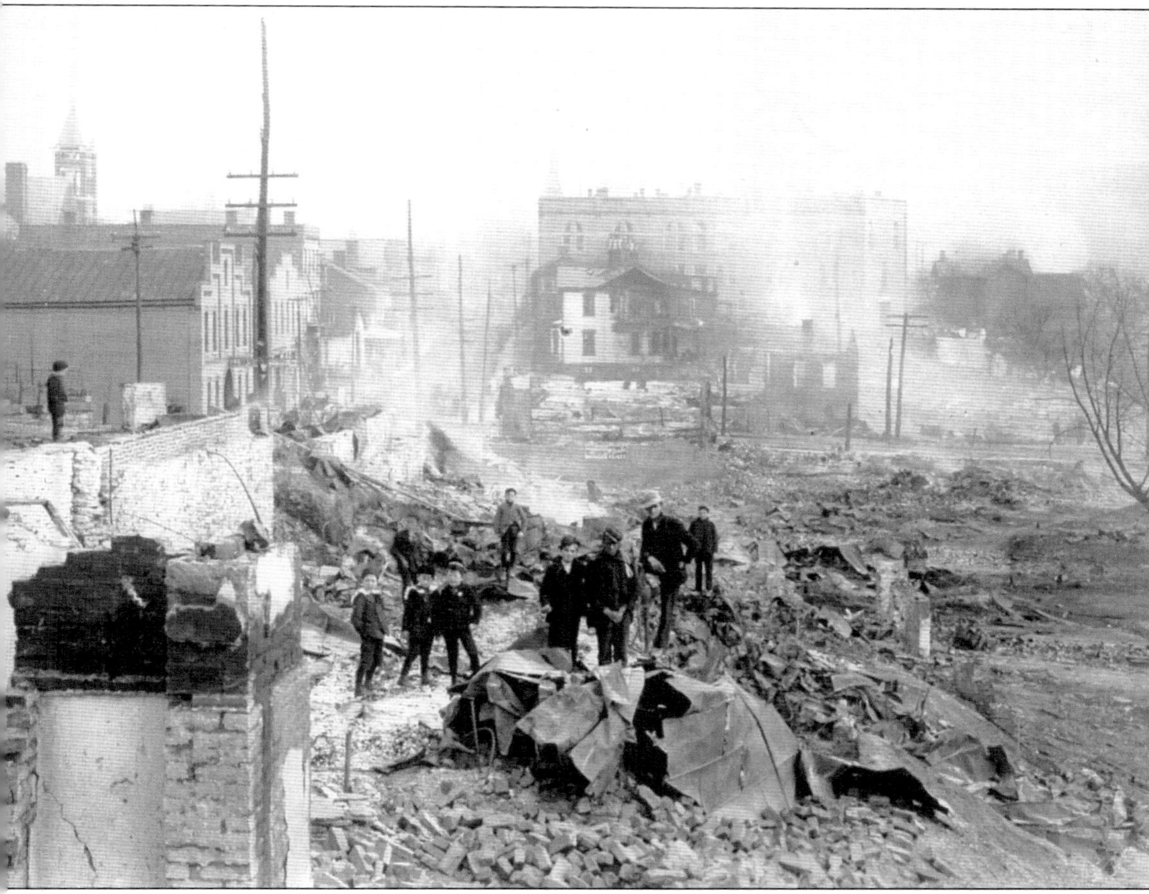

Canonsburg's most destructive fire occurred on November 13, 1898. The blaze began on West Pike Street and consumed more than a third of the town's business district, including the town's borough building. Dynamite was eventually used to bring the flames under control, along with the assistance of townspeople who formed a bucket brigade. This photograph from the following morning shows some of the debris still smoldering. Ironically, the fire came just days after a unanimous council vote to purchase new chemical equipment. Following the fire, the town moved quickly to purchase a Holloway soda-engine cart, which consisted of two large 30-gallon tanks of water. The town actually had its new firefighting equipment in place before a formal fire company was reorganized, as no official company had existed since 1890. Prior to the reforming in 1900, it was merely up to passersby to begin bucket brigades when a fire was underway. (Force C. Dunlevy.)

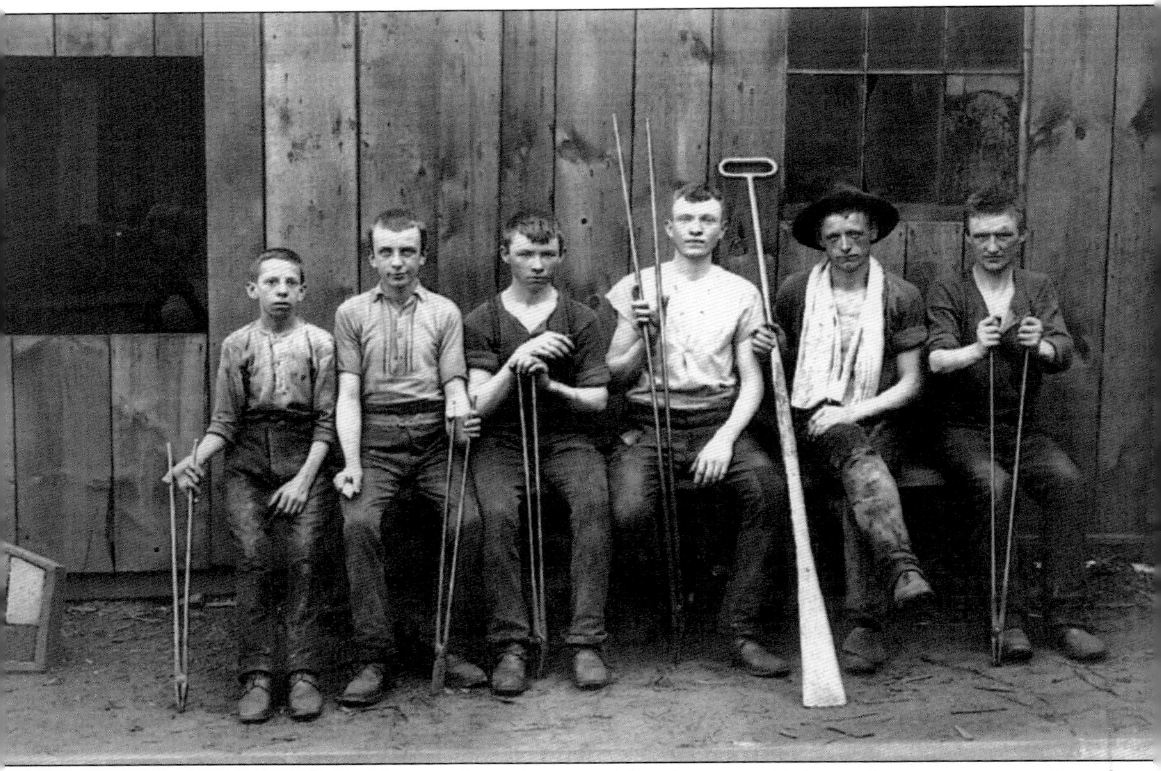

In an effort to fill the financial void created by the loss of the college, representatives for Canonsburg solicited a partnership with a Pittsburgh-based firm looking to produce sheet iron. Investors successfully raised the needed funds, and a deal was completed. A new factory was built on the western border of Canonsburg, and by the end of 1882, workers were in place as the Canonsburg Iron Company was up and running. The factory expanded in 1884 by purchasing the Budke Manufacturing Company, which produced kegs. The Budke plant owner, John F. Budke, stayed on as the new manager of the expanded mill, which soon became the Canonsburg Iron and Steel Company. With Budke at the helm, the company prospered until selling out to National Steel Company in 1899. Iron mill workers from 1886 include, from left to right, John Arthur Tolley, H. Bell Thompson, James McNamara, Frank Cole, Gwilym Price, and Joseph Dean. (Ruth Lesso.)

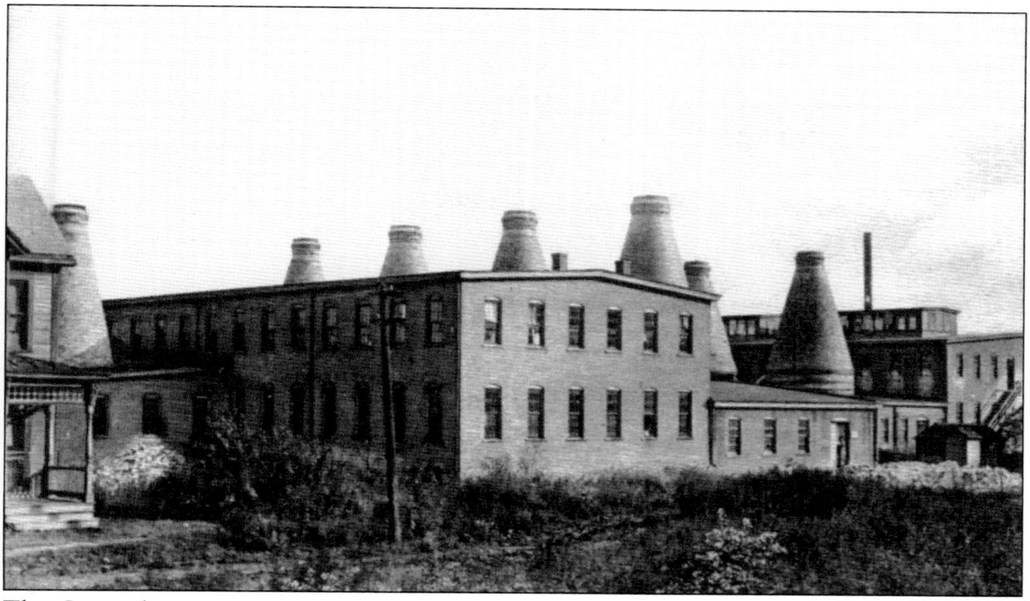

The Canonsburg Pottery Company began when Ohio businessman W. S. George opened a pottery in South Canonsburg in 1901. Initially called the Canonsburg China Company until 1909, the pottery specialized in mass-produced dinnerware. Later split into a second business called the W. S. George Pottery (seen in this postcard), both companies continued to thrive for many decades, until the Canonsburg plant finally closed its doors in 1976.

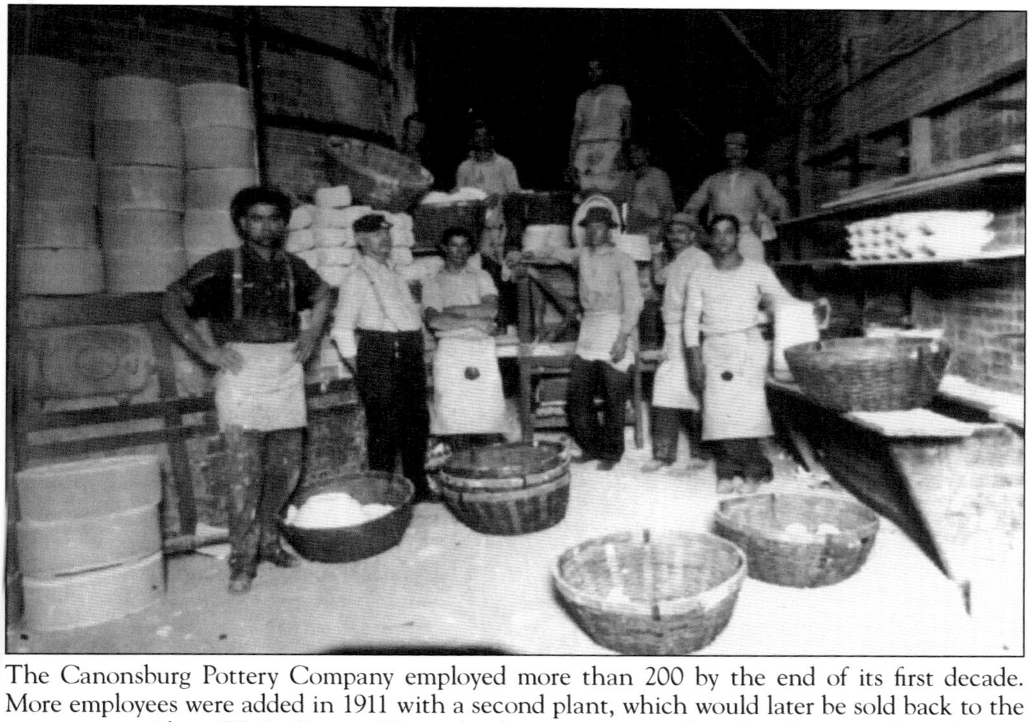

The Canonsburg Pottery Company employed more than 200 by the end of its first decade. More employees were added in 1911 with a second plant, which would later be sold back to the company president, W. S. George. Water for the pottery came from local sources, but clay was imported from various eastern states. (Canonsburg Pottery.)

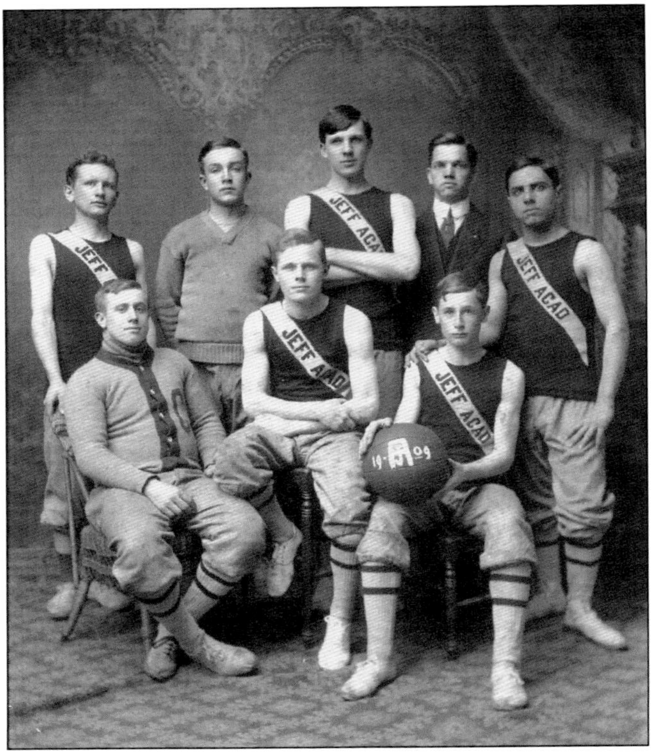

In the late 1890s, enrollment at Jefferson Academy was shrinking. Addison Craig, who became principal in 1901, tried to entice new students by increasing an emphasis on athletics. Featured here are members of the 1909 Jefferson Academy boys' basketball squad. (Weller Studio.)

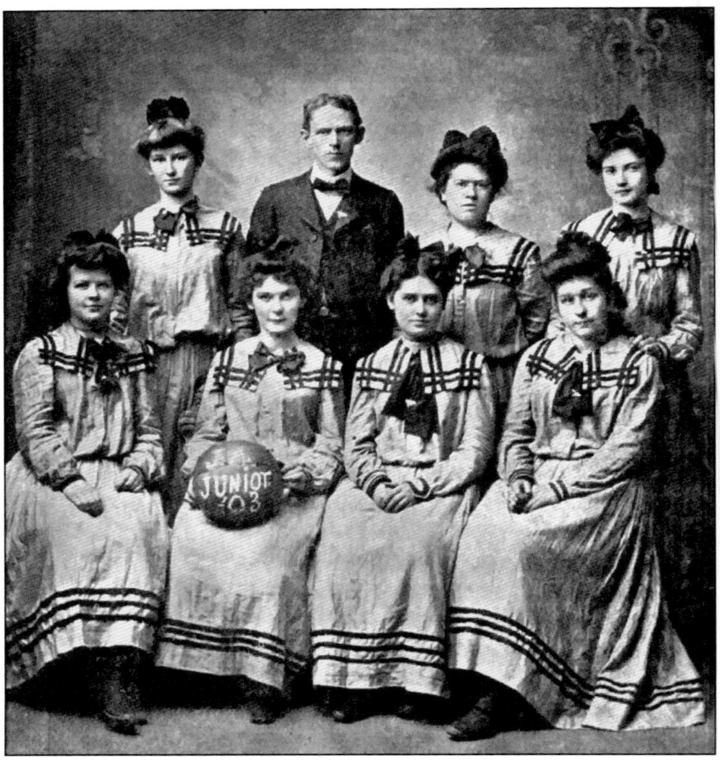

Jefferson Academy also sported teams for women students, with games scheduled both on the intramural level and in contests against other local teams. Pictured here is the well-dressed 1903 version of the junior girls' basketball team. (Weller Studio.)

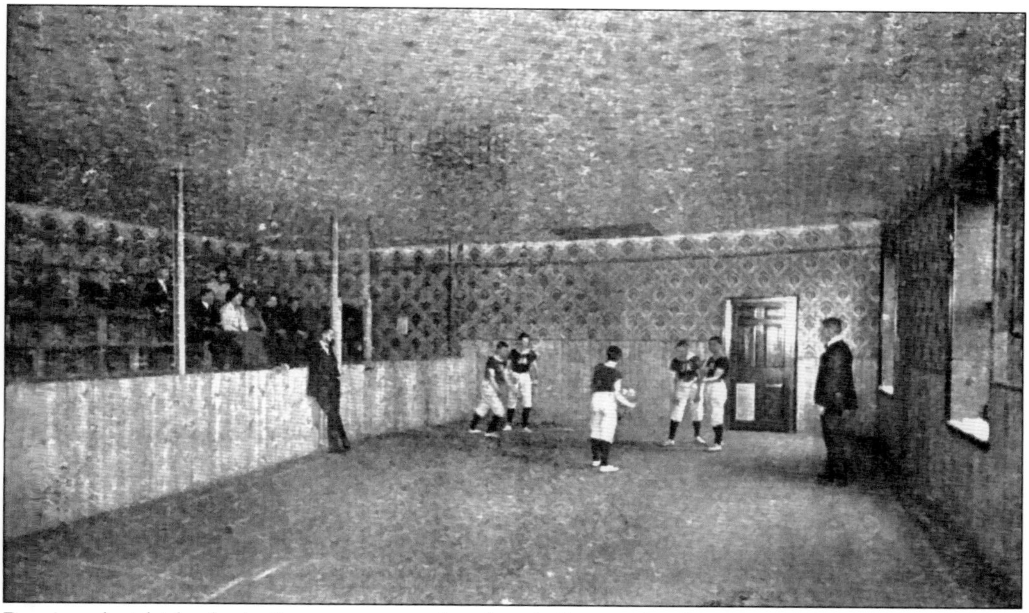

Boys' and girls' basketball games were played at Jefferson Academy in a renovated room that had formerly been used for the Philo Literary Society suite and the Goat Hall passageway. The basketball court in Providence Hall featured electric lights, a rarity on the campus. Classrooms were still using gas lamps. (Weller Studio.)

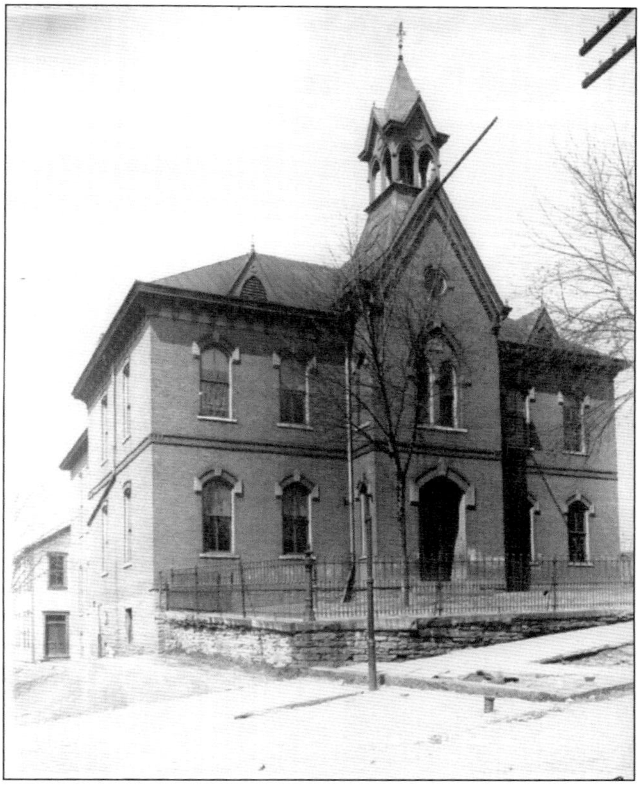

The origins of Canonsburg High School can be traced back to this brick North Central Avenue school building. Constructed in just three months over the summer in 1884, it went through several expansions over the next 20 years, adding classrooms, a new foundation, and electricity. The building remained in use until the 1960s. (Martin Estep.)

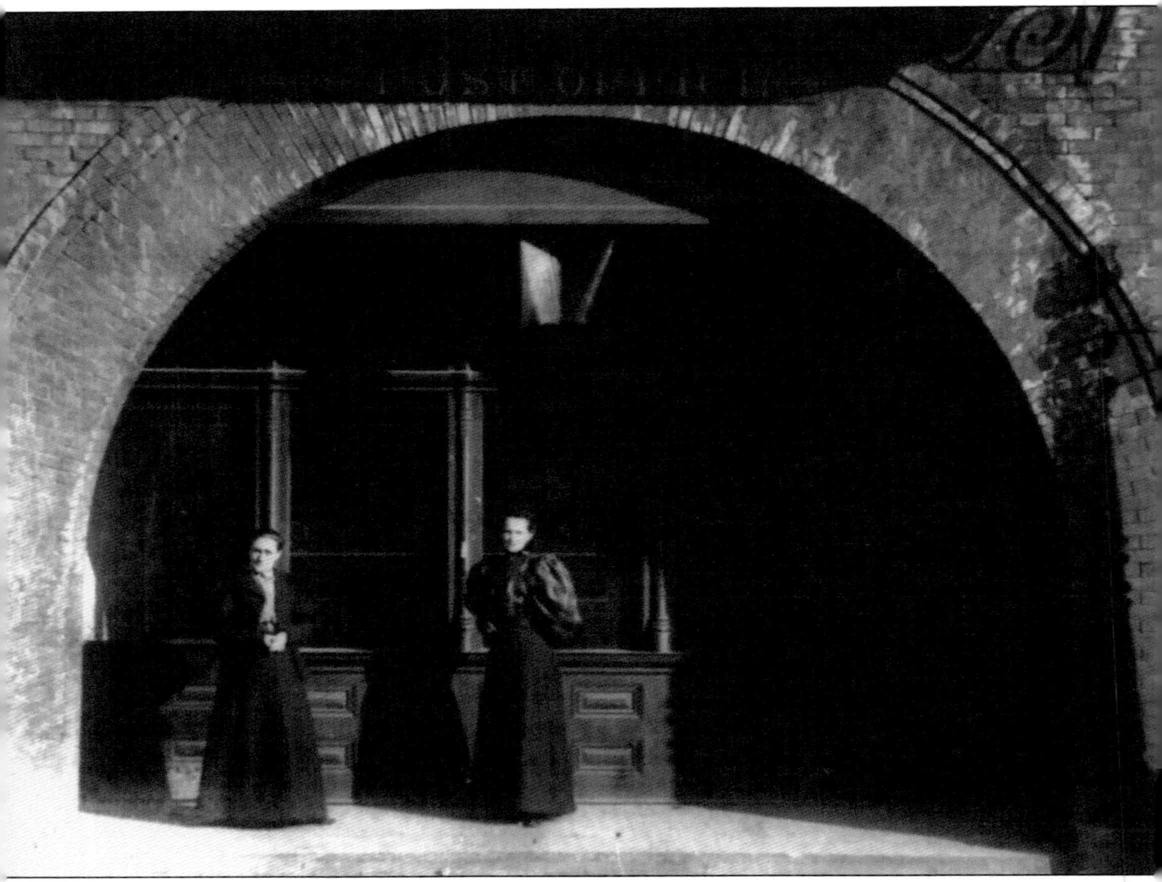

In the early years of postal service in Canonsburg, post offices were typically run out of the postmaster's home or place of business, although it routinely was found on Pike Street. The national post office department was responsible for the temporary change in the spelling of the town's name to Canonsburgh in 1849. A new guideline aimed to unify the spelling of all other *burgs* to *burgh*. The original spelling returned in 1890. Sisters Sarah and Catherine Perritte, seen here, served as assistant postmasters in the 1890s and posed for this photograph in front of the post office in the Morgan Building. Rural delivery began in Canonsburg on March 8, 1900, with home delivery following on November 1, 1903. Business increased so rapidly during this period that the post office was forced to expand its office several times, including purchasing the adjoining popular barbershop operated by George C. K. Sluby.

Three

Turning 100 and Beyond

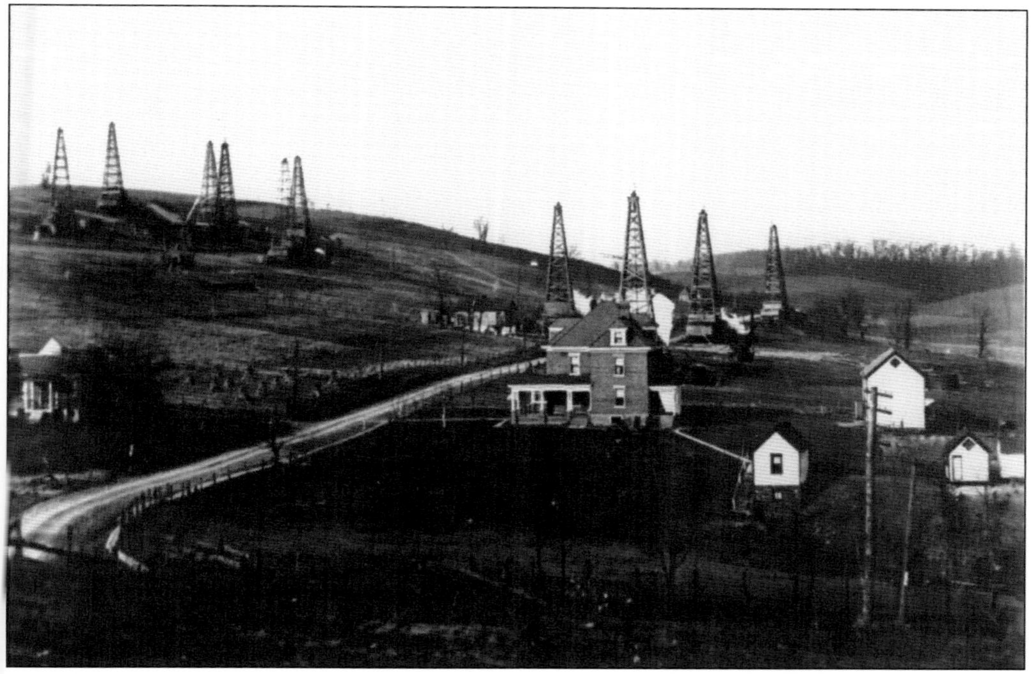

Derricks were frequently seen over the landscape of Canonsburg in 1911–1912. Rich petroleum fields were found on many properties, including those of Ridge Avenue homeowners, as seen in this 1912 photograph. Oil wells and derricks were quickly built. The Valvoline Oil Company piped the oil from the wells, with daily production peaking at 550 barrels. The boom barely lasted a year, though, and by May 1912, the digging was finished.

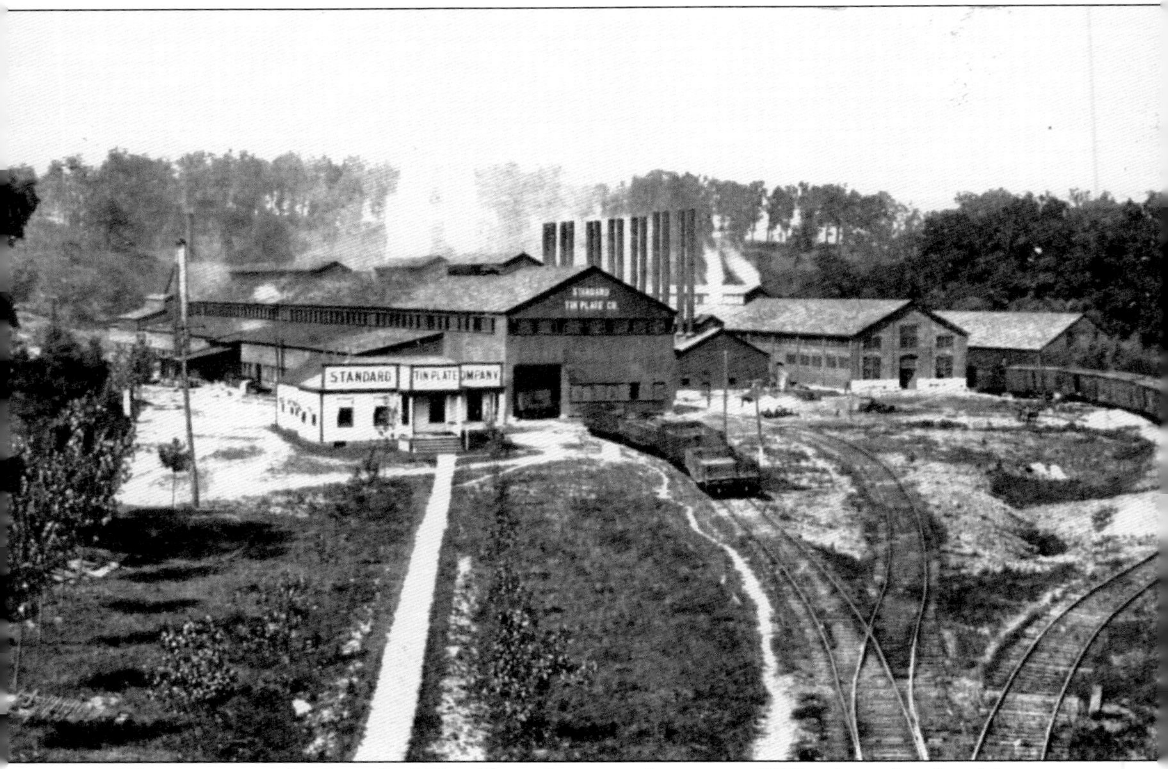

The origins of the Standard Tin Plate Company began in 1902, when the Cecil Improvement Company purchased farmland to use as a steel mill. Standard Tin Plate bought a portion of the property, with the rest of the former farmland sold as residential land. The new steel mill initiated operations in 1903 with less than 100 employees producing tin sheets usually used as roofing material. Within just a few years, the factory had grown as one of several prosperous businesses bringing much-needed new life—and new workers—into the area. The output at the factory reached new heights with the arrival of World War I, as tin cans were needed to ship food to American troops in Europe. The entire production line was turned over to tin can production. Employees now numbered more than 2,300 with 23 mills in use.

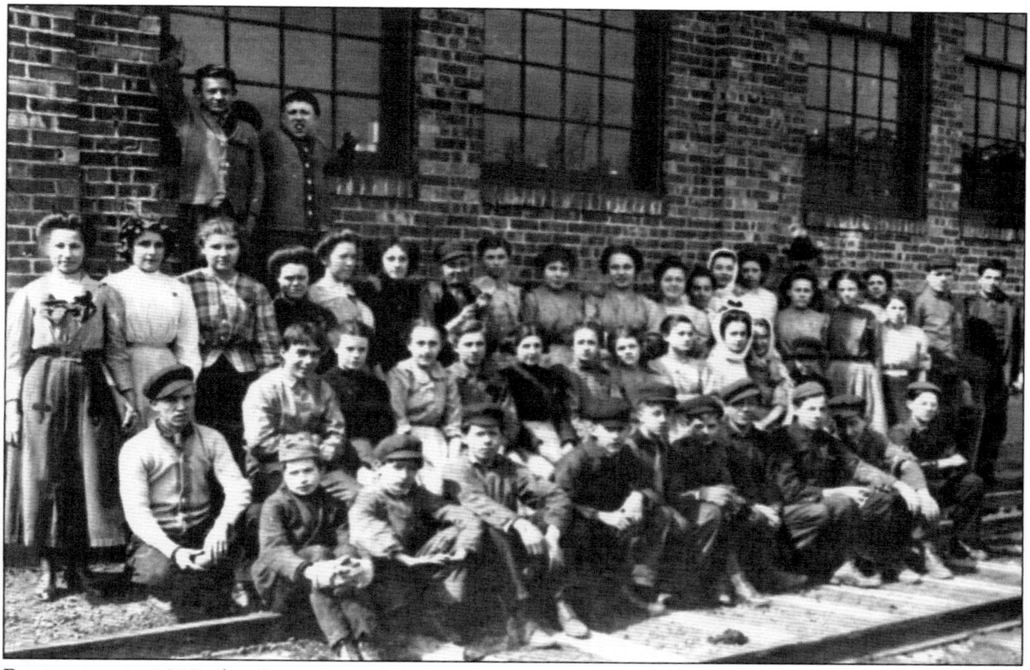

Beginning in 1910, the Continental Can Company, based in New York, operated a factory next to the Standard Tin Plate Company. In 1919, the company refined its plant to produce only can lids, while the production of cans was moved out of the state. An example of one shift from 1910 is pictured.

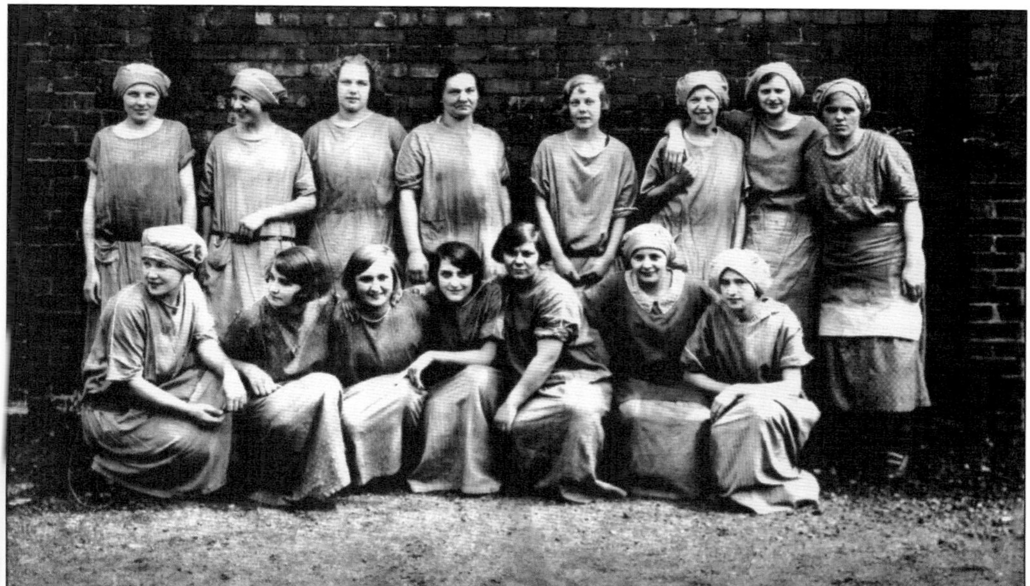

By 1925, Continental Can had purchased Standard Tin Plate, increasing the production of can lids and exporting tin sheets to other plants. The plant appeared to be depression-proof, as business remained profitable through the era. The plant also featured a heavy female workforce, in addition to the young males in the previous photograph. (Tom Ondrik.)

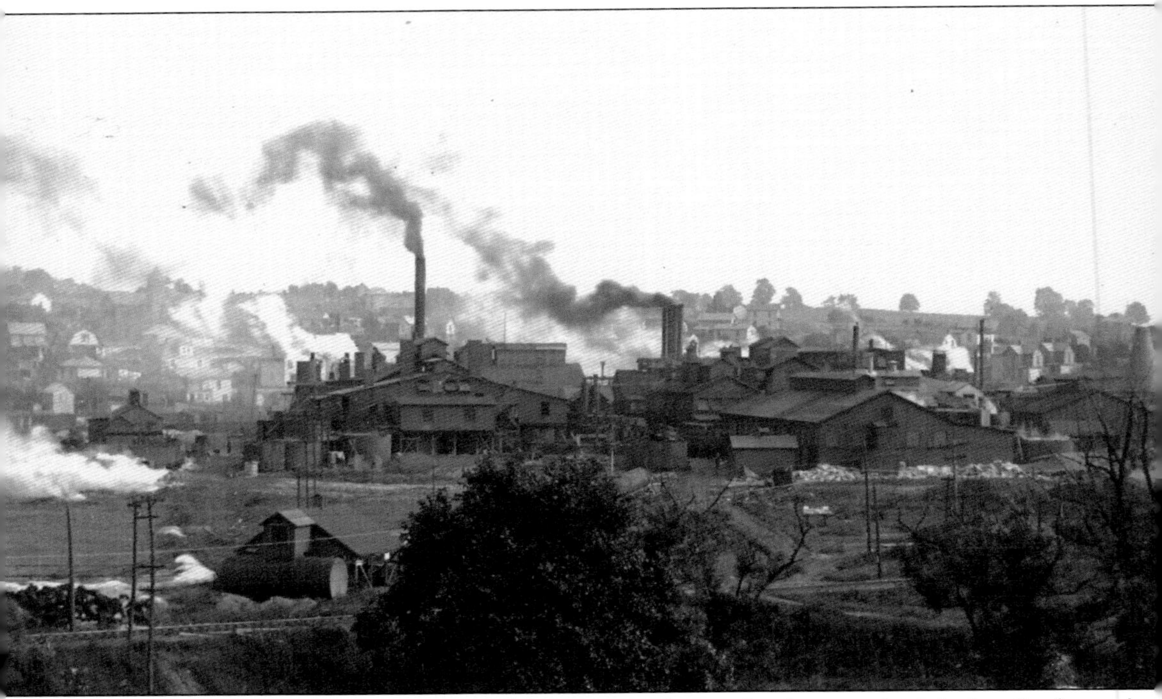

Around 1909, the Standard Chemical Company took over this factory, which had earlier housed the short-lived Simpson Stove Works. Standard Chemical was opened as a plant to produce vanadium as a by-product of carnotite ore that was produced at an outside plant. The process of refining the ore produced uranium, as well as small amounts of radium. Neither element was considered very important until it was determined they had other uses. Radium was found to be effective in the treatment of cancer, while uranium was an element vital in the production of atomic weapons. By 1914, Standard Chemical's output of radium equaled the production of the rest of the world. Marie Curie, who discovered radium, visited the plant in 1921. By 1923, the factory was sold to a Belgian radium factory. In the 1940s, the plant became the Vitro Rare Metals Company and focused shifted to uranium, with locally produced uranium being delivered to the government's atomic bomb production as part of the Manhattan Project. (R. N. Sandberg.)

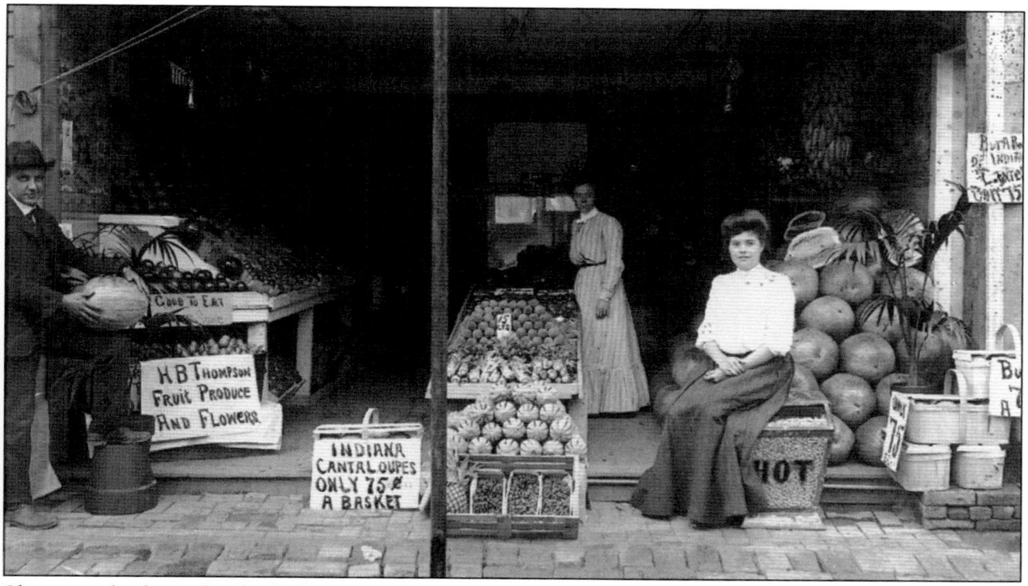

Shoppers looking for fresh fruit, produce, and flowers in Canonsburg would likely have visited this stand owned by Herbert Thompson on East Pike Street. (Ruth Lesso.)

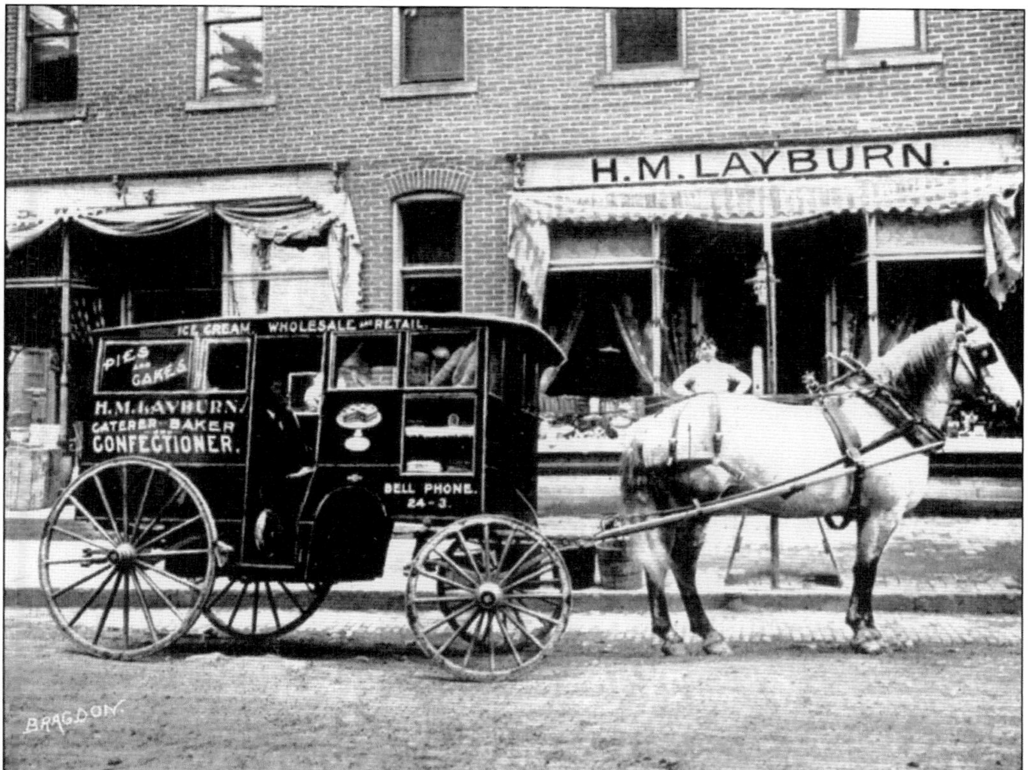

H. M. Layburn specialized in wedding and reception catering from his Layburn Café location on West Pike Street. Note the telephone number notice on the cart, likely among the first of this kind of advertising in town.

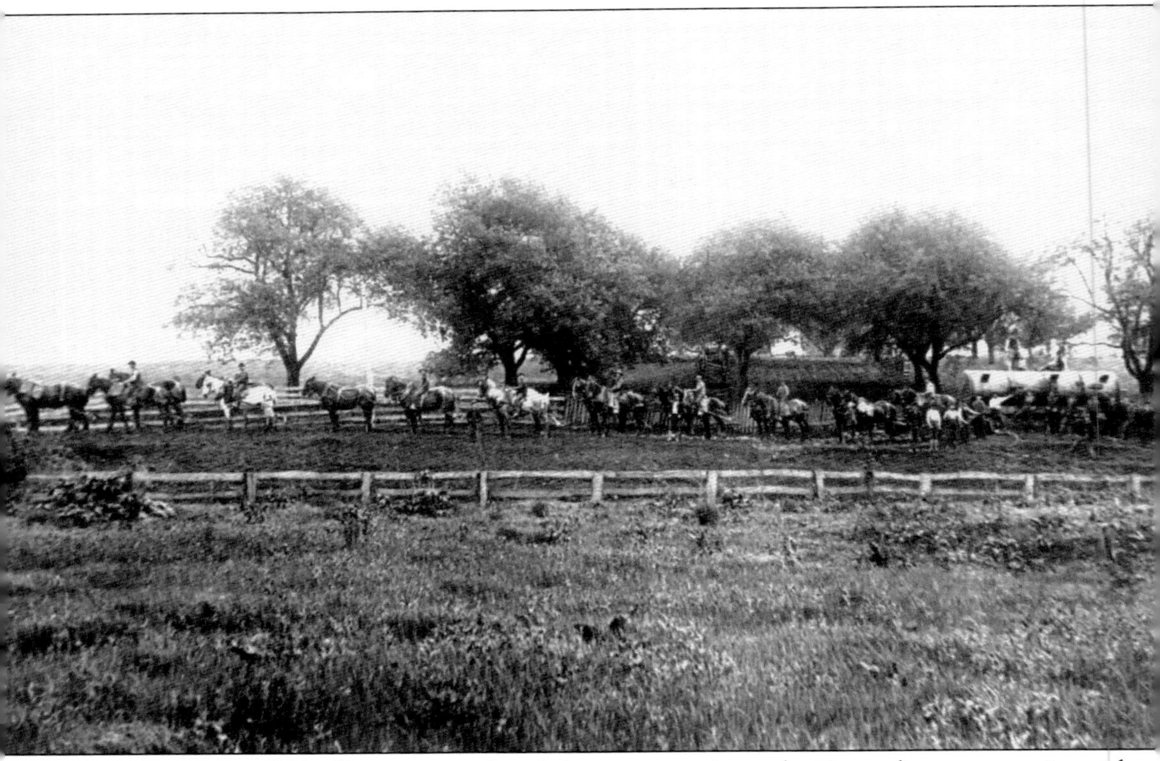

Beginning in 1901, efforts were made to bring water service to the Canonsburg community, with the purchase of land and the construction of a new dam and pumping station. In 1902, water service was offered by the newly formed Peoples Water Company, which would later be known as the North Strabane Water Company. In addition to supplying water to home customers, a special tank was provided to service the local fire departments for emergency. Over the course of the next decade, though, water service was frequently shut down and service interrupted. By the end of the second decade of the 20th century, many customers were still utilizing the more efficient town water pump for their needs. In the photograph above, an 11-team hitch was necessary to transport the new steam engine boiler to its destination at the Linden Pump Station.

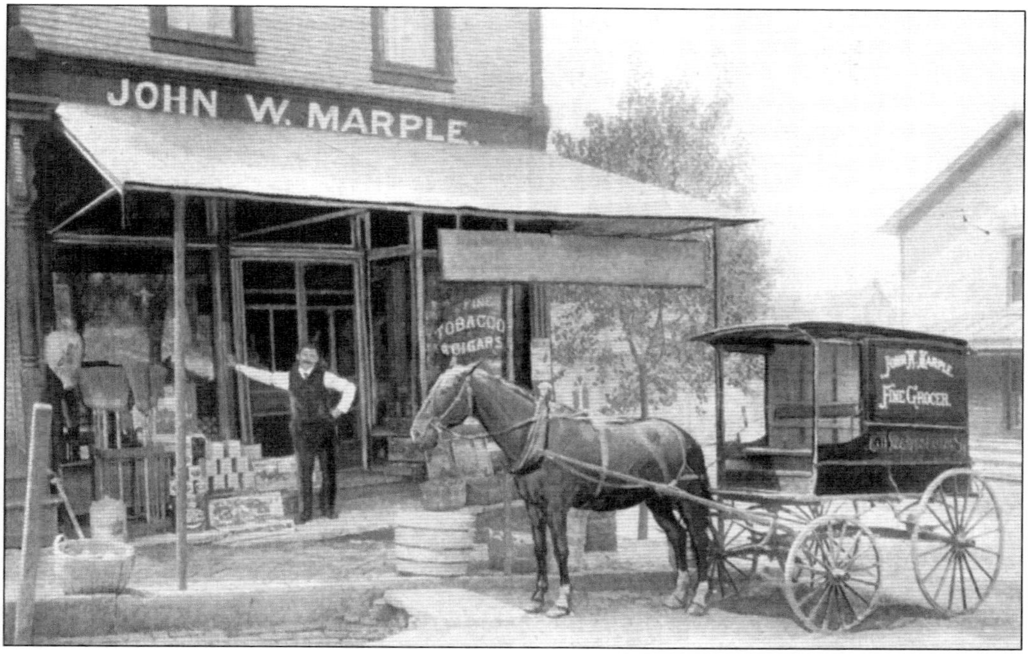

An example of an early successful grocery store in Canonsburg was John W. Marples's business at Jefferson Avenue and College Street. Delivery service was available via the store's horse and buggy. (Canonsburg centennial booklet.)

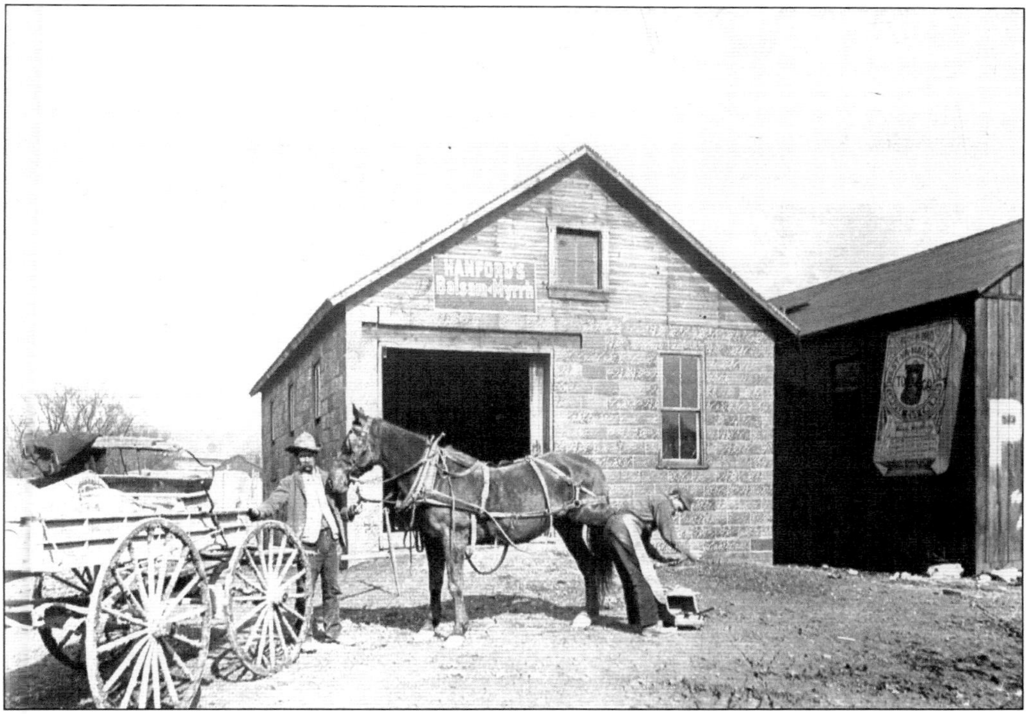

Blacksmith work was performed at the Crouch Blacksmith Shop on South Central Avenue. Joe Weaver is the gentleman shoeing the horse.

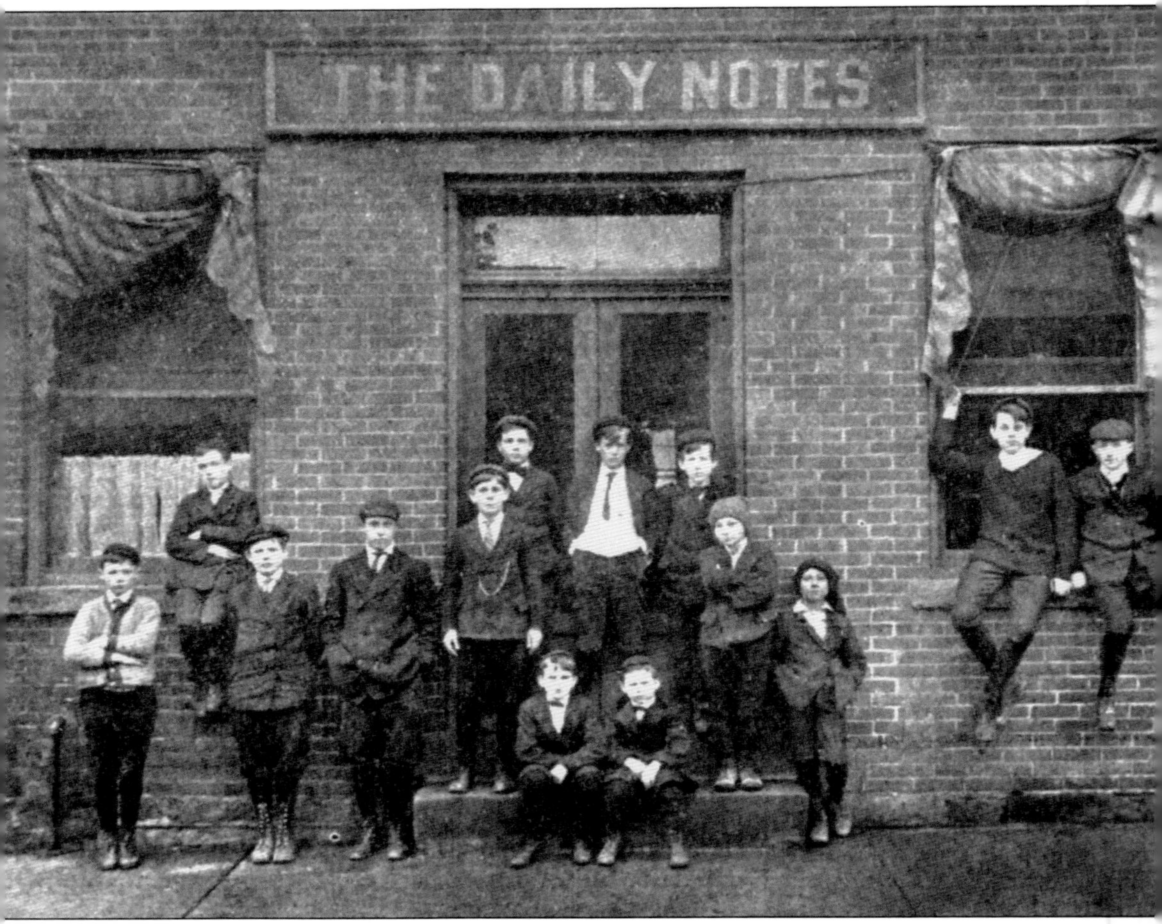

An early competitor to Maxwell Potts's the *Herald* was *Notes by F.P.*, a publication issued by Fulton Phillips in 1875, initially just 10 by 14 inches in size and printed in Phillips's home. The paper began a legacy that would last more than a century until the paper ceased in 1980. The name of the paper went through several changes, retitled from its original name to *Rural Notes*, *Canonsburg Notes*, *Daily Notes*, and lastly the *Chartiers Valley Notes*. An attempt to restart a paper under the same name in December 1980 proved to be fraudulent. This photograph shows the team of delivery boys in 1909 gathering in front of the Tannehill Building. Pictured are, from left to right, (first row) John Krafcic and Archie Smith; (second row) George Patterson, Roy McPeake, John McNutt, Harold Schade, Gilmore Blose, Ernie McNary, Charlie Dickson, Hobart Donaldson, Jack Fofigian, Alex Fofigian, Donald Roach, and John Ingram. (Daily Notes.)

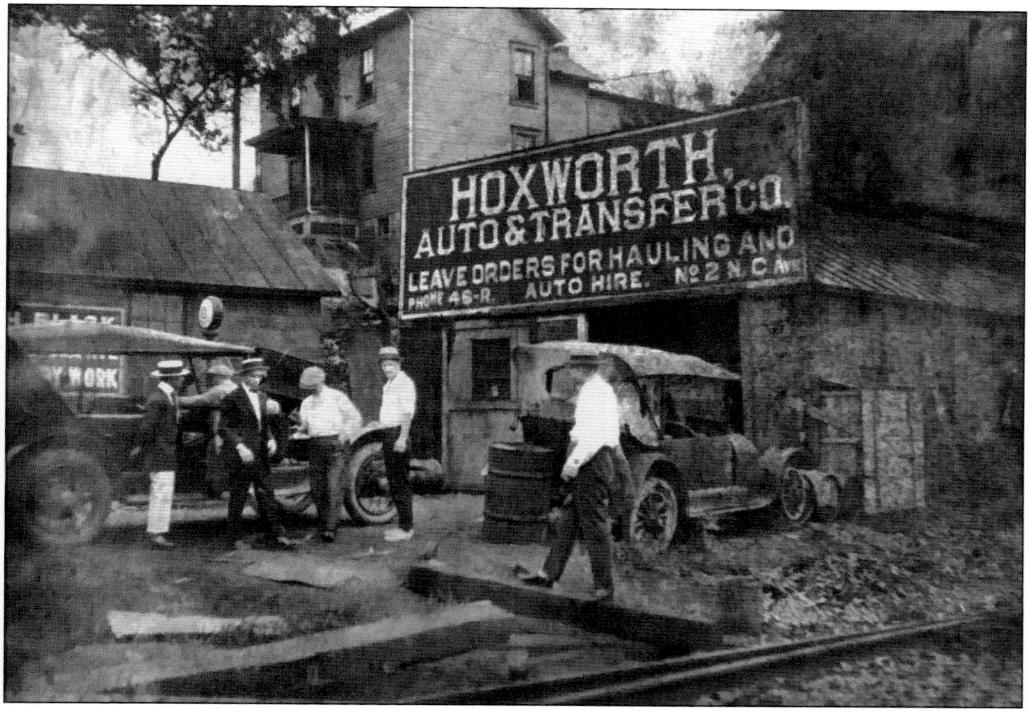

Automobiles started to become a regular sight in Canonsburg around 1905–1906. A speed limit of 10 miles per hour was established in 1906. John A. "Shorty" Hoxworth owned and operated the Hoxworth Auto and Transfer Company at 10 Murdock Street, providing some of the earliest automobile sales and repairs in Canonsburg.

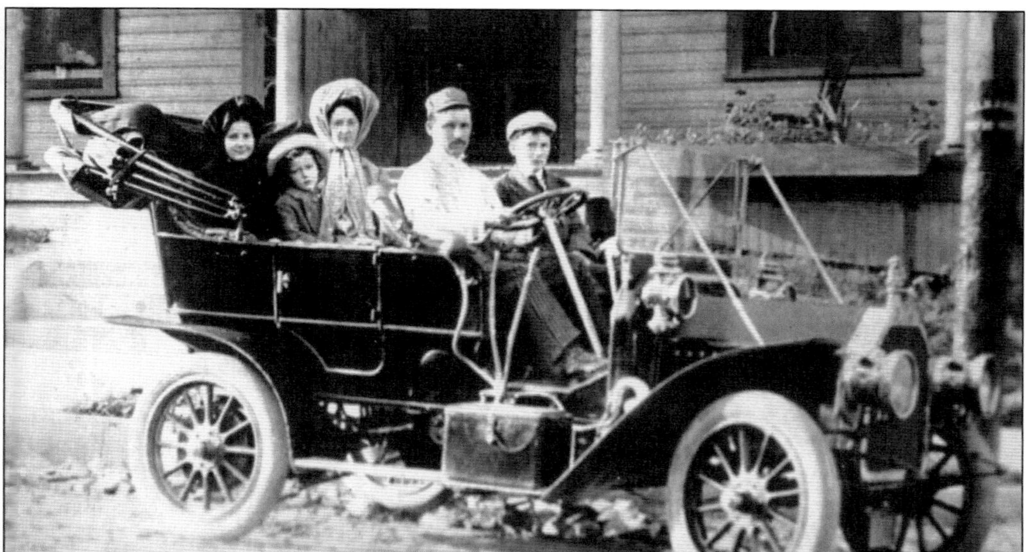

Shorty Hoxworth was also a licensed Buick dealer and is seen here with the first Buick in Canonsburg. Joining Hoxworth (at the wheel) for the ride are (from left to right) Norine, George, his wife Maude, and Porter.

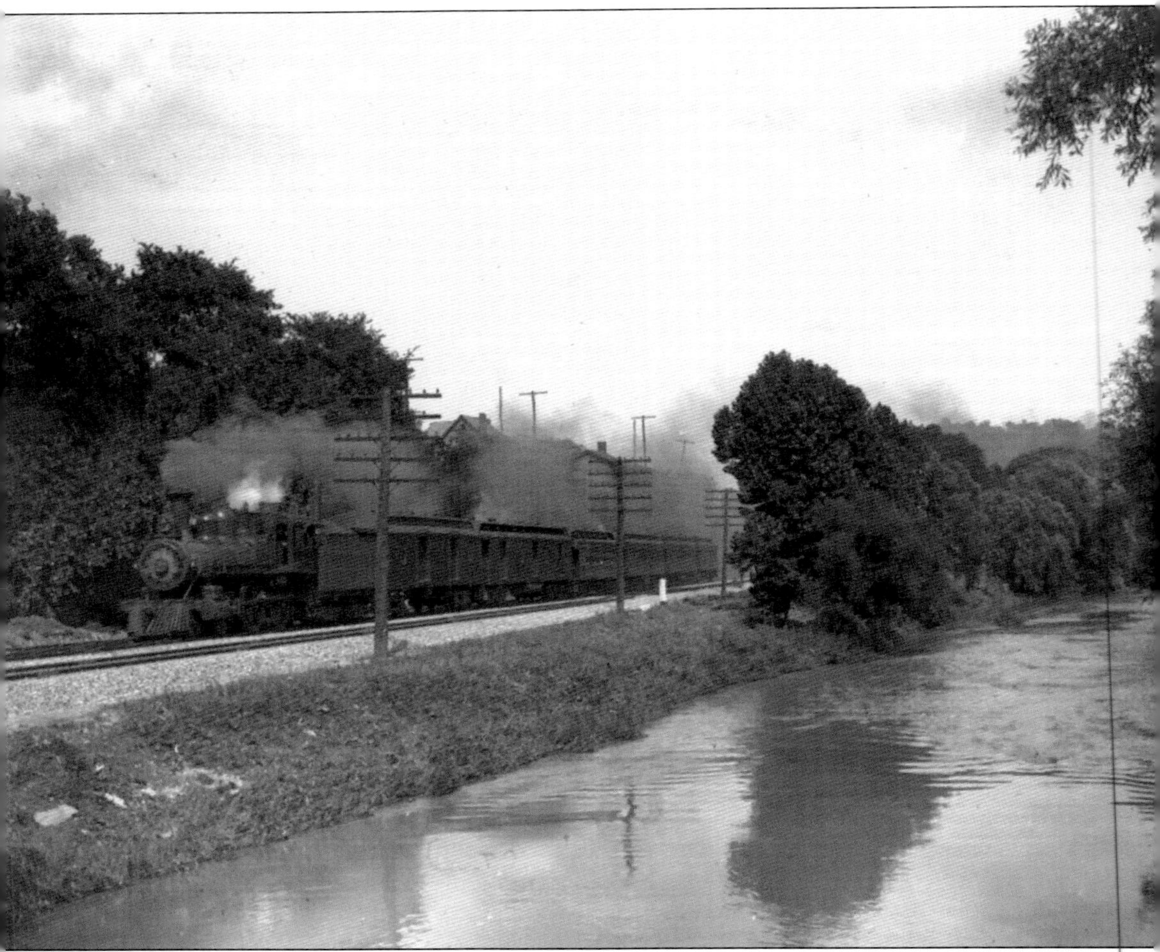

The arrival of the railroad system played a big part in the industrial growth of Canonsburg in the late 18th century. Although charters had been granted to prospective railroad companies as far back as 1831, it was not until late 1870 that connections were finally completed between Canonsburg and Pittsburgh, with regular service to Mansfield (now Carnegie) beginning in May 1871. The success of the railroad system was felt for decades, bringing new business for farmers, while creating new opportunities for mining and milling operations. The Cannonball, seen here, was an express that began in July 1889 between Pittsburgh and Washington with stops only in Canonsburg and Bridgeville. The Canonsburg town council, however, believed the Cannonball, running up to 60 miles per hour, was actually too fast, and attempted to curtail its speed with an imposed speed limit. For parts of 1893 and 1894, the railroad responded by eliminating the stop in Canonsburg. The protest succeeded, and the stop was returned to local commuters. (Martin Estep.)

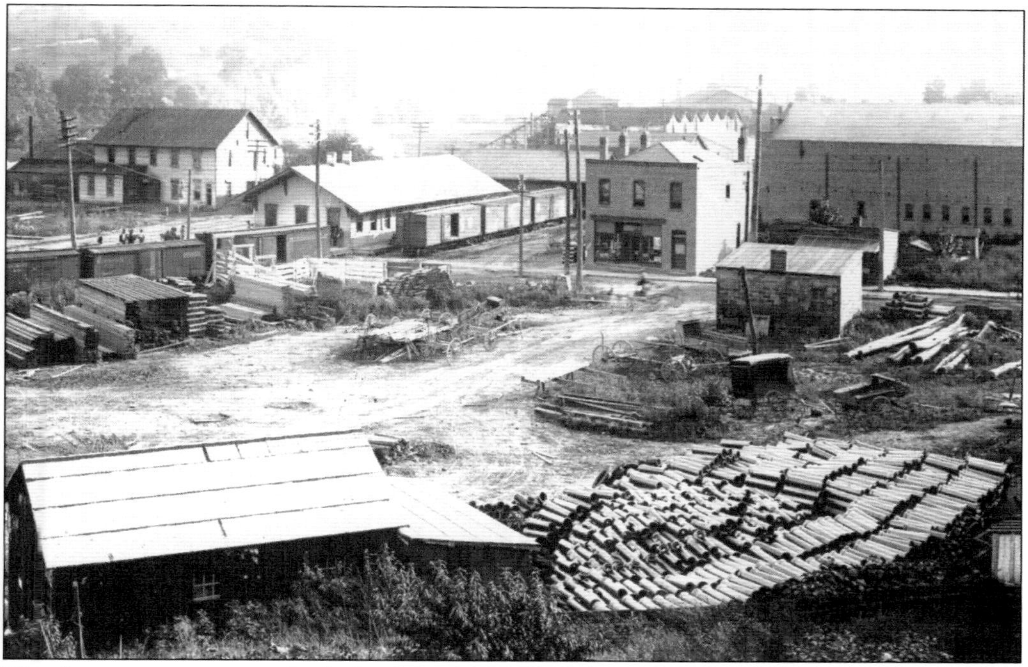

This first image captures the look of Canonsburg's first train depot in 1903. Much of the area surrounding the depot was destroyed in the fire of 1898. The wooden depot was built in 1871 to service the growing railroad traffic between Canonsburg, Washington, and Pittsburgh. (Force C. Dunlevy.)

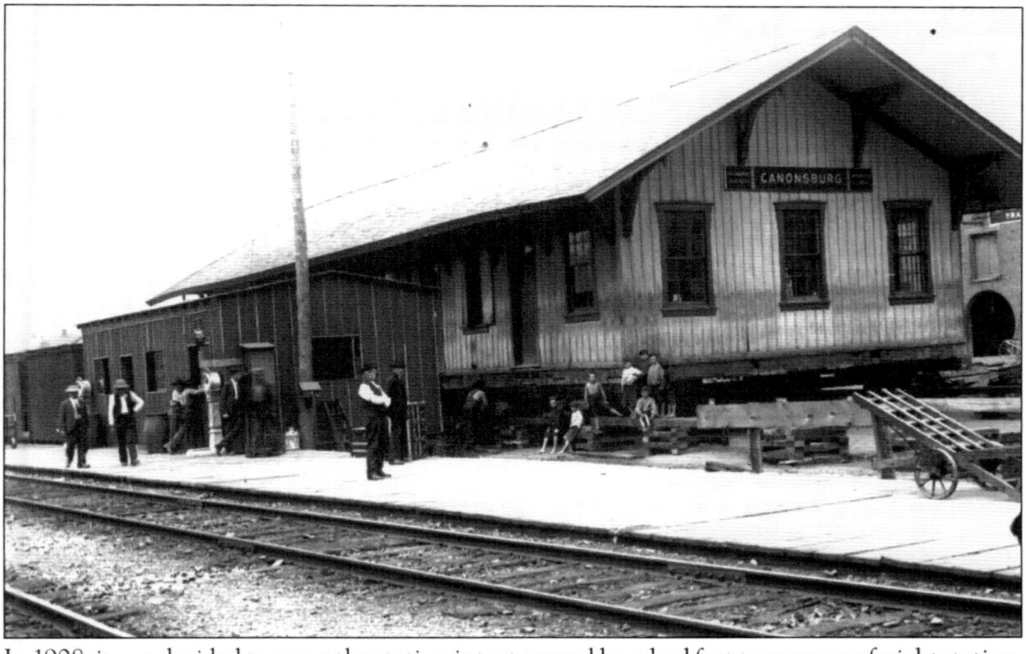

In 1908, it was decided to move the station intact several hundred feet to serve as a freight station. The structure was raised and moved along tracks to its new location several hundred feet to the west, while temporary ticket windows were erected to handle transactions. (Martin Estep.)

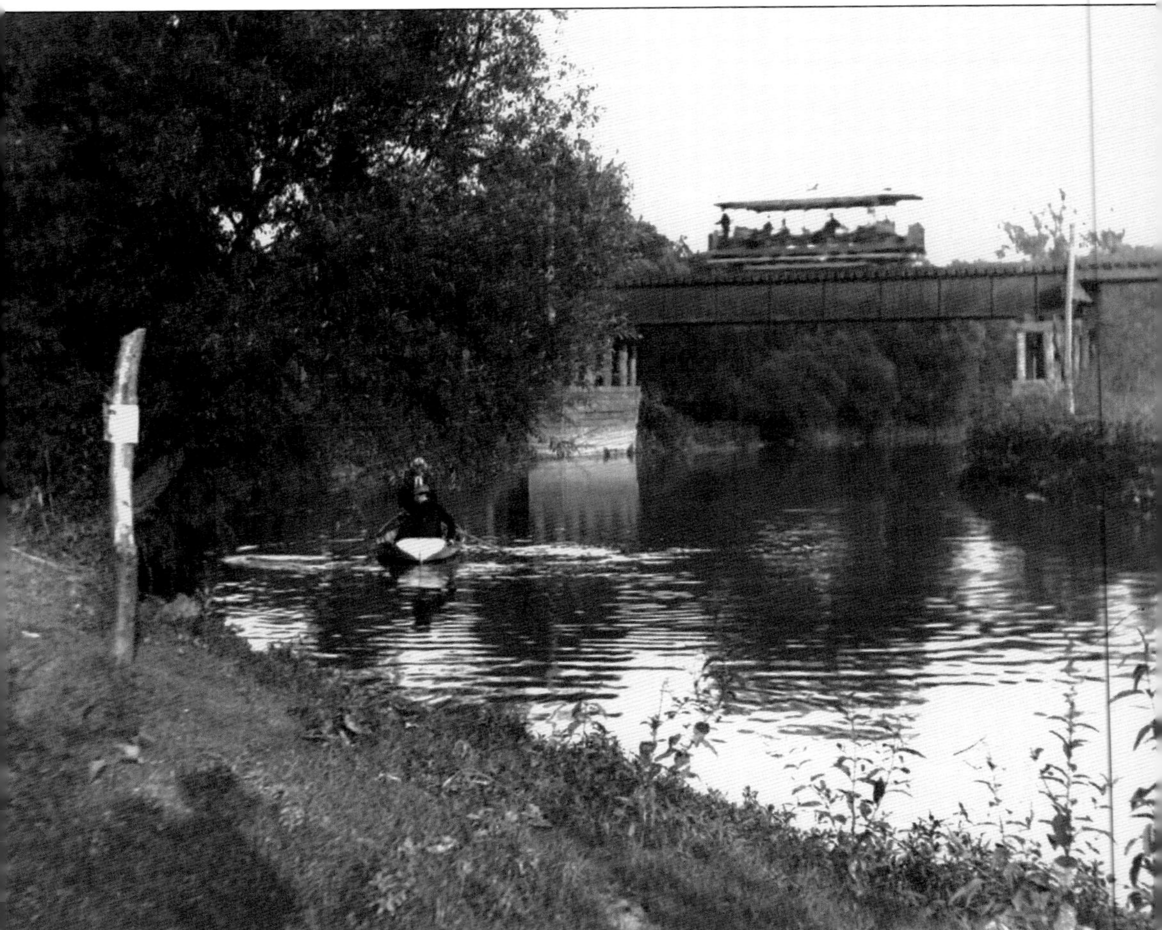

The first attempt to initiate trolley service began in 1898, although the effort failed. In 1902, though, the Washington and Canonsburg Railway Company began construction on trolley lines, and the first regular trolley service to the area was finally in operation in 1903. An early open-sided trolley car is seen riding over a trestle at the milldam. Open-sided cars were used in warmer months on local trips around town. The company was purchased in 1906 by the Philadelphia Company and eventually became the Pittsburgh Railways Company. Service was extended to Pittsburgh in 1909, and the first driver to complete the trip was motorman Hugh Dillie, who previously had captained the first journey from Washington to Canonsburg. The popularity of the self-driven automobile, though, soon started to take its toll on trolley service. By the 1940s, freight service had been eliminated, and all trolley service to Canonsburg came to an end on August 29, 1953. (Martin Estep.)

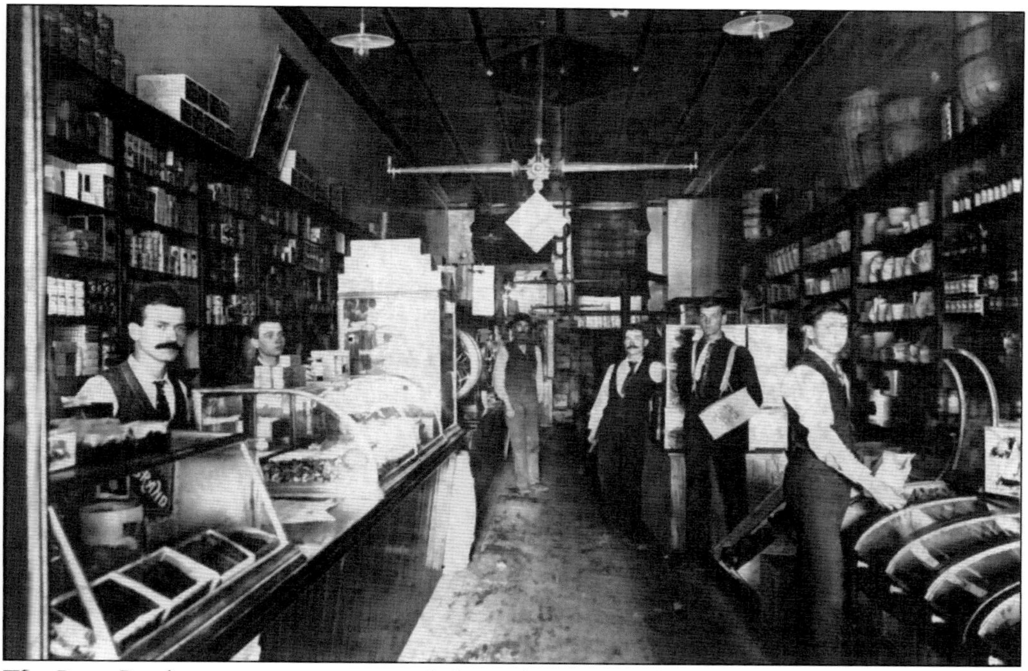

The Potts Brothers grocery store provided a wide range of dry goods on Pike Street. William Louis Potts is seen manning the counter at the left. Brother Miller Potts is at the rear of the right inner aisle.

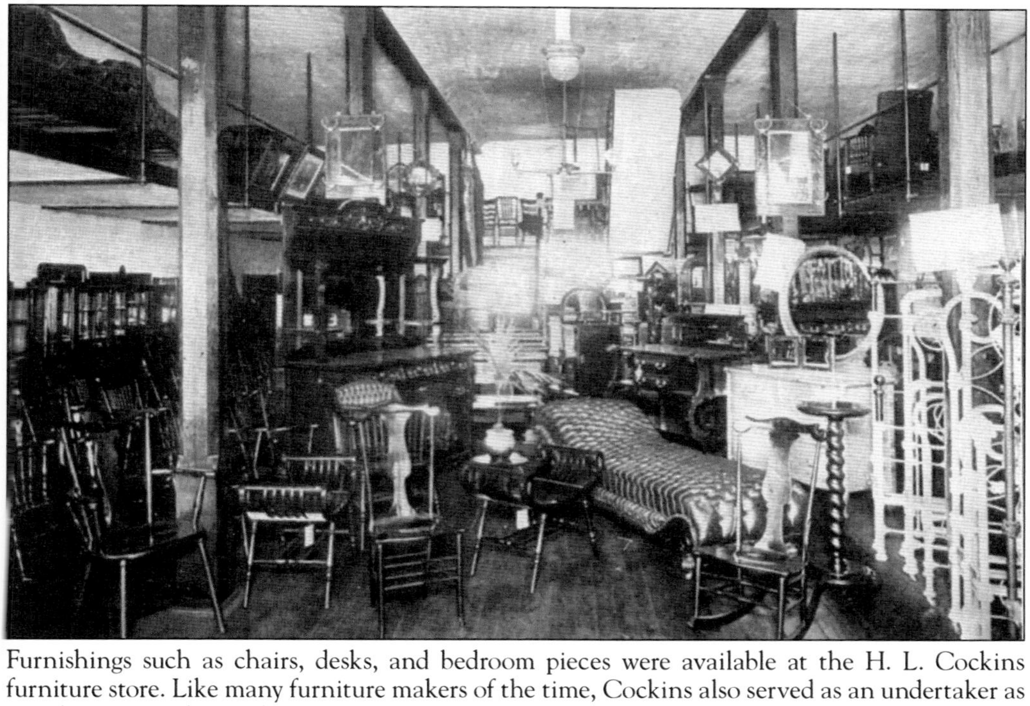

Furnishings such as chairs, desks, and bedroom pieces were available at the H. L. Cockins furniture store. Like many furniture makers of the time, Cockins also served as an undertaker as an adjoining trade. Cockins was also among the first businesses to offer Sperry and Hutchinson (S&H) green trading stamps.

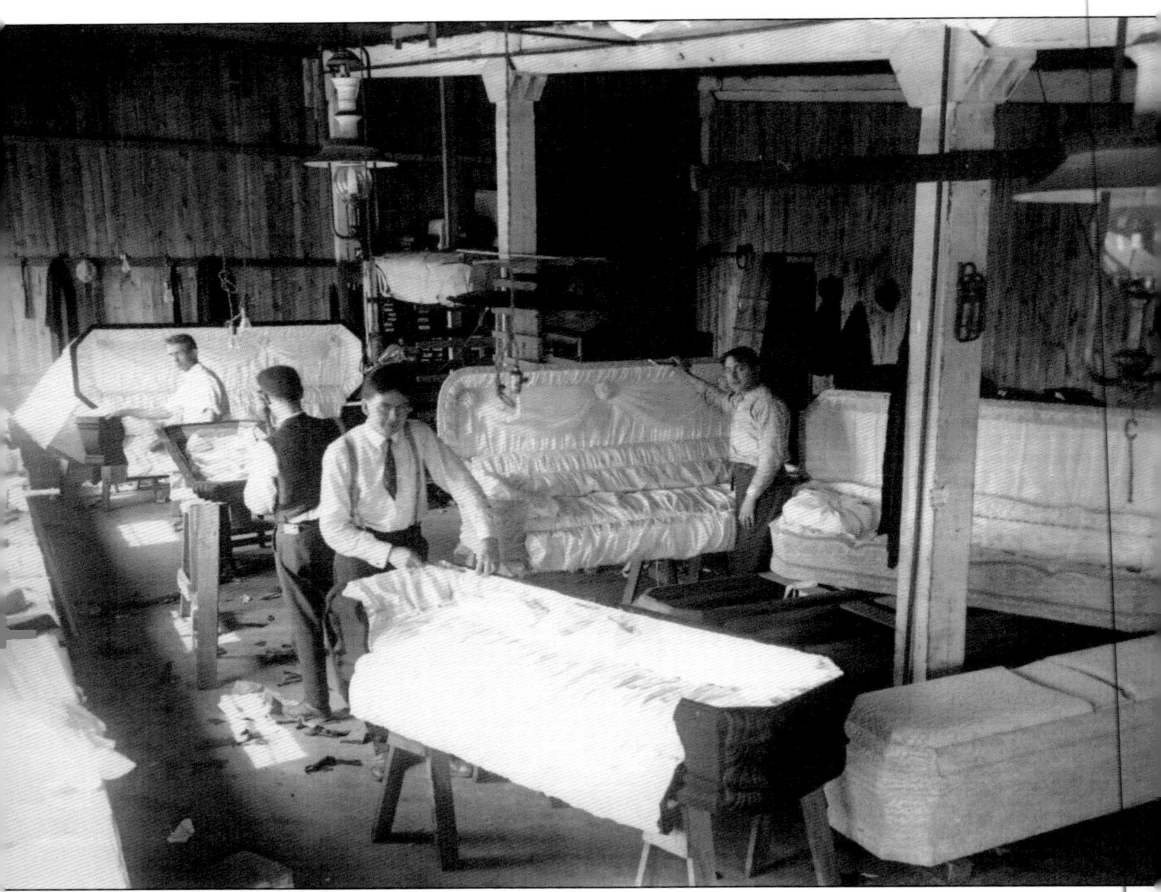

From 1905 through 1909, the Pittsburgh Casket Company ran a successful casket-making company in Canonsburg. The factory had been used previously by the Canonsburg Planing Mill from 1869 through 1882 on land to the rear of John Canon's original mill property. In 1882, the factory was purchased by McDowell and Dickson, which produced housing material, such as mouldings, windows, and doorframes. The building was damaged in the town's blaze of 1898 but stayed in business as the steam engine was spared. The Pittsburgh Casket Company bought the plant in 1905 and operated it for several years, although financial failures forced the business to close in 1909. The Pennsylvania Stock Paper Company purchased the site in the 1920s, although the building was mostly used for storage. The company left the premises following a fire in 1935. Another fire struck the plant in 1937. No business was using the property at the time. (Martin Estep.)

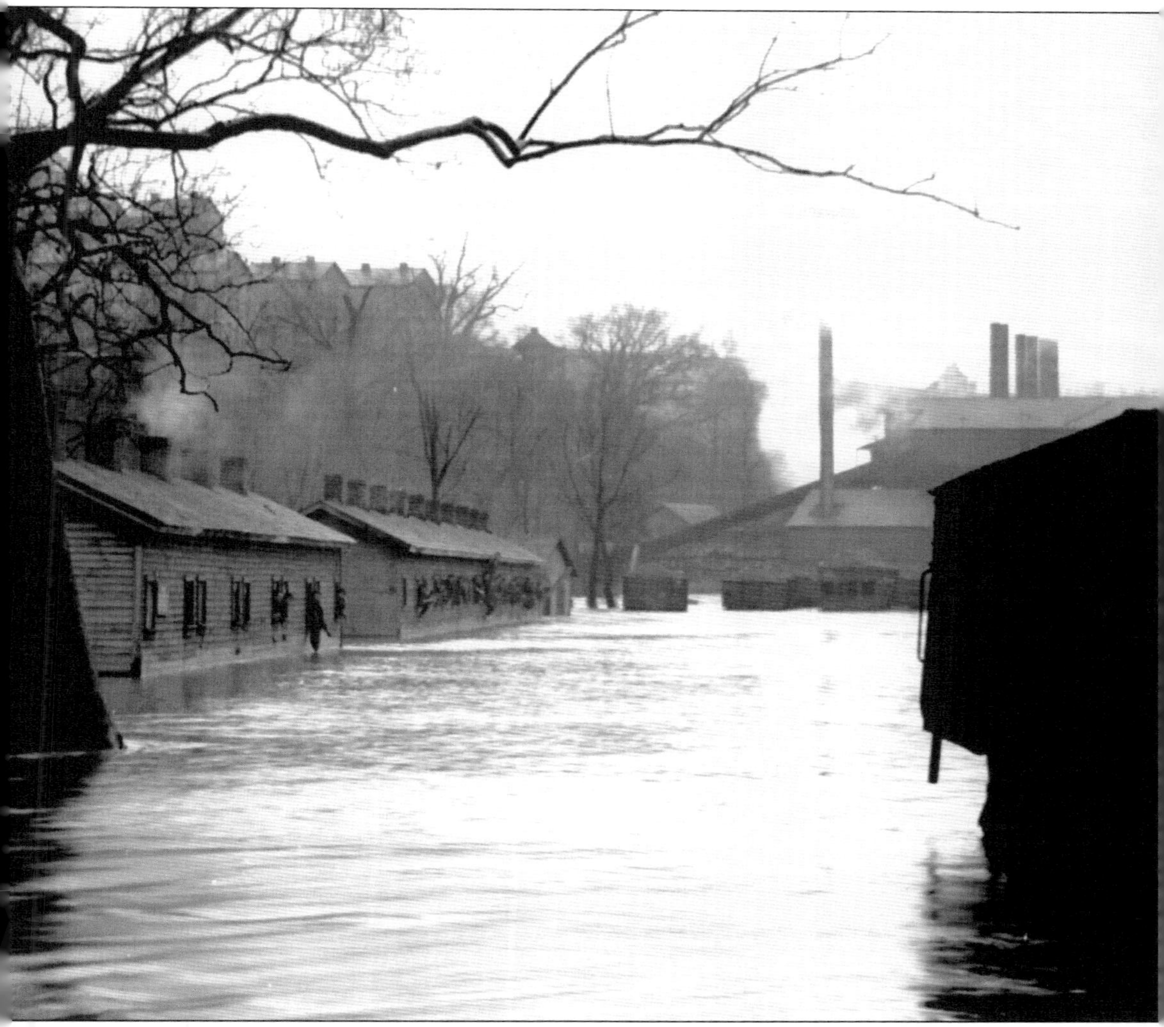

The development of the railroads into Canonsburg saw many businesses expand, including the coal-mining industry. Mines that flourished in this new era included the Pittsburgh Coal Company and Shupe and Stoner. In 1900, James Jones and Sons purchased coal mines in North Strabane Township and adjacent surface land in Canonsburg. The combined, two-township operation became known as the Hazel Mine. Jones tried to promote modern techniques in mining in an effort to increase production and eliminate injuries. The mine employed more than 800 workers, second only to Standard Tin Plate as the town's largest employer of the time. The devastating flood of 1912 brought work in Canonsburg to a halt, including that of coal-mining operations at the Hazel Mine, seen here. The mine was not financially profitable, and debt forced the mine to close in 1915. The Chartiers Creek Coal Company took over the site in 1916 and was quite successful, producing coal for World War I efforts, but frequent strikes in the 1920s and the Great Depression produced little in terms of future profit. (Martin Estep.)

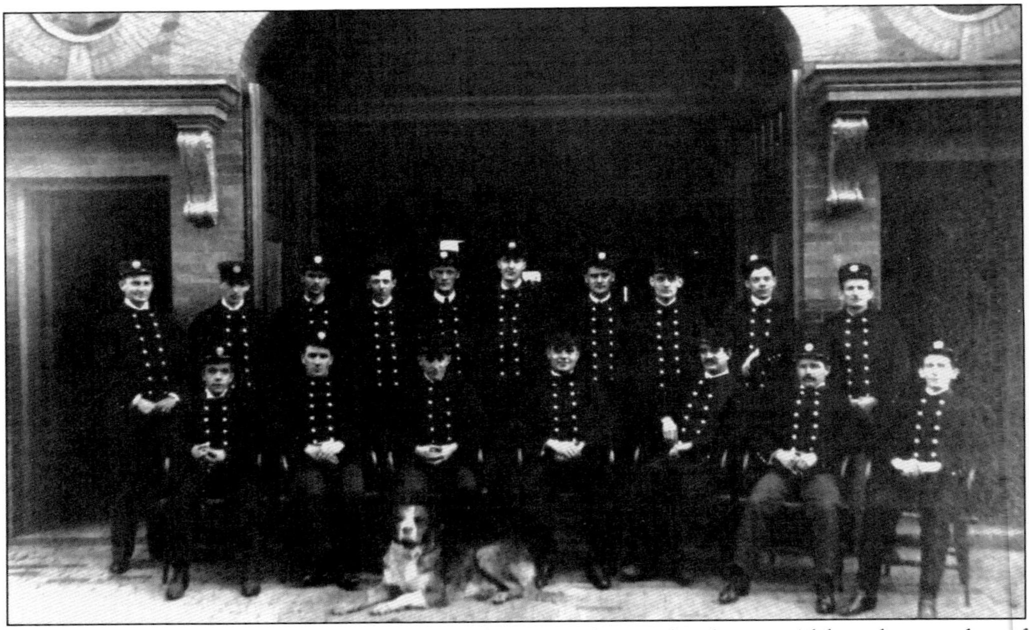

The creation of a firefighting force in Canonsburg was slow in developing. Although a number of volunteer troops existed throughout the 1800s, they were limited in equipment. A new force was finally organized in 1900, but only after the great 1898 blaze that destroyed more than a third of the town's downtown businesses. The volunteers who manned Engine House No. 1 were the first to use pressurized water from pipes as a means of fighting fires.

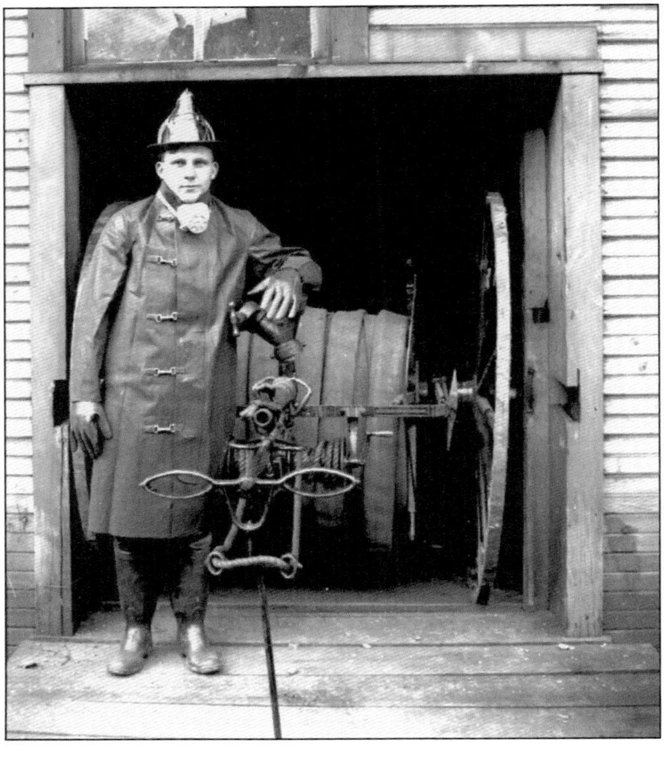

Firefighter John Grubbs, a member of Canonsburg Fire Company No. 2, models the uniform and equipment used in 1912. Fire Company No. 2 was located behind the Elm Street School. The helmet, boots, and coat were the only parts of the uniform provided by the borough to the firefighters. Firefighters were aided with the arrival of the town's first motorized fire truck in 1918. (Howard M. Taylor.)

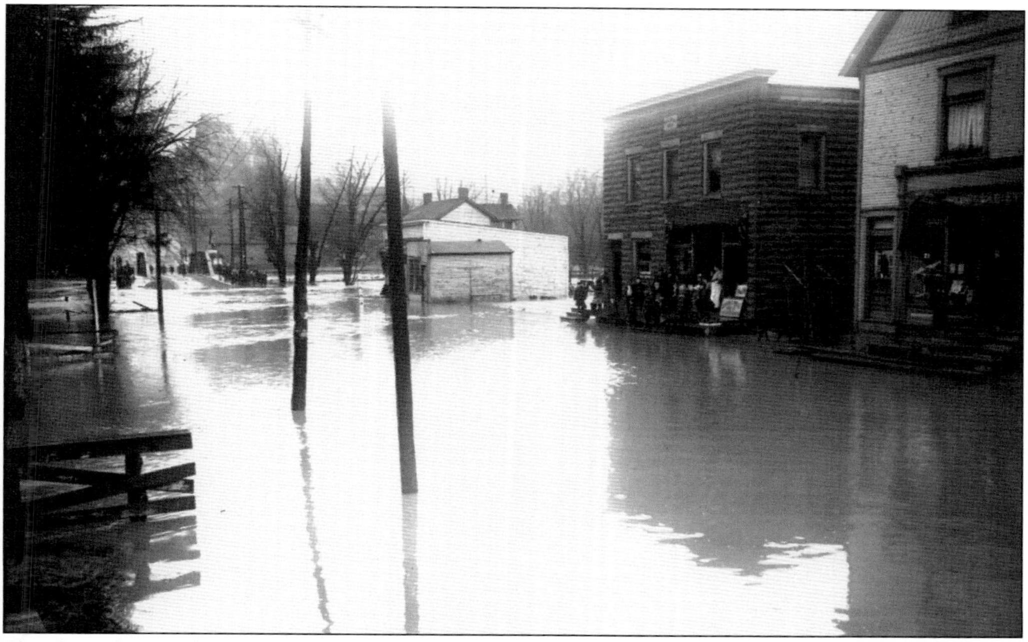

Flooding from Chartiers Creek brought life in Canonsburg to a standstill on a number of occasions over the decades, frequently caused by heavy summertime rain or winter snowmelts. The worst of the floods came in 1888, 1912, and 1956. Bridges were swept away in both the 1888 and 1912 floods. The image above, from 1912, shows the rising waters in front of several Central Avenue businesses. Below, travelers wade their way across East Pike Street. It would not be until the 1970s that urban renewal and land redevelopment would attempt to deal with the Chartiers Creek flooding issues by relocating the flow of the creek. (Martin Estep.)

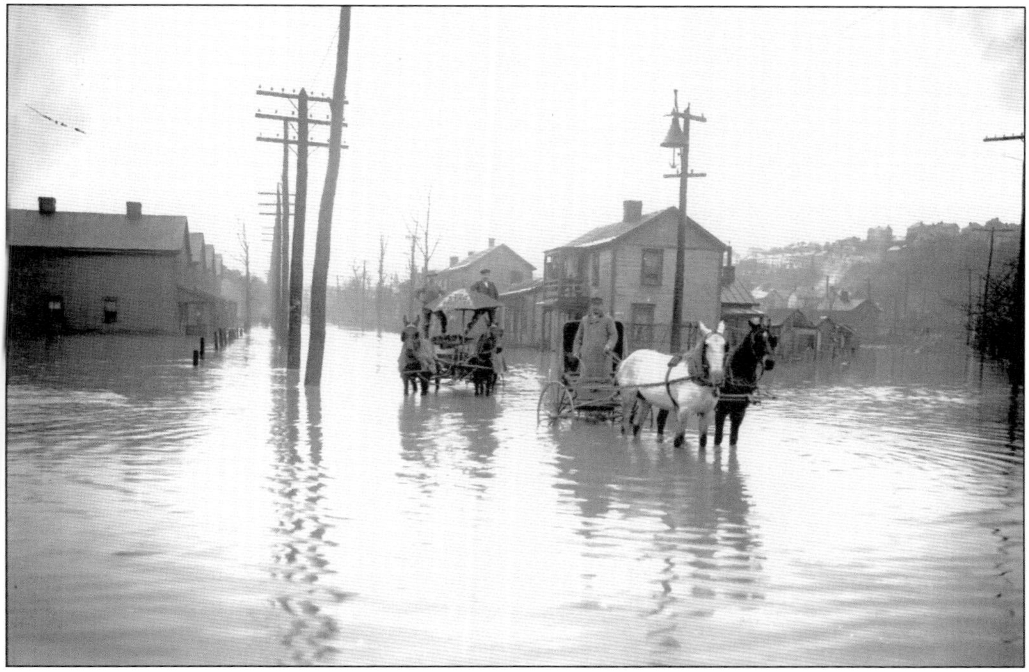

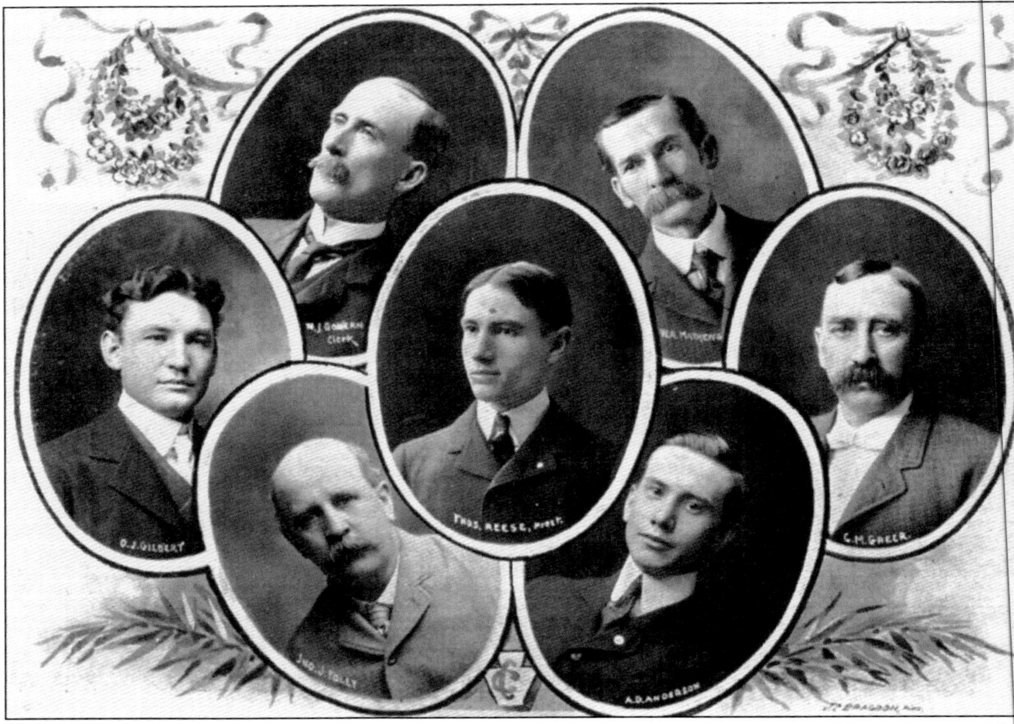

An early depiction of the Canonsburg town council is seen in this montage from 1902. In the center circle is council president Thomas Reese. Surrounding him (clockwise, from far left) are O. J. Gilbert, W. J. Gowern (clerk), W. A. Mathews, C. M. Greer, A. D. Anderson, and John J. Foley.

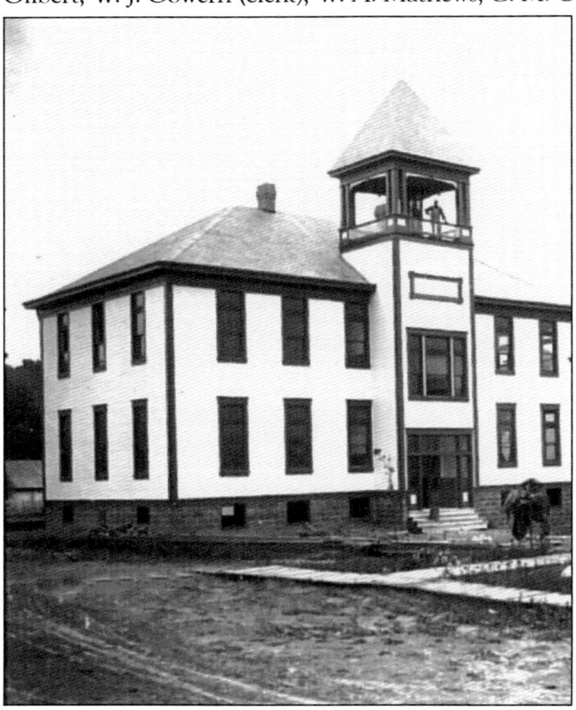

This White Lawn School building provided classrooms for more than 20 years until it was closed as a school in 1929. Canonsburg acquired the school from the Chartiers Township School District in 1923. The school would eventually be replaced by the Hawthorne School. The Scouts continued to use the property until it was razed in 1933. (Martin Estep.)

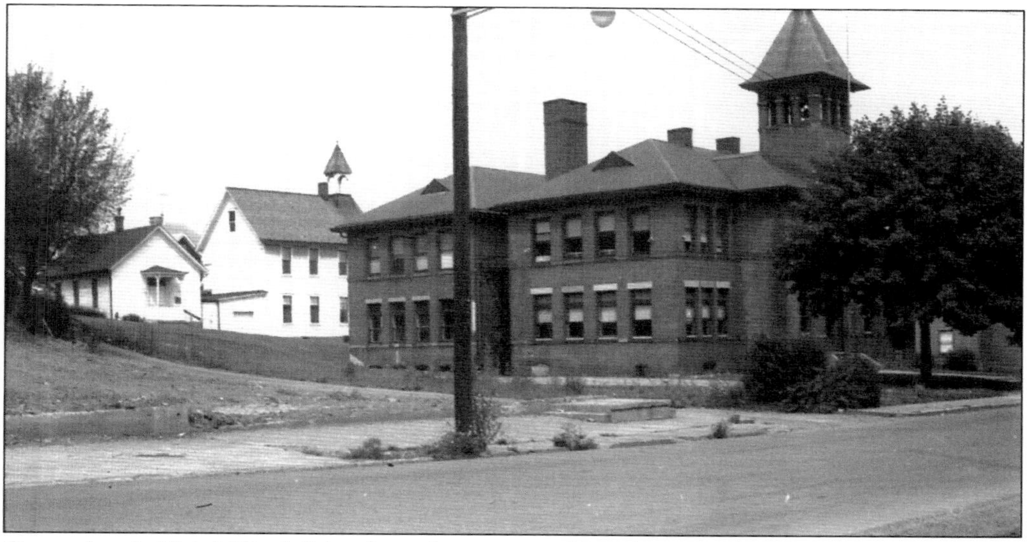

Canonsburg's Third Ward School on the corner of South Central and Elm Streets actually consisted of two separate buildings constructed in 1902 and 1907 to serve the expanding student enrollment. The buildings were joined in the middle by an additional hallway. It remained in use through the 1960s. (Ducky Swan.)

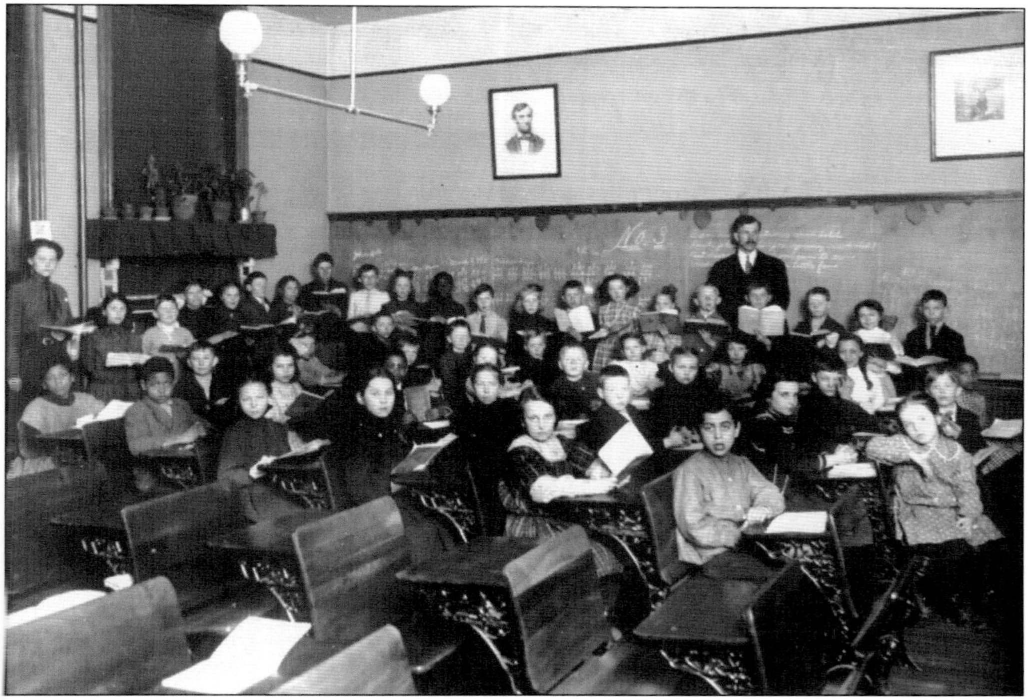

Third-grade students are seen in this example of classrooms found in the Third Ward School in 1906. Principal S. P. McWilliams is standing by the blackboard.

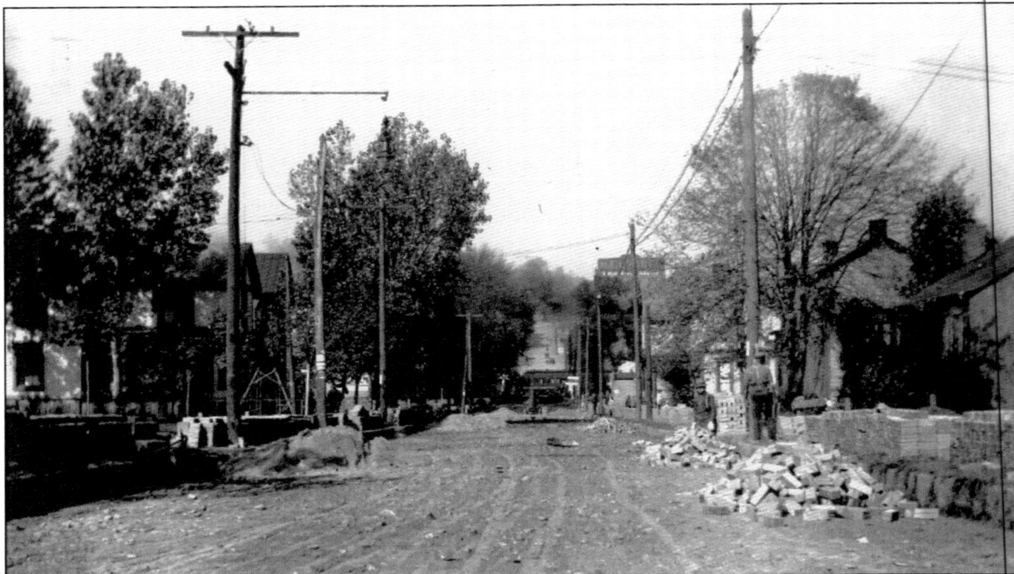

Road paving was first instituted in Canonsburg in 1903, with a plan devised to split the cost evenly between the borough and the landowners adjacent to the respective roads. Roads were initially paved with concrete and brick. All the major roads were completed by 1909. This photograph from October 27, 1911, shows work in progress on South Central Avenue. (Howard M. Taylor.)

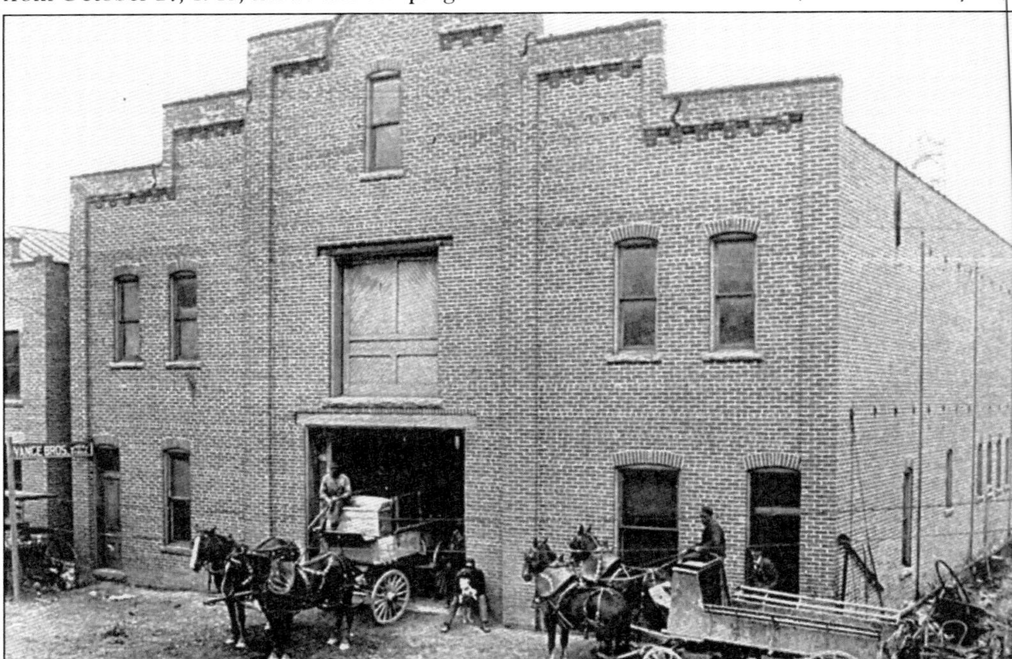

As the town expanded in the early 1900s, moving to a new location could have been just as much of a headache as it is today. To help with the process, the Canonsburg Transfer Company, owned by W. R. Enlow, offered a full range of services, including personal or business relocation, property transfer, and even plowing and fertilizing. One advertisement offered teams to transfer "anything moveable." (Canonsburg centennial booklet.)

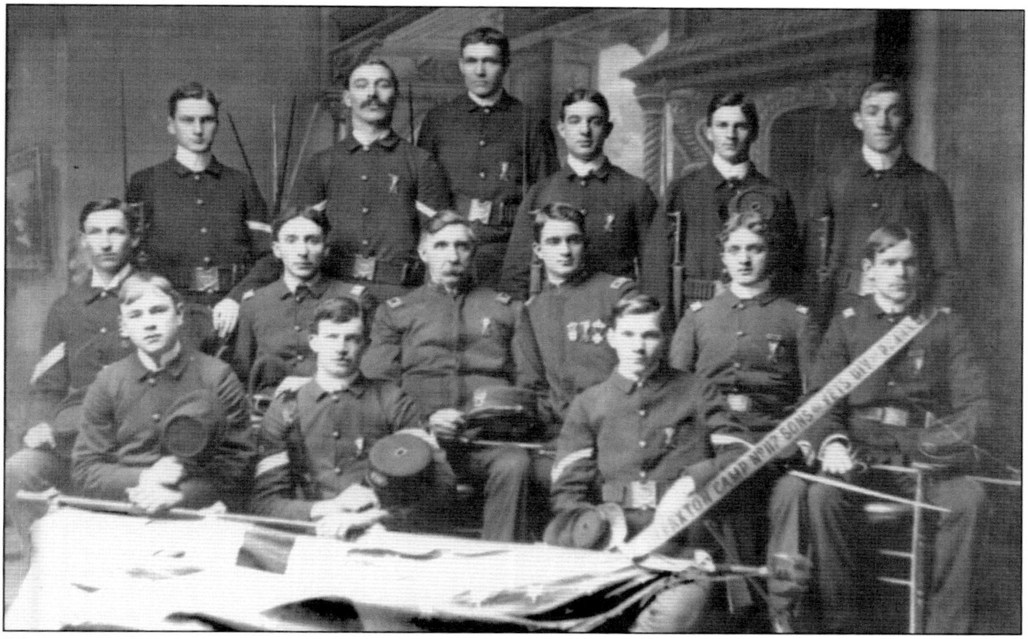

The Sons of Veterans was a society group that assisted the aging members of the Grand Army of the Republic (GAR) local branch. Among their duties was helping the GAR, which was made up of Civil War veterans, in honoring deceased members by decorating graves on Memorial Day.

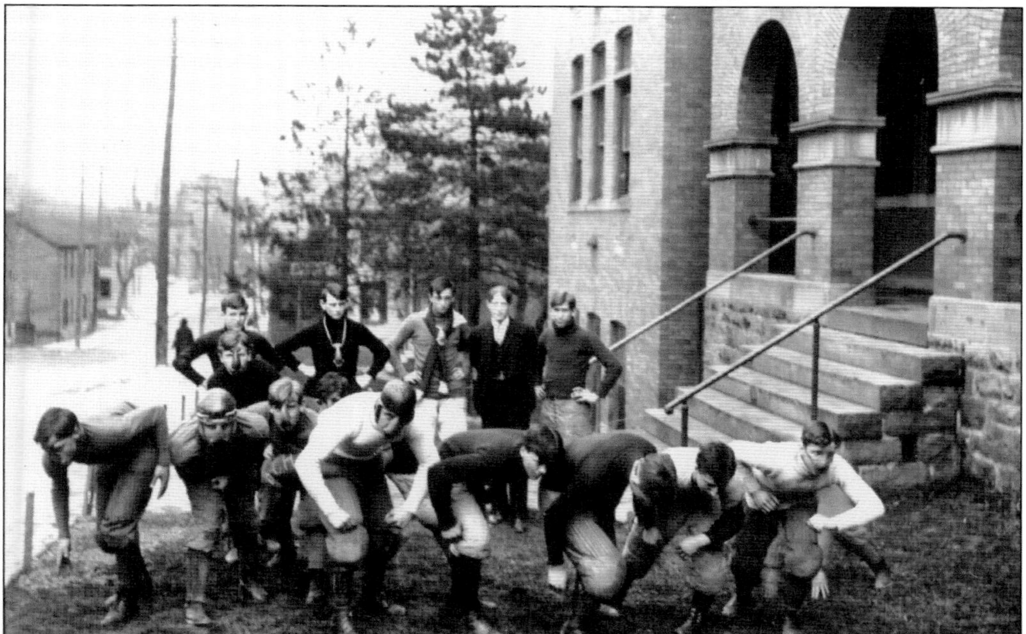

Canonsburg High School featured this lineup of players on its 1905 football team. From left to right are (first row) Howard Crane, Roy Richards, Sam Munnell (holding the ball), Bill Farrar, Art McPeake, John McWilliams, Waldo Whitely, and Fergus Smiley; (second row) Earl Forsythe, Paul Templeton, Harry Wassum, Walter Smith, and Russell Marple.

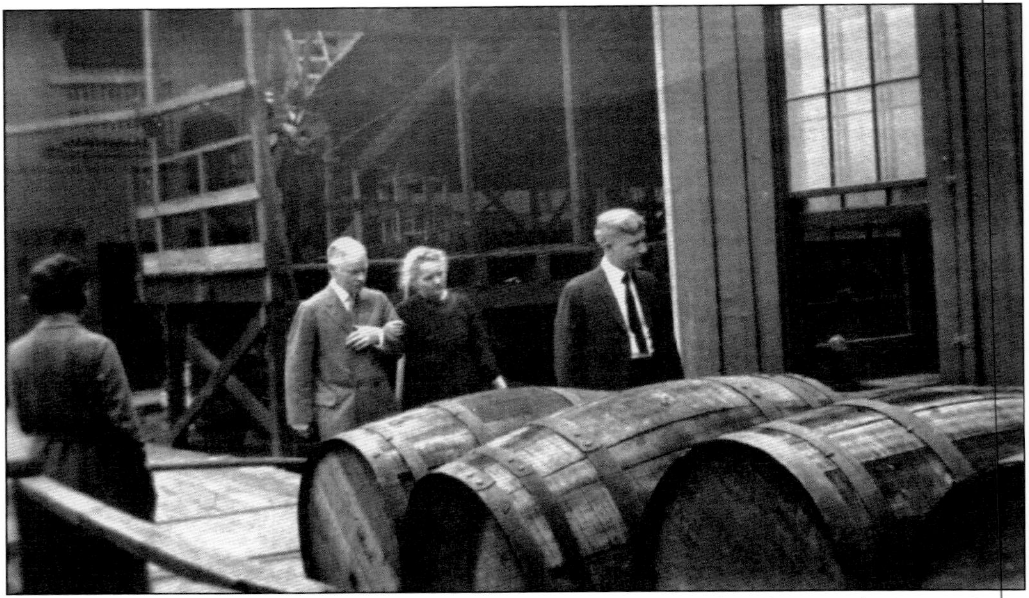

The employees of the Standard Chemical Company were honored with a visit by Marie Curie on May 21, 1921. Along with her husband Pierre, Curie is credited with discovering radium in 1898. As part of her tour of the United States, Curie was given a gift of one gram of radium by Pres. Warren Harding. (James T. Herron Sr.)

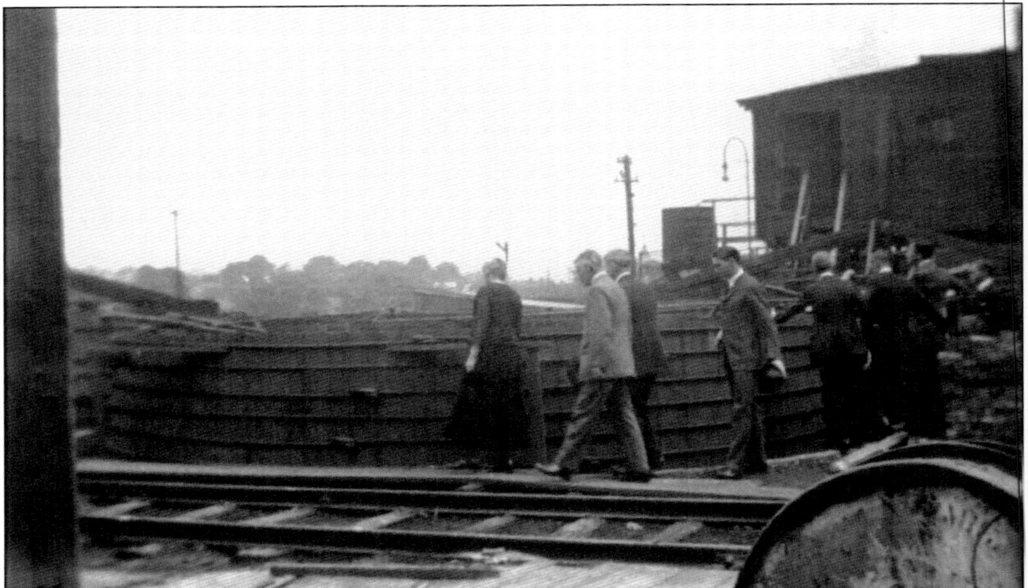

As part of the tour, Curie inspected the tank of vanadium acid liquor, a by-product of refining carnotite ore. She was joined on the tour by James G. Gray, president of Standard Chemical, and L. F. Vogt, works manager. Curie's daughter Irene accompanied her on the visit to Canonsburg. (James T. Herron Sr.)

Four

INDUSTRIAL ADVANCEMENTS

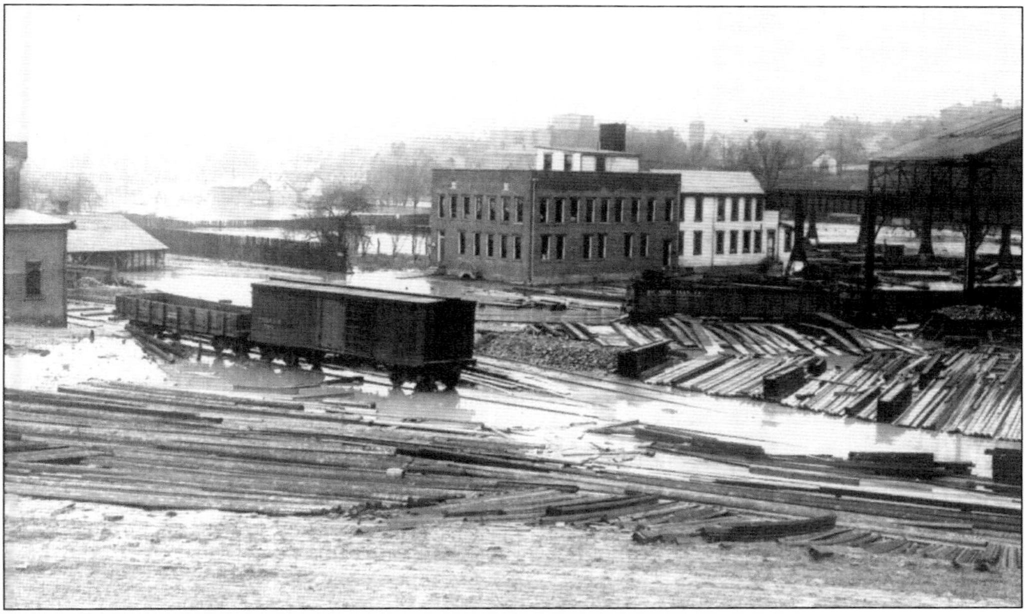

As with the Canonsburg Iron Mill, citizens formed a committee to bring another industrial plant into town in 1884, when a deal was struck with the Pittsburgh Architectural Iron Works. In 1896, the new plant began business as the Fort Pitt Bridge Works. Work remained steady through the decades, but the plant, seen here after the 1912 flood, finally closed its doors on September 30, 1981.

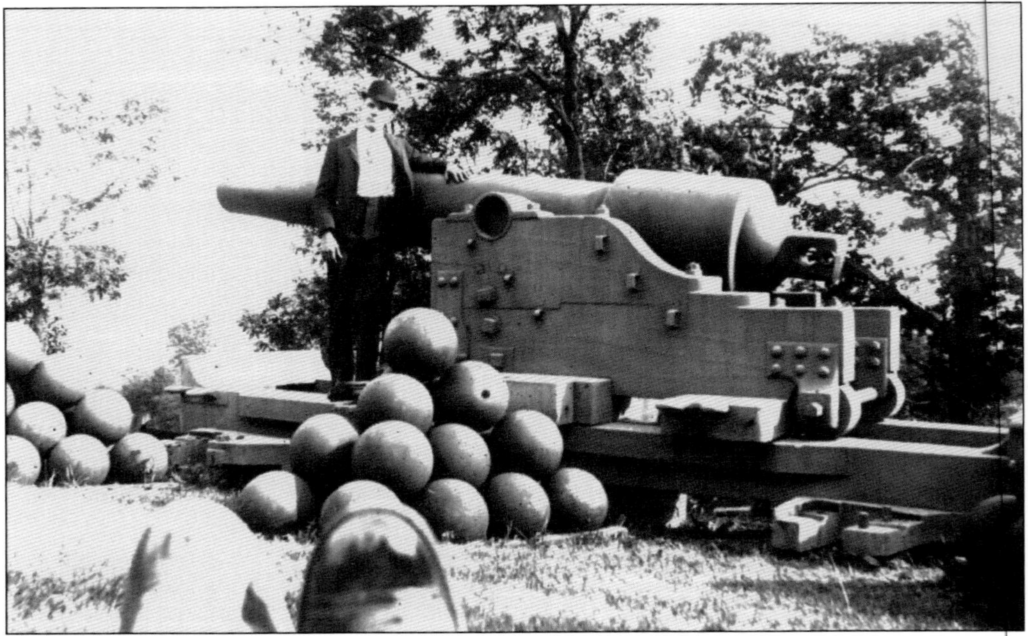

Although the town is named after John Canon, Canonsburg has actually displayed a number of cannons over the years. This Civil War parrot gun is seen in a photograph from around 1900. The gun resided in the cemetery until the 1940s, although the gun carriage and wheels were removed sometime soon after this photograph was taken, leaving only the barrel.

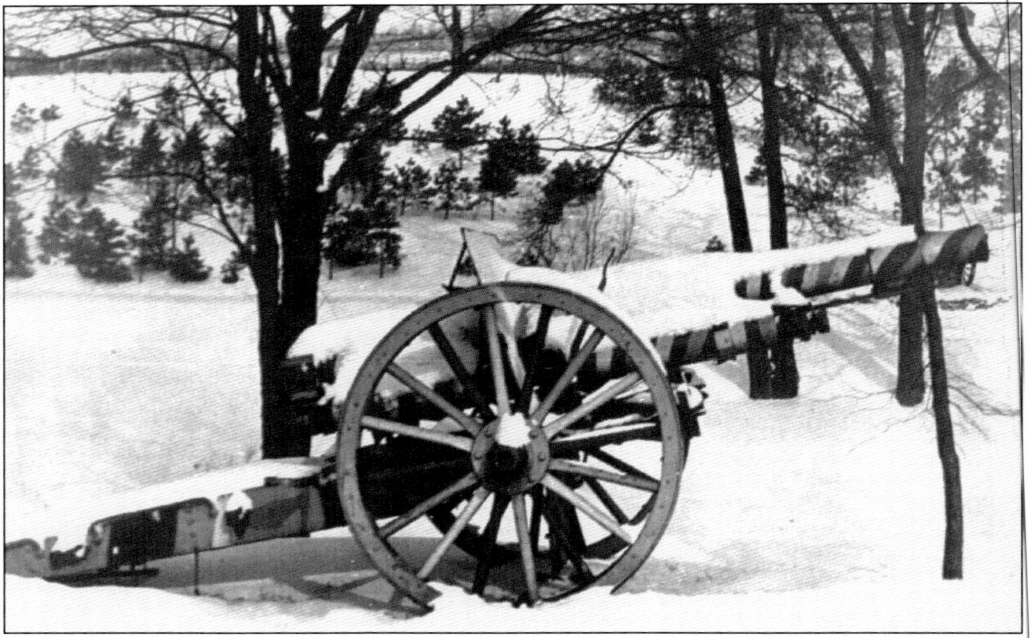

The town also had two World War I–era German cannons on display in the 1930s, as shown in this wintry photograph, given by a congressman from the Aberdeen Proving Grounds. However, all three canons were taken away to be melted down for scrap during the early days of World War II. (Chuck Springer.)

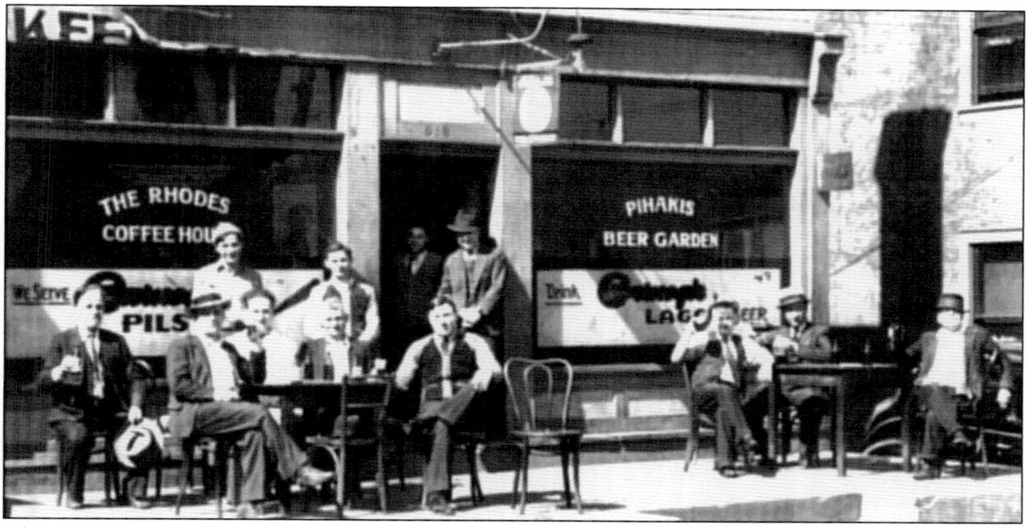

The Pihakis Beer Garden, owned by Michael Pihakis, was a popular destination for Greek men in the East End neighborhoods. (Manuel Pihakis.)

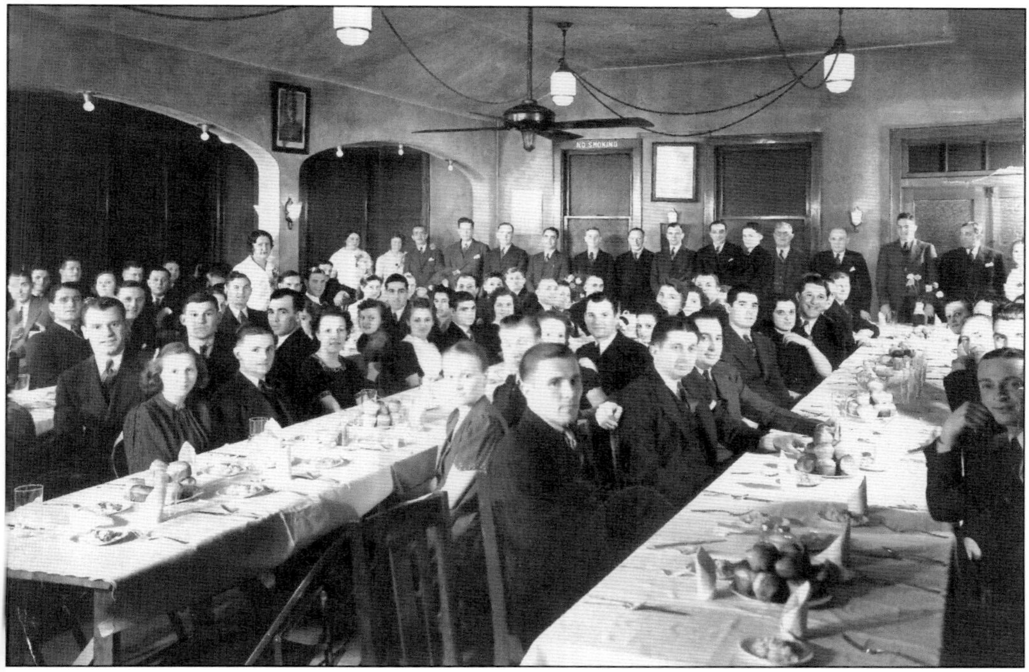

The Hofbrau on Highland Avenue has been a popular site for meetings and banquets, including this athletic dinner from 1939.

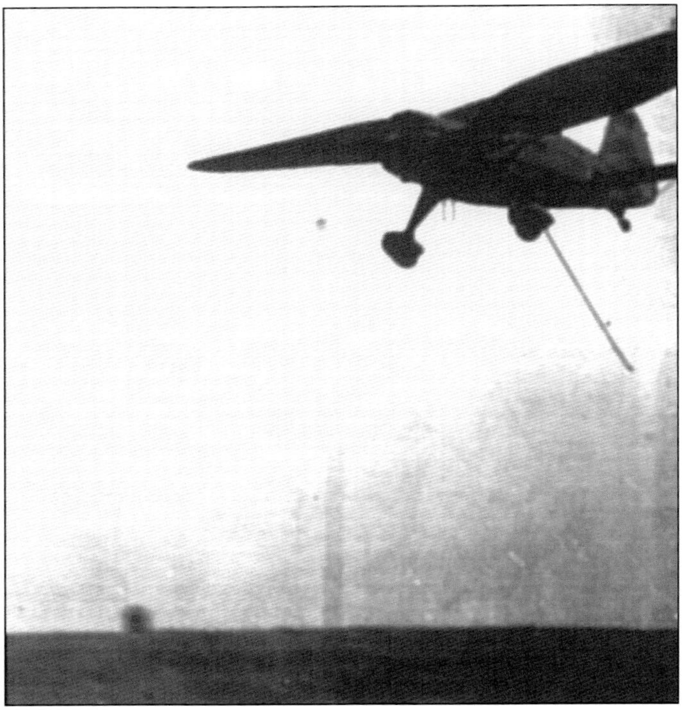

Although Canonsburg never had its own airport, the town still found a way to participate in airmail service. Canonsburg became one of 22 locations to feature the Adams Pick-up Mail System for the All-American Airlines, beginning in November 1940. Mail would be hung in a sack between two poles and subsequently snatched by the pilot of a low-flying Radiant or Cessna-style mail plane. (Virginia Arnal.)

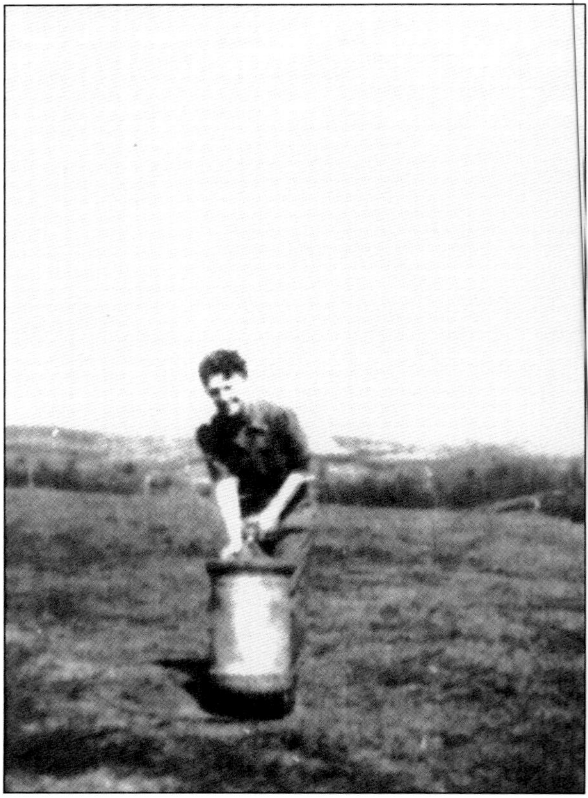

On a return flight, mail would be dropped in special postal bags. The service also included stops in Pittsburgh, Ohio, West Virginia, and Kentucky. All-American Airlines employee Virginia Arnal is seen here picking up one of the special mail sacks dropped by the plane. The service continued until 1949. (Virginia Arnal.)

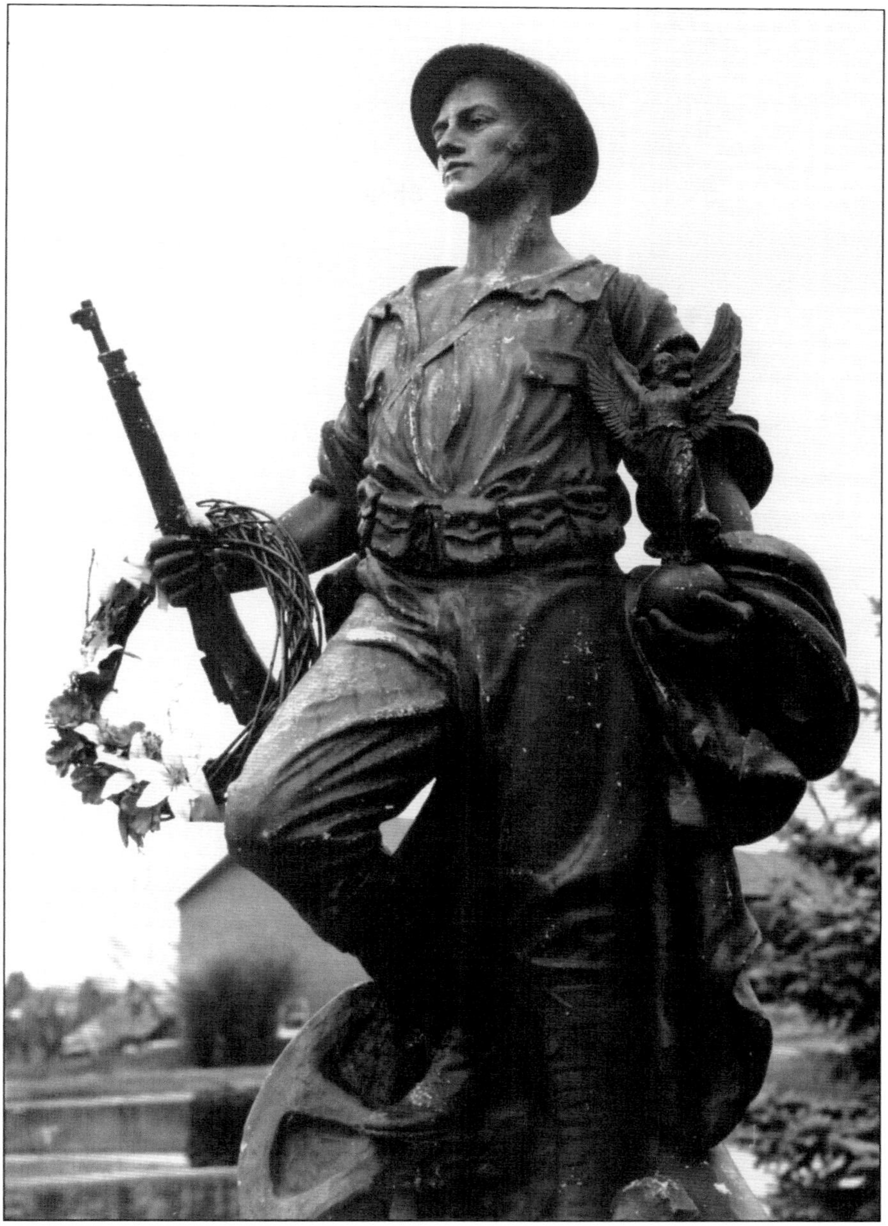

On Memorial Day 1924, a statue was dedicated to honor Canonsburg's veterans. The statue was commissioned by the Mothers of Democracy, a local women's organization formed in 1918 to support soldiers and their families. Donations were solicited to help pay for the tribute. The figure was designed by Giuseppe Moretti, a noted sculptor of statues in Pittsburgh. Moretti surprised the Mothers of Democracy with his interpretation. The women's group had expected a statue featuring a fierce soldier in battle, although Moretti's model was a more casual young man returning home. The soldier also carried a winged victory in his left hand, a symbol of victory. At the dedication ceremony in 1924, three World War I veterans were honored for their service. A Memorial Day service is conducted each year at the statue, located at the corner of College Street and Central Avenue. (James T. Herron.)

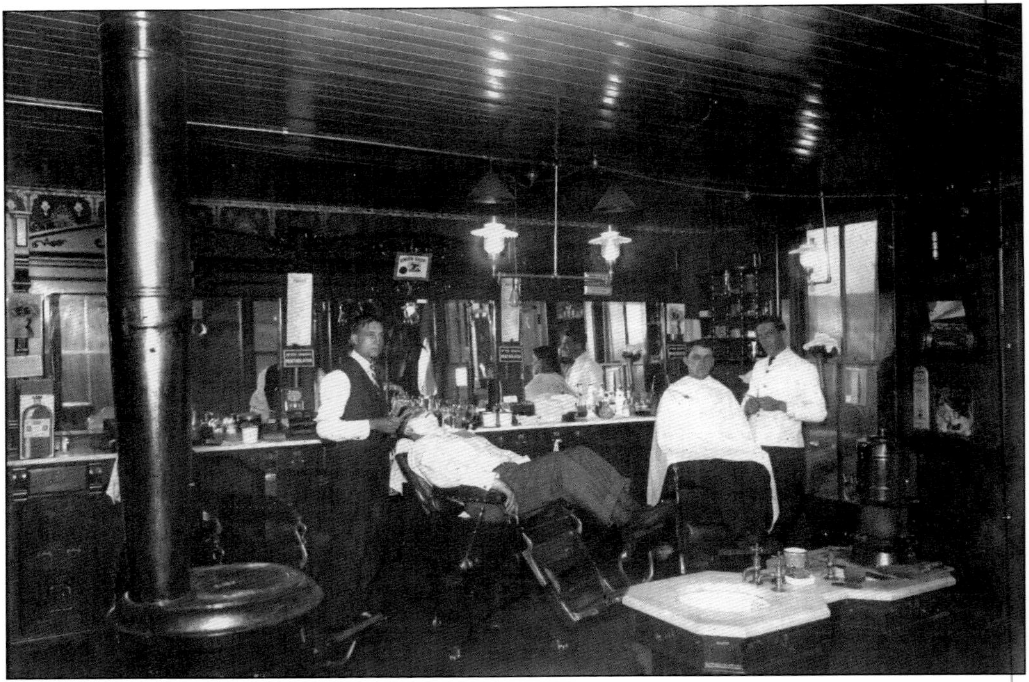

Canonsburg has always enjoyed a rich tradition of barbers, dating back to Thomas Bishop Sluby around 1859, who was followed in succession by son George and grandson Paxton. This 1912 photograph shows the staff and customers of the Swihart Barber Shop. Ernest Hampson Sr. is on the left, preparing a razor shave. (Lloyd Hampson.)

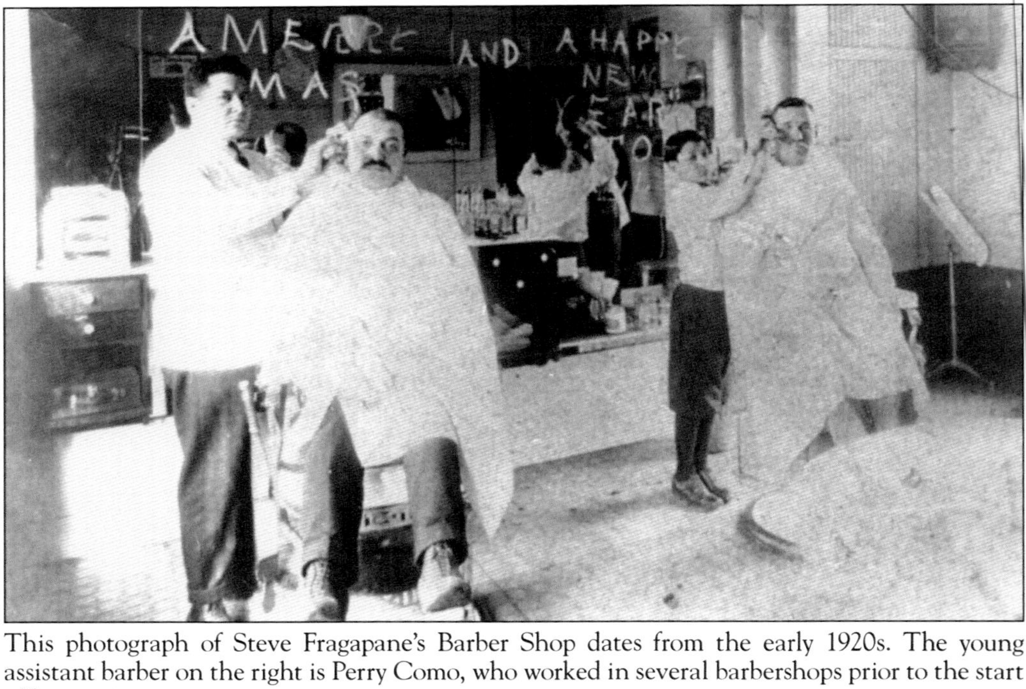

This photograph of Steve Fragapane's Barber Shop dates from the early 1920s. The young assistant barber on the right is Perry Como, who worked in several barbershops prior to the start of his singing career.

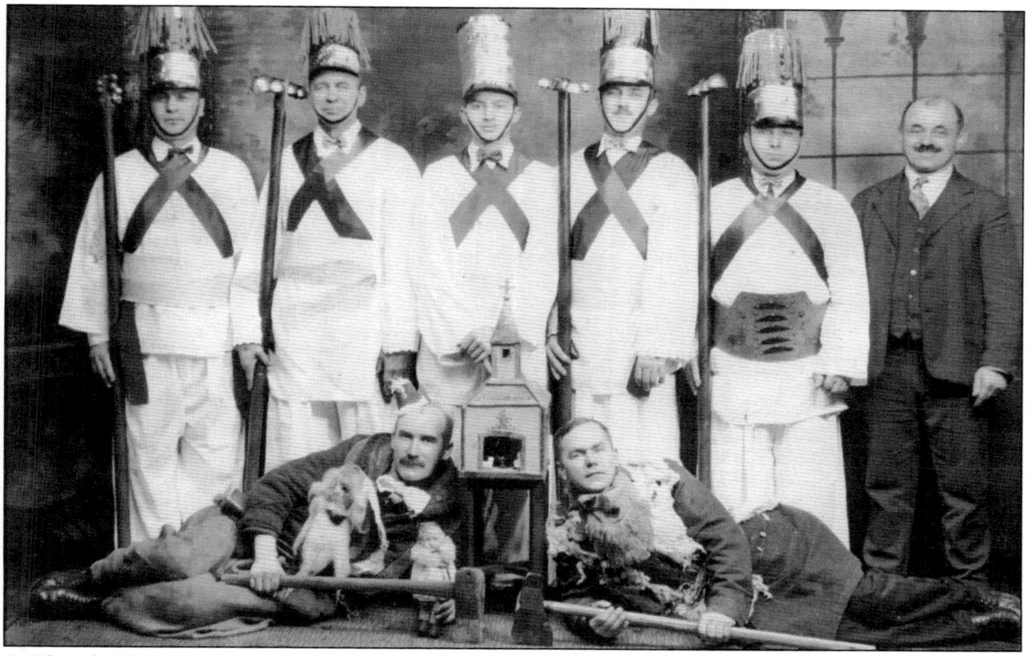

A Slovak Christmas program is captured in this photograph from around 1930. Portraying the shepherds in the rear are, from left to right, Joseph Kacvinsky, Mr. Franko, Martin Gonglik, unidentified, Vincent Shimko, and Mr. Petros, the show's director. The gentleman on the bottom right is identified as ? Spilak, while the name of the bottom left is unknown. (Joseph A. Solobay collection.)

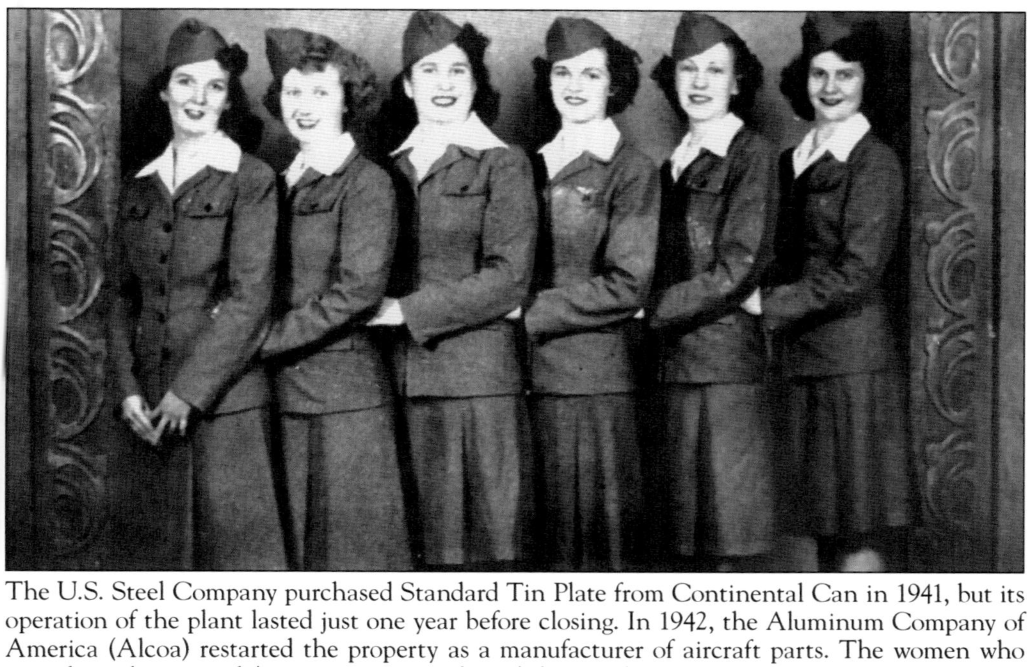

The U.S. Steel Company purchased Standard Tin Plate from Continental Can in 1941, but its operation of the plant lasted just one year before closing. In 1942, the Aluminum Company of America (Alcoa) restarted the property as a manufacturer of aircraft parts. The women who served as plant guards/receptionists are, from left to right, M. J. Russ, M. McQuade, Helen Babyak, B. Kauffield, G. Osiechi, and K. Superich. (Alcoa.)

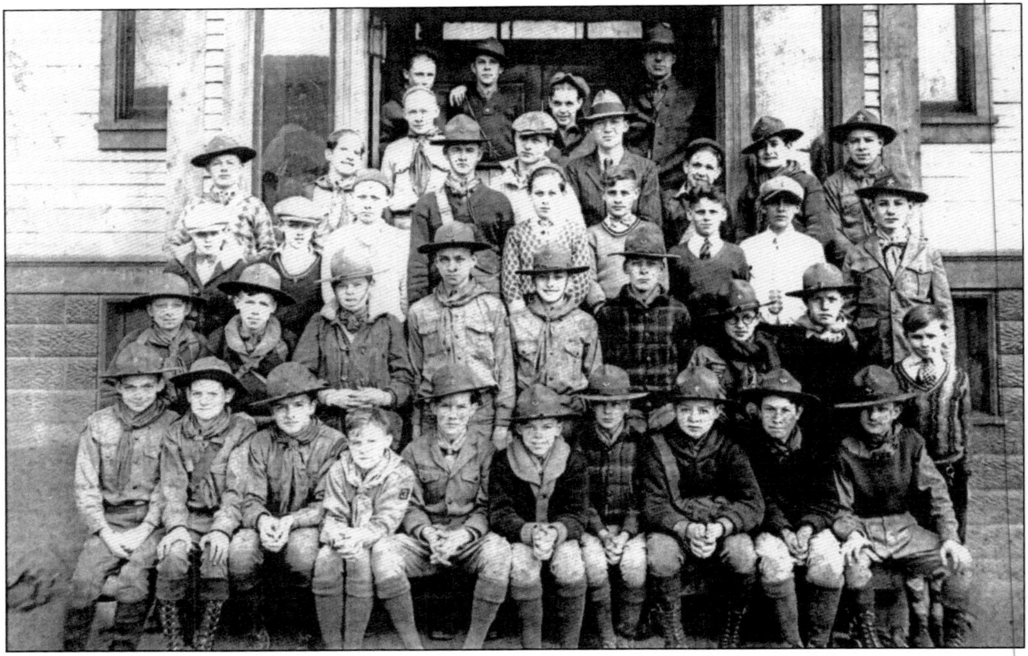

The Boy Scouts of America in Canonsburg dates back to the early years of the organization in the second decade of the 20th century. This troop photograph dates from around the 1930s, when the number of boys in one troop even exceeded national limits. O. Northen, seen in the back upper right, served as scoutmaster of this troop. (Daily Notes.)

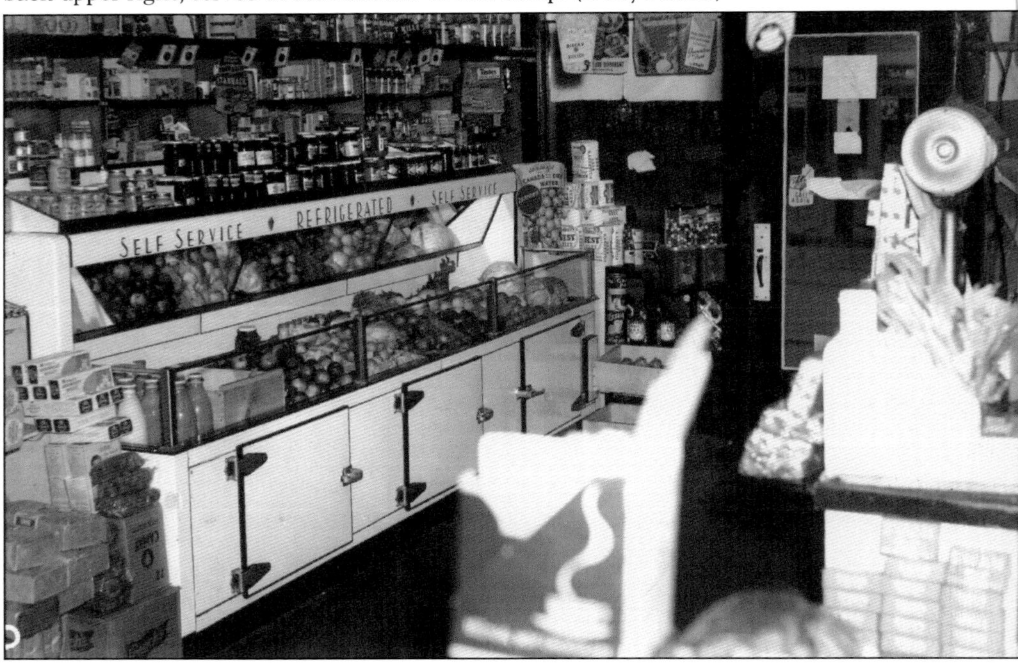

This image of the aptly named Tiny Store provides a glimpse of the interior of a traditional mom-and-pop grocery market of the 1930s and 1940s. The store continues to operate into the present day on West Pike Street. (Sylvia DeFilippo and Joan Prince.)

Five

PROMINENT LANDMARKS

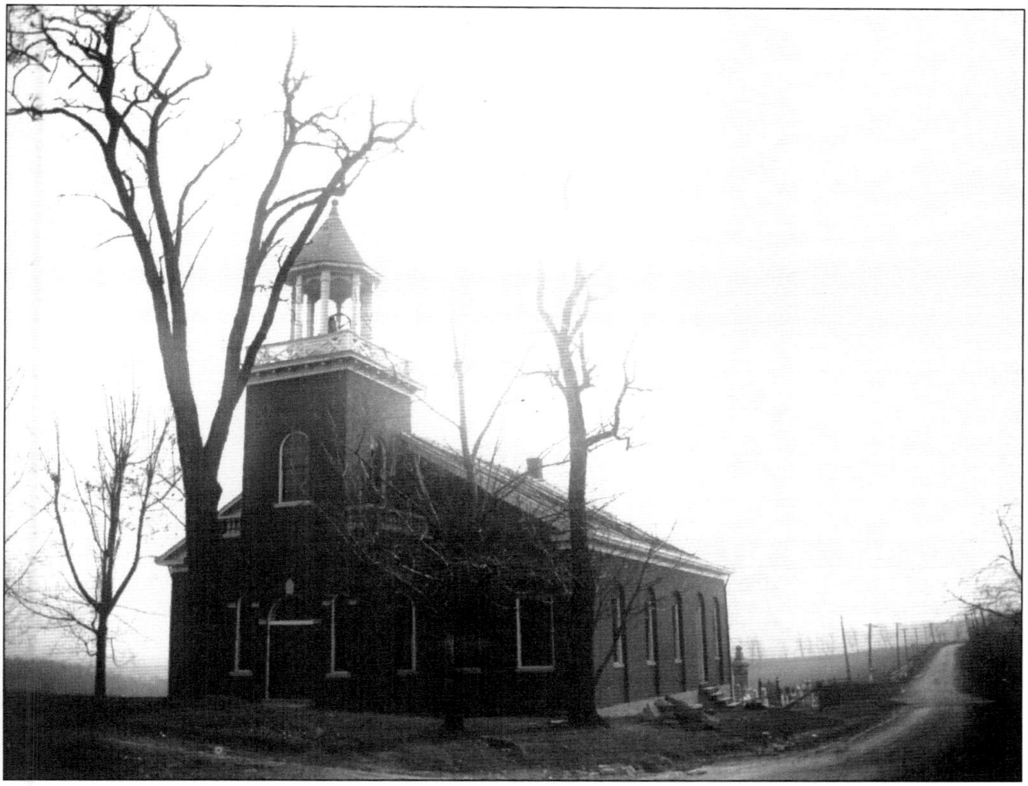

Rev. John McMillan started the Chartiers Hill Presbyterian Church in 1775 and served as pastor for 54 years until his retirement in 1830. The church's present building was constructed in 1841 and is seen here in a photograph from the early 1900s, long before the nearby road became the busy Route 19 that exists today.

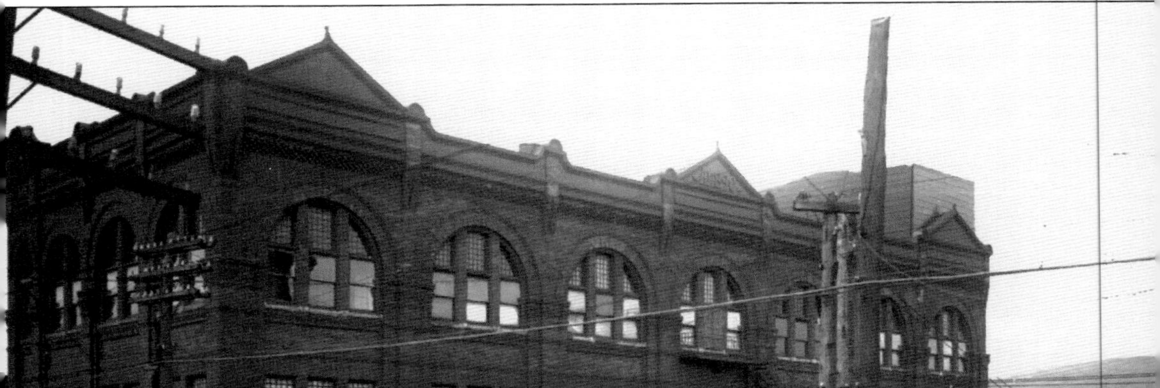

The worst disaster in Canonsburg's history came on August 26, 1911, when 26 people lost their lives at the Morgan Building Opera House, located at Pike Street and Central Avenue. The building had been opened since 1890, offering a variety of entertainment presentations. During an early-evening film presentation of *The New Church Carpet*, a spectator misinterpreted a spark that had been displayed from the movie projector. There had never been any actual danger, as a new fireproof projection booth had been installed six months prior to the events of the tragedy. When the spectator cried out "Fire!" a panic ensued in the outer lobby among customers waiting for the later show. Inside the theater, the show continued, although the panicked crowd in the halls rushed toward the one available staircase to the street below, resulting in a fatal pileup of bodies. There had been theories that the outer door only opened inward, adding to the tragedy, although this was proven to be untrue. (Martin Estep.)

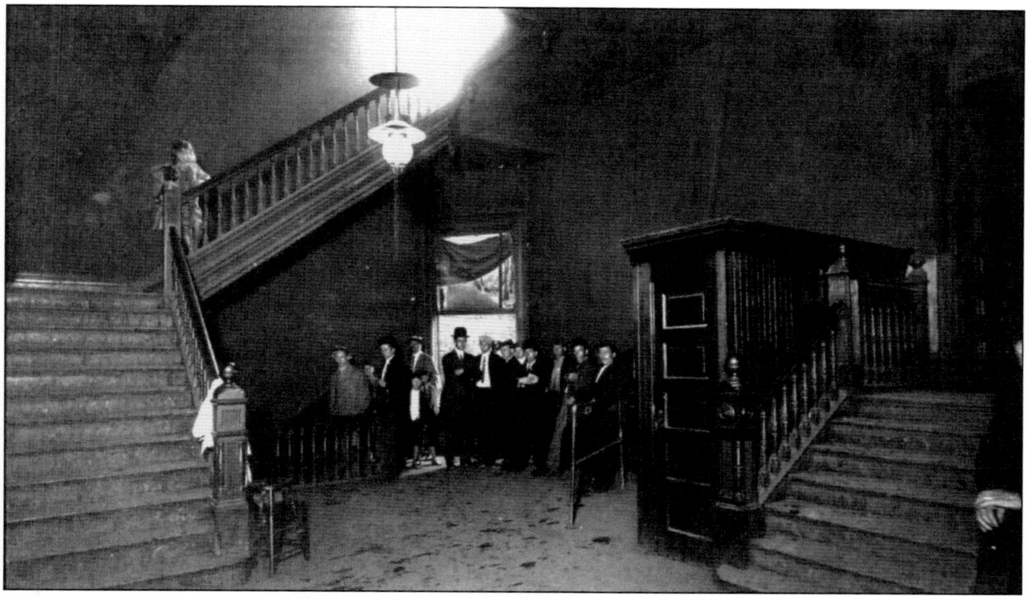

The second-floor lobby of the Morgan Building Opera House was the site of the start of the panic among customers. Attendees for the second showing would often mingle in the center of the lobby or line up along the edges of the balcony and gallery staircase to the left, or on the short auditorium staircase to the left. When the alert was yelled, the awaiting customers stampeded down the center staircase, leading out of the theater. (Weller Studio.)

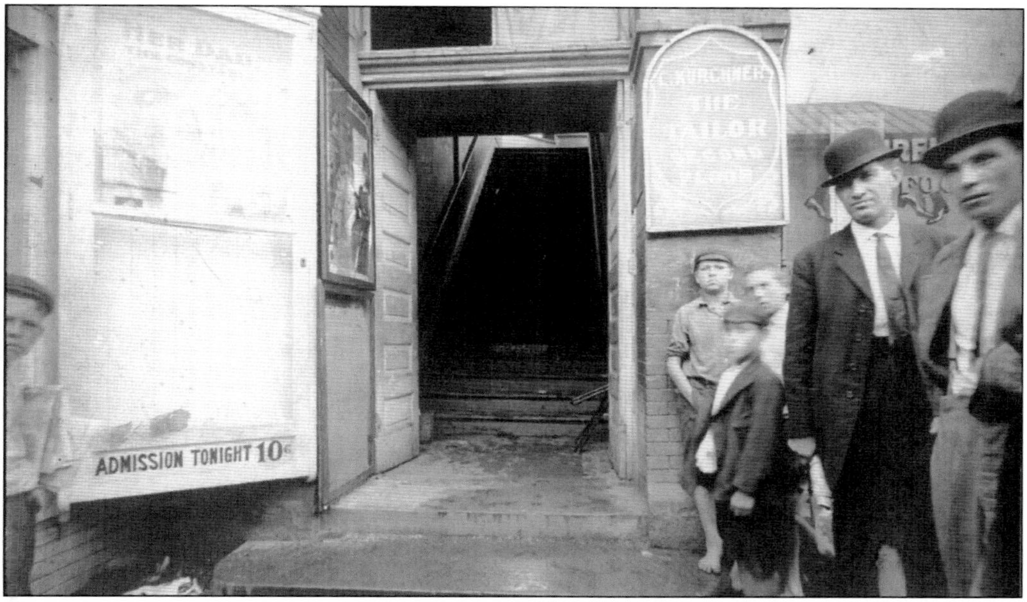

This one staircase provided the escape for most of the panicking crowd, although some may have used an outer fire escape staircase. Fleeing customers tripped over each other and piled on top of each other, resulting in deaths that the coroner's ruling described as due to suffocation and internal injuries. One death was even to a passerby attempting to enter and provide assistance. The opera house never reopened as an entertainment venue and was later renovated into apartments. (Weller Studio.)

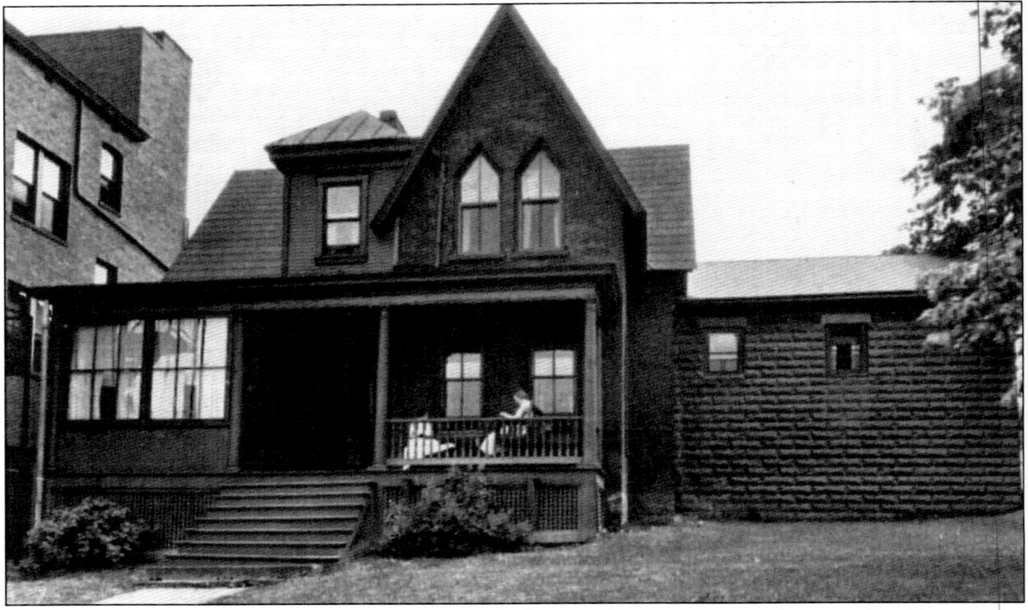

Canonsburg's first hospital came in the form of a house that was previously owned by Rev. James Barr. It was purchased by the Canonsburg General Hospital Association, which was formed in 1903. By 1904, the house had been converted into a hospital with just two patient rooms, although another four rooms would be added in 1907. (Canonsburg General Hospital.)

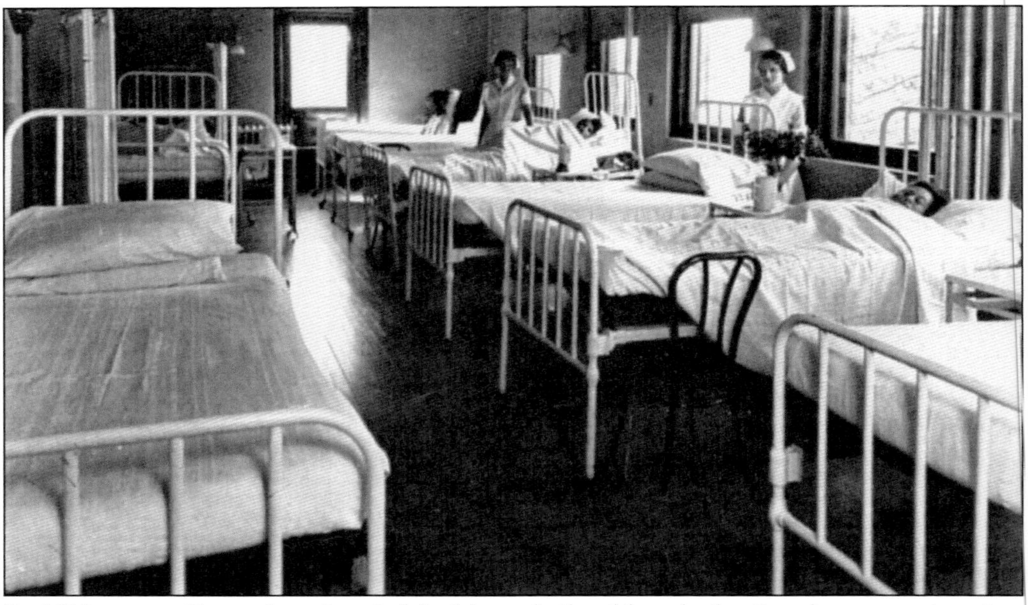

By 1915, a new Canonsburg hospital had been built, although the Barr house continued to remain in use as a nursing school and students' residence. A women's ward from its days as a hospital is seen here. (Canonsburg General Hospital.)

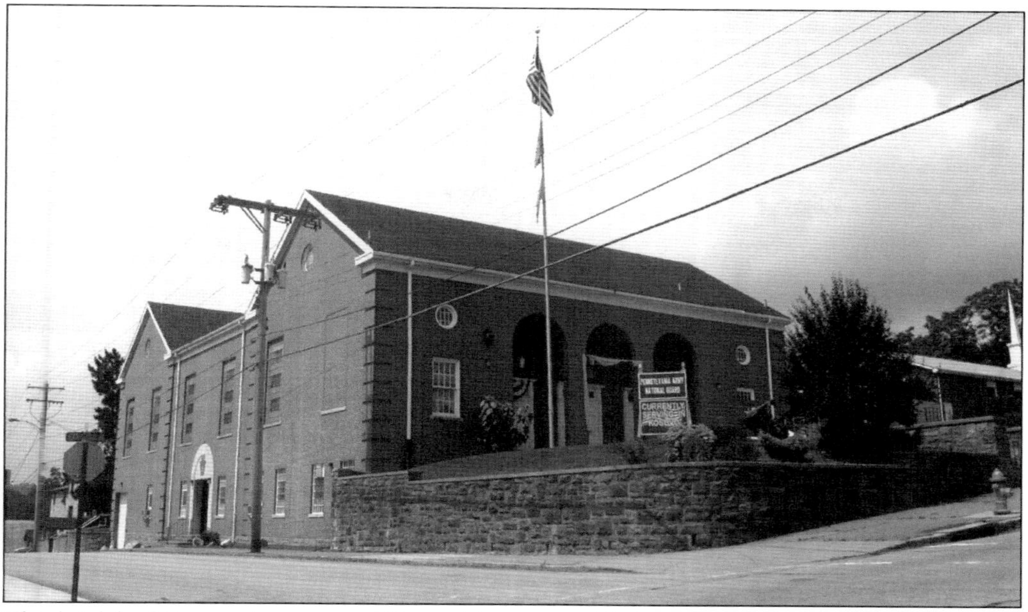

This brick building on the corner of Central Avenue and College Street served as the new armory for the 108th Hospital Company of the 103rd Medical Regiment. Opened in 1938, it provided facilities for drill and training exercises. In recent decades, it has served as an auditorium for school events, trade shows, and athletic competitions. (James T. Herron.)

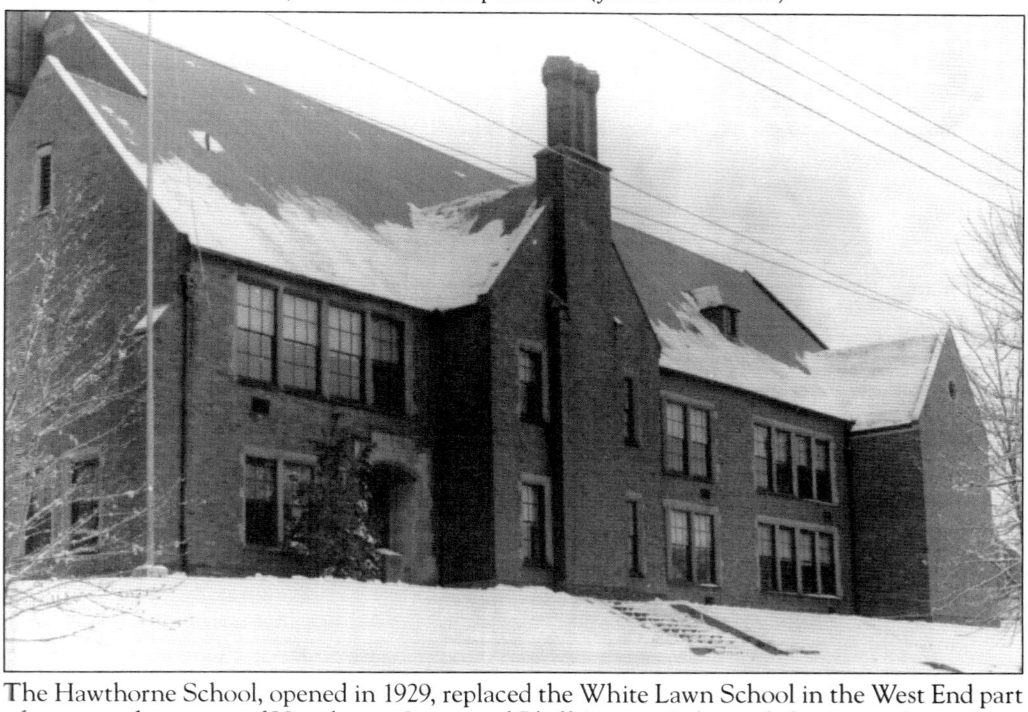

The Hawthorne School, opened in 1929, replaced the White Lawn School in the West End part of town on the corner of Hawthorne Street and Bluff Avenue. It housed classrooms for students in grades one through six. The upscale-looking, Tudor-style building was designated as a historic landmark in 1986.

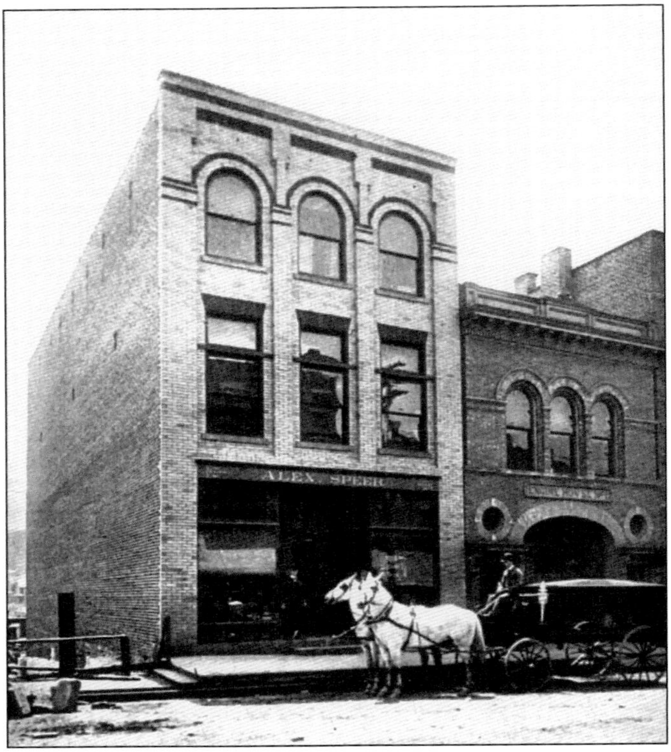

The only elevator in Canonsburg in 1902 could be found in this location, the Alex Speer Building, located adjacent to the borough building and fire station. Speer had purchased the undertaking business from Daniel Day in 1894 and eventually moved the business to this new structure following the 1898 fire. (Ern Weller.)

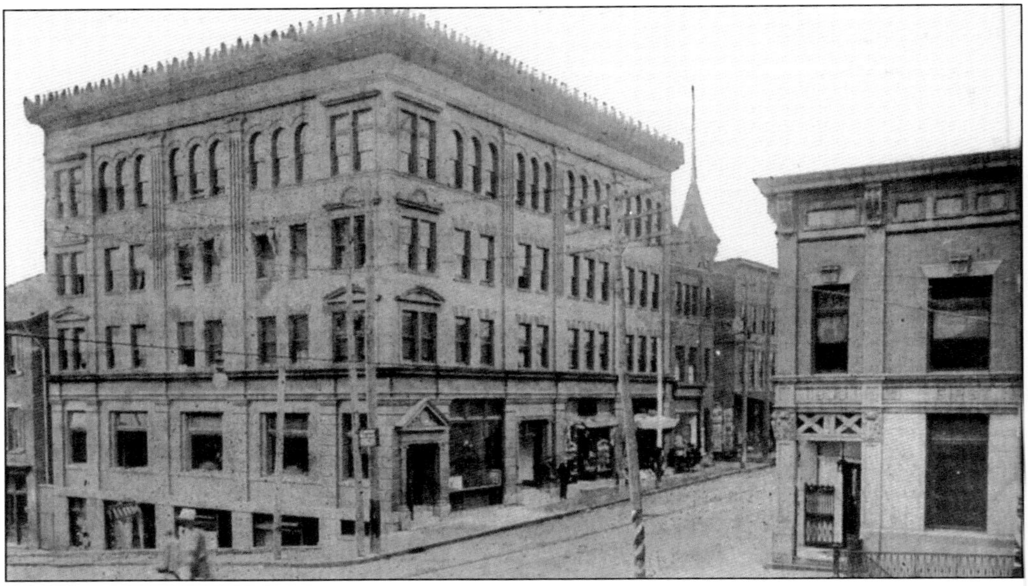

Two notable financial institutions shared the corners of Pike Street and Central Avenue. The building on the left housed the Citizens' Trust Company, while the building on the right was home to the First National Bank of Canonsburg. As with other banks, First National was crippled by the stock market crash of 1929 and the runs on currency that followed. Despite a slight change in name designed to create a new line of credit in 1933, the bank eventually closed for good in 1940.

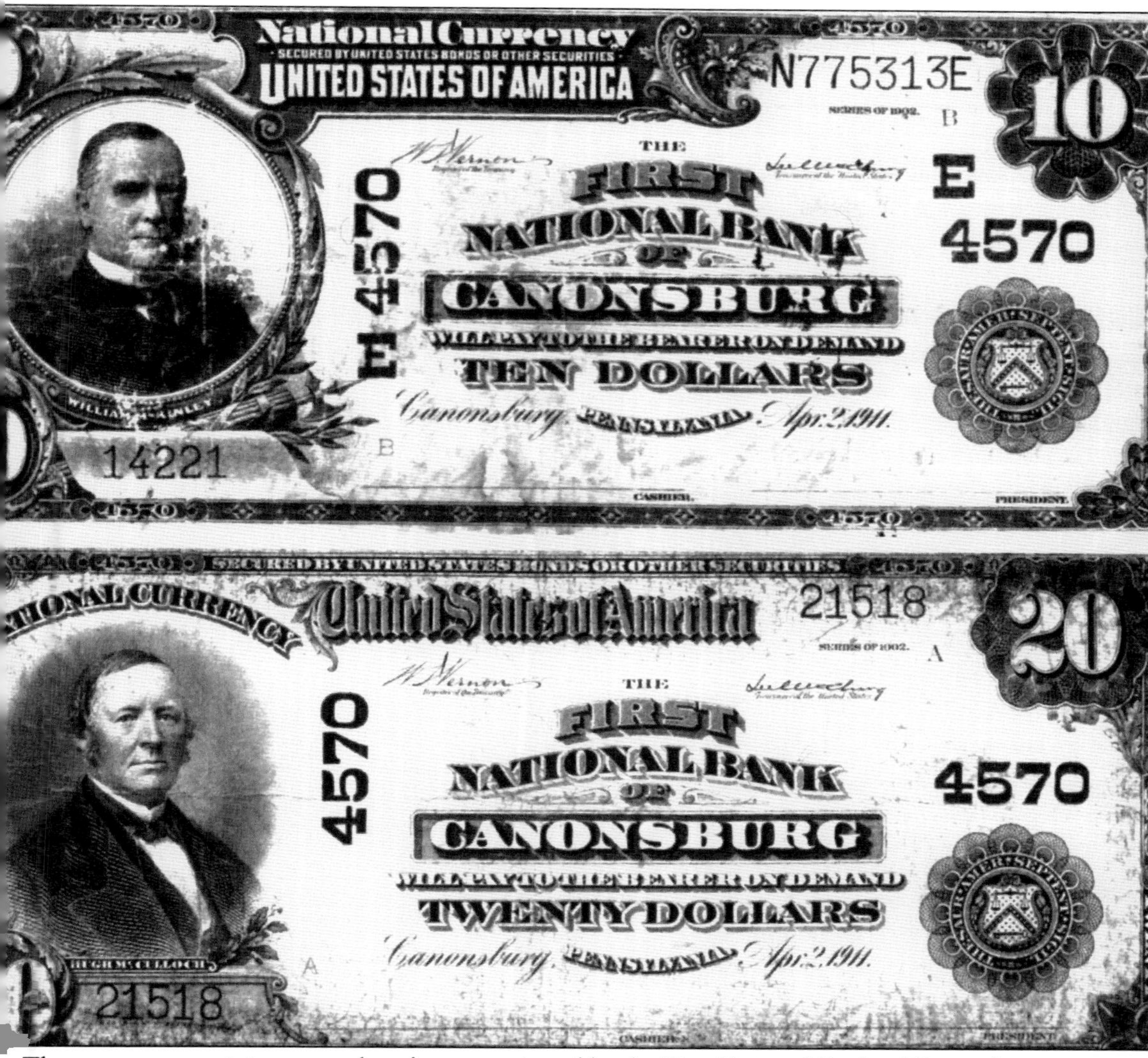

These are rare surviving examples of currency issued by the First National Bank of Canonsburg in the early 1900s. These bills featured the images of Pres. William McKinley on the $10 note and Hugh McCulloch, secretary of the treasury in the last days of the Abraham Lincoln administration, on the $20 bill. (Raymond E. O'Shinski collection.)

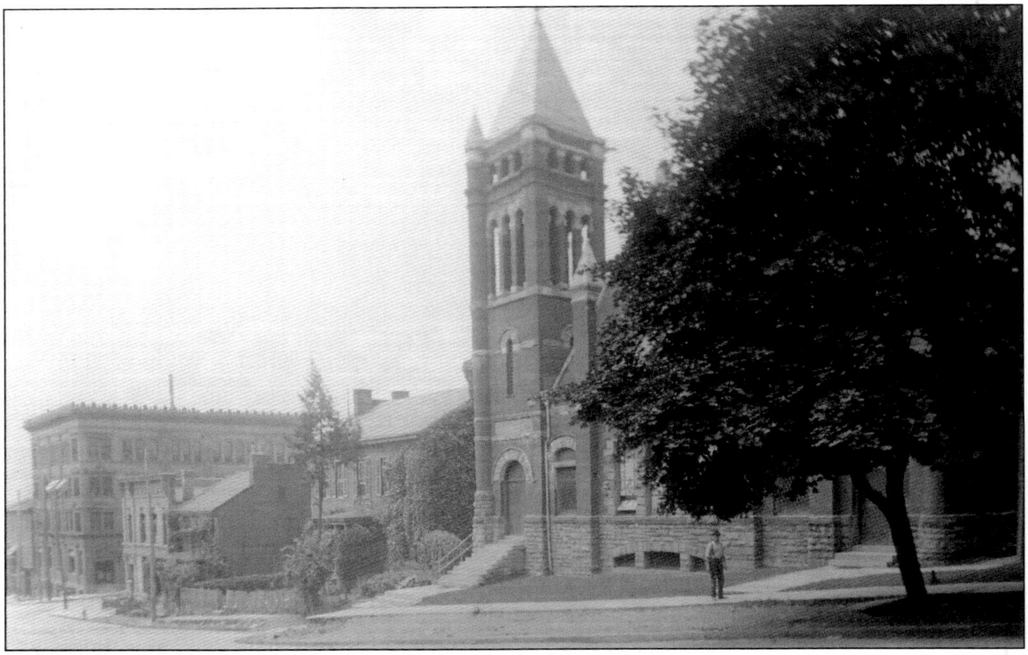

The First Presbyterian Church was formed in 1887 when members of the Canonsburg Presbyterian Church elected to rename and move off the college campus. After several years of meeting at a nearby skating rink, this new church building was opened in 1880 with its first pastor, Rev. Charles H. Pridgeon. (Martin Estep.)

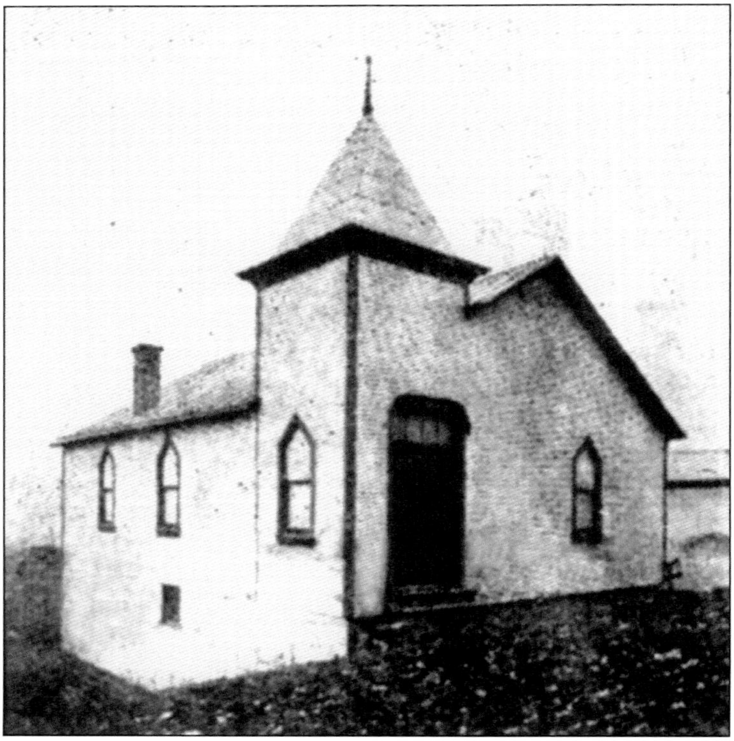

From 1908 until 1970, this Vine Street church served as the home of the Mount Olive Baptist Church. Although its Canonsburg roots date back to 1901, the church was not granted a charter until 1946. The congregation relocated to the vacant former United Presbyterian Church on Greenside Avenue in November 1970. (Daily Notes.)

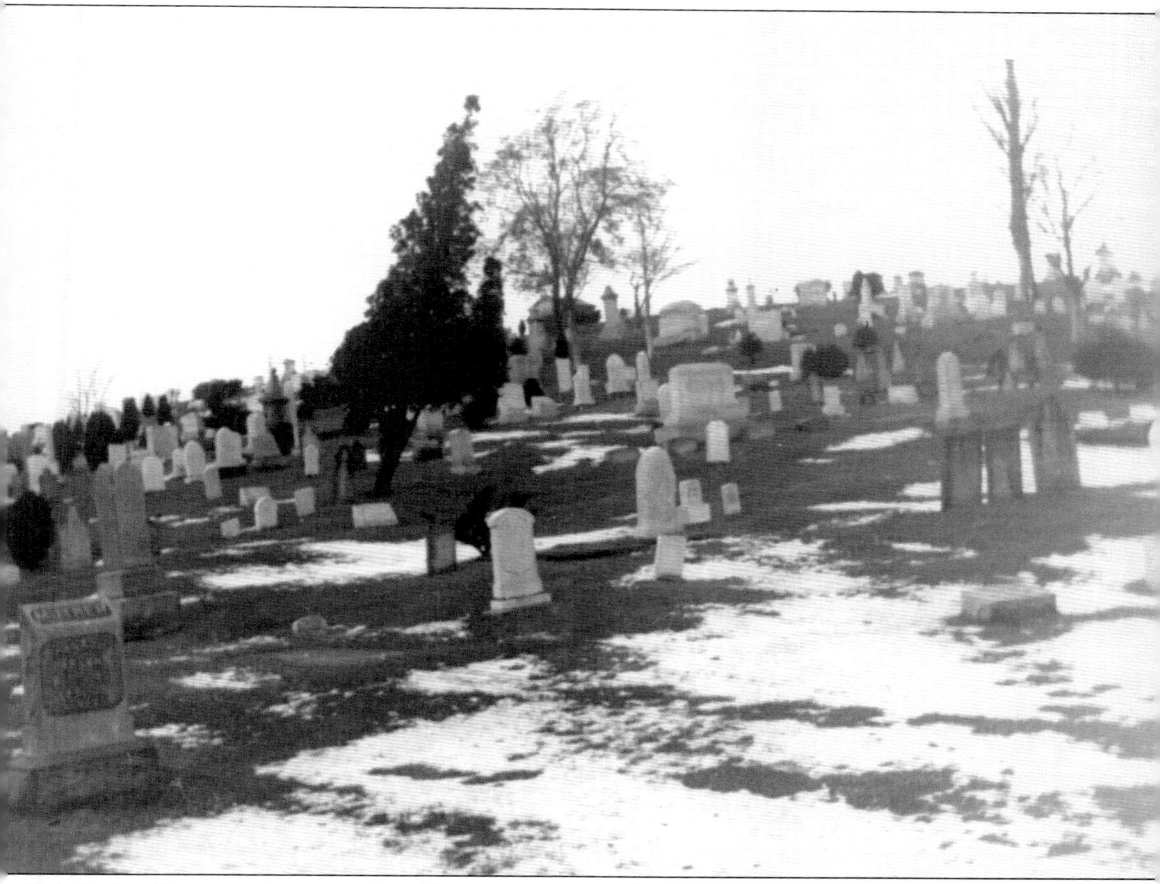

Oak Spring Cemetery is among the oldest cemeteries in Canonsburg. Its first known burial took place in 1780. At the time, the land was part of the property of Chartiers Associate Congregation Church. When the church moved to West Pike Street in 1869, the cemetery was placed under the control of the newly formed Oak Spring Cemetery Company. Since its beginnings, the property has expanded from a mere 6 acres in size to nearly 100 acres. Improved systems for grave allotments have been implemented as well. Special sections are designated for veterans of various battles, and several church groups have private sections. The view here is of "the Old Yard," containing some of the oldest graves in a lot near where the old Congregation church used to stand. All told, more than 20,000 burials have taken place in Oak Spring Cemetery. During the history of the cemetery, five generations of the Wilson family have served as caretakers. (Joseph A. Solobay collection.)

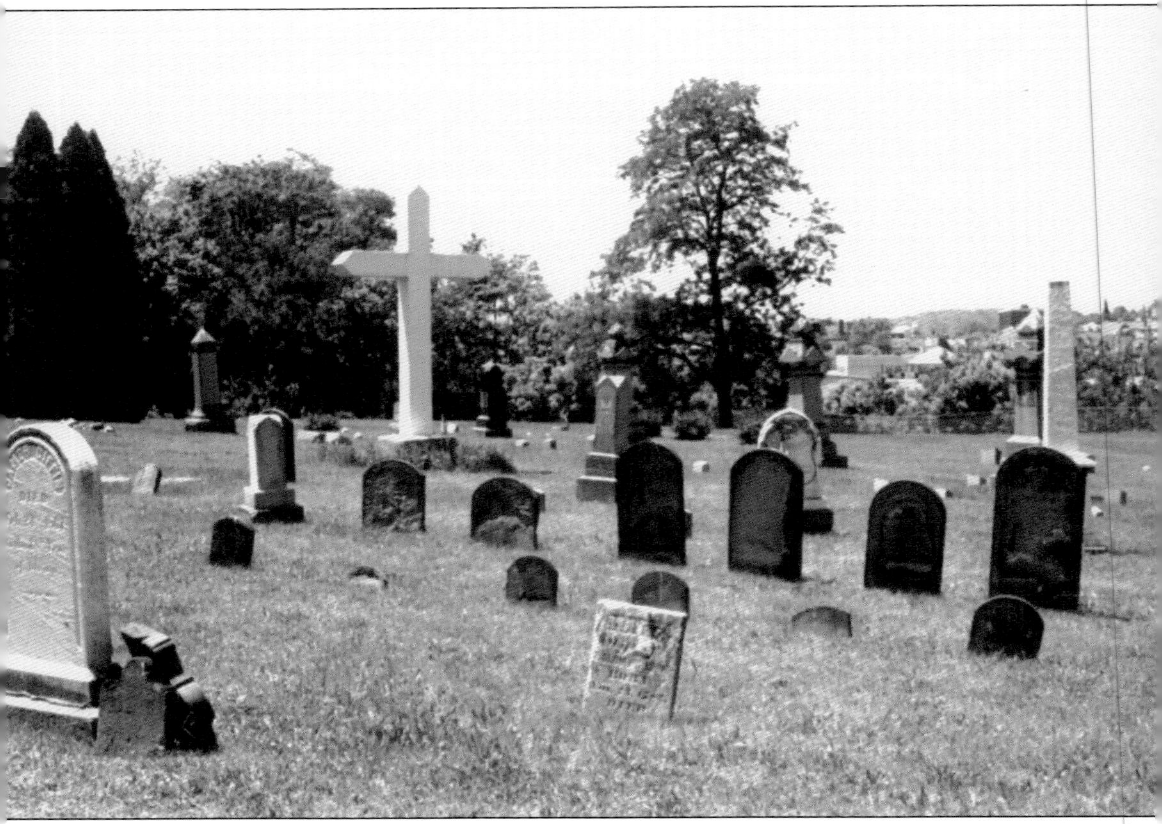

The Speer Spring Cemetery was created in 1832 as part of the Speer Spring Associate Reformed Presbyterian Church, with its first burial being officiated in 1834. The adjoining Old Bridge Church was closed in 1885 when the congregation moved to a new location on Greenside Avenue. In 1889, the Speer Spring Cemetery Company was formed to handle the property when the church relocated. Over the decades, the cemetery has fallen into periods of disarray, with little maintenance provided to the grounds. Several efforts have been made to clean up the cemetery. The last major cleanup effort took place in 1977, when the large white cross, seen here, was erected to honor the unidentified remains buried in the cemetery. A local group of volunteers now regularly cares for the grounds. The last burial on the grounds took place in 1967, and many victims of the Morgan Building Opera House tragedy are also interred at the cemetery. (Gina Nestor.)

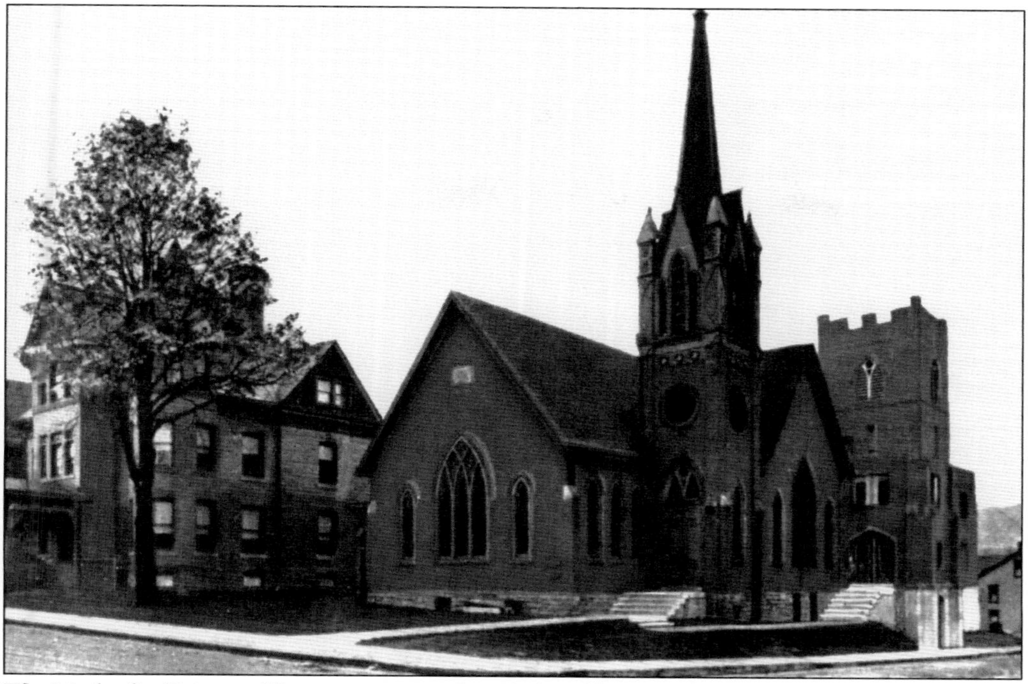

The Methodist Episcopal Society originated in 1842 and became the Methodist Episcopal Church three years later. As part of a merger in 1939, it became the First United Methodist Church. In 1968, yet another merger resulted in a change to the United Methodist Church. The church has been located on the corners of Iron Street and Pike Street since 1888. This 1914 image predates the removal of the church's distinctive 95-foot spire. (First United Methodist Church.)

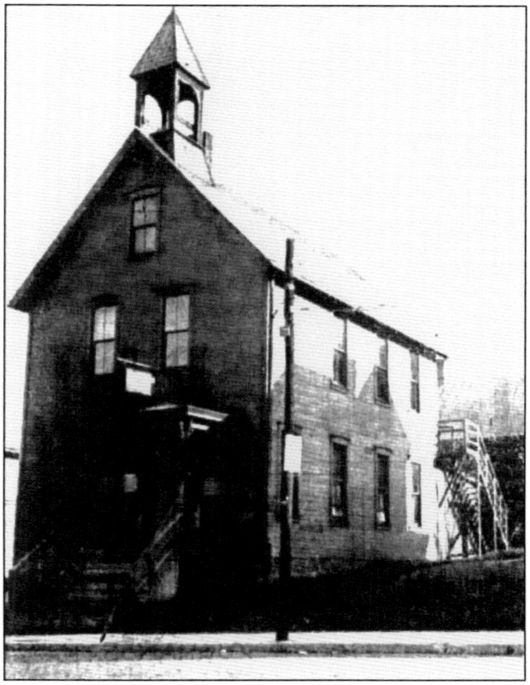

Originally built in the late 1890s as a school, this small building was used by a number of religious and social groups by the mid-1930s. By 1935, ownership was given to the Russian Evangelical Christian Church, which used the building for more than two decades. In 1960, the Gospel Way Church bought the property and was located there into the present century. (Pittsburgh Sun-Telegraph.)

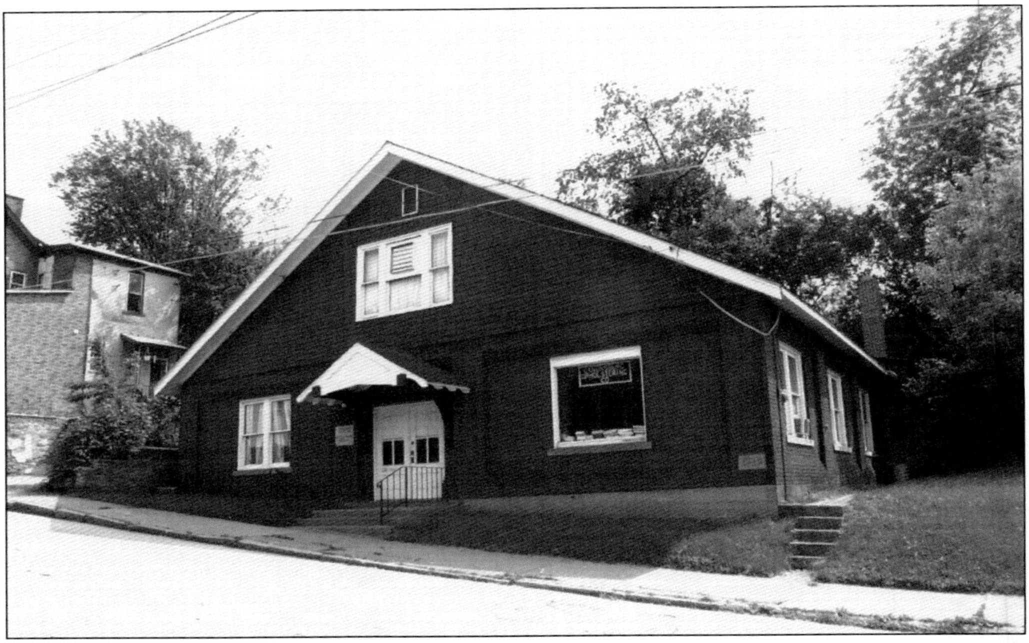

Although the First Christian Church dates back to 1903 in Canonsburg, it had owned no church of its own until this small, brick structure was constructed on North Jefferson Avenue in 1925. The church remained in use in 1959, when new property was purchased in North Strabane Township. (James T. Herron.)

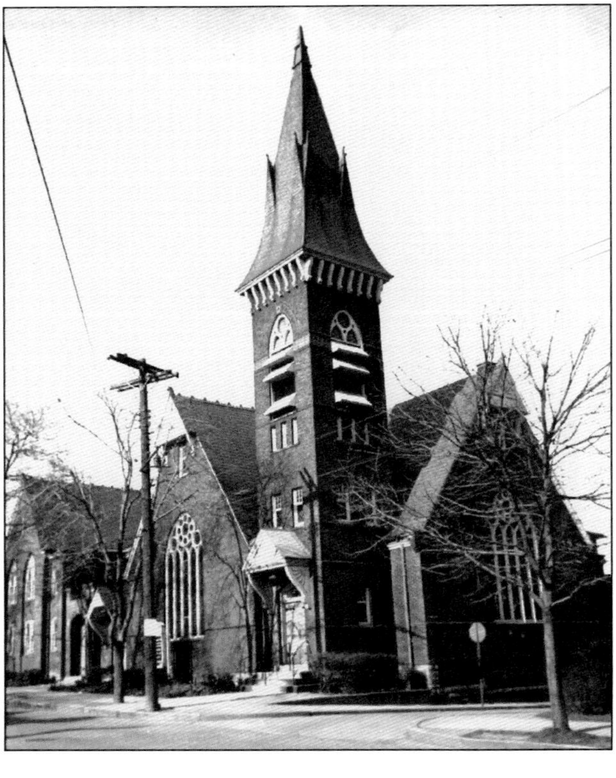

This church has been home to two congregations. From 1885 to 1967, it was the place of worship for the Canonsburg United Presbyterian Church, which began as the Speer Spring Congregation of the Associate Reformed Presbyterian Church in 1930. After the four various Presbyterian churches in Canonsburg merged in 1967, the church was eventually sold to the Mount Olive Baptist Church, which moved from its outdated Vine Street location. (Ducky Swan.)

Members of the Polish Roman Catholic faith decided to form their own church in Canonsburg in 1916, the St. Genevieve Roman Catholic Church. The community opened its new church building in 1922, which included the first Catholic school in Canonsburg. The school closed in 1969, and the church merged with St. Patrick's Church in 1993, although masses are still held in the St. Genevieve Church.

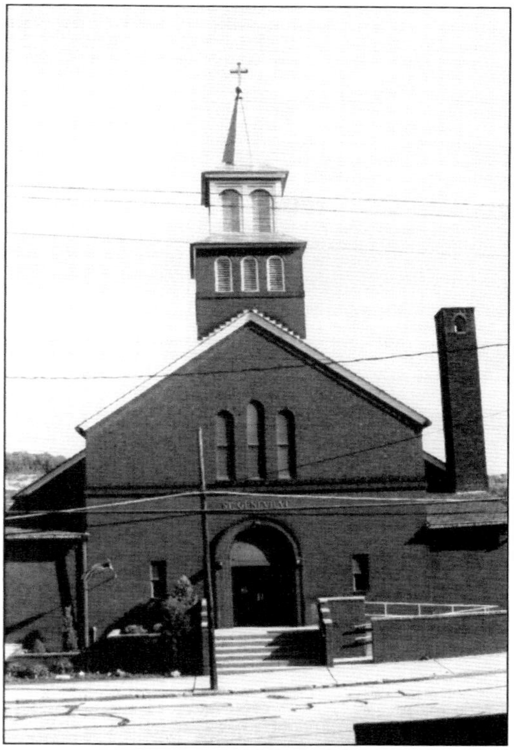

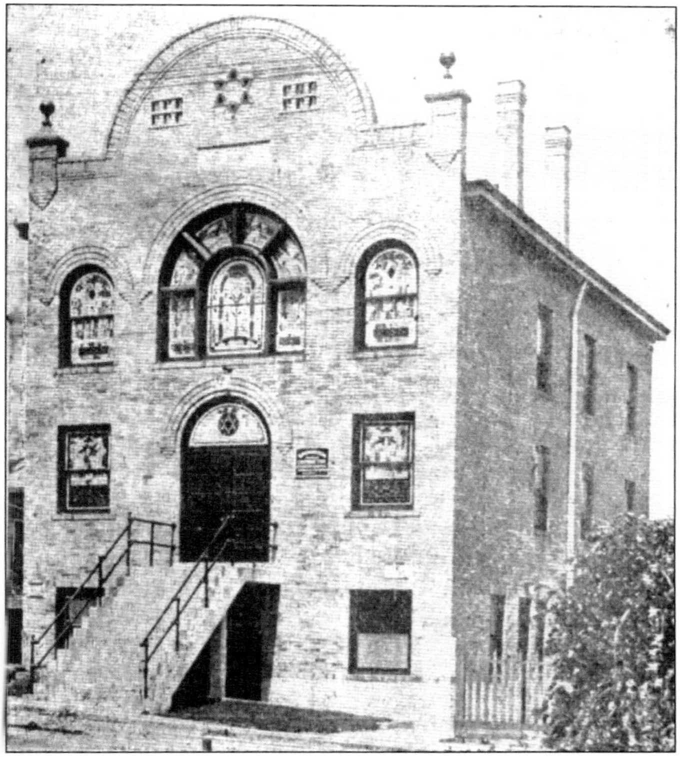

Members of the Jewish religion first started arriving in Canonsburg in 1901, although they had no synagogue until the completion of the Tree of Life Synagogue in 1914. It served as a place of worship until decreasing numbers of members forced its closing in 1960. The building on Ashland Avenue was razed in the 1970s. (Daily Notes.)

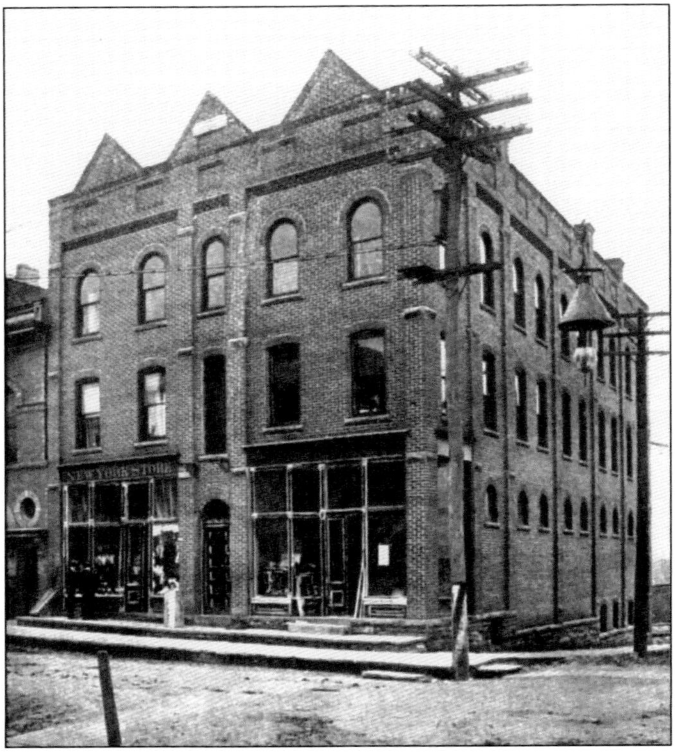

The McNary Building, located on the corner of West Pike Street and North Jefferson Avenue, was built following the destructive fire of 1898. It served as the location for William McNary's undertaking and furniture business. Victims of the Morgan Building Opera House tragedy were brought to this location, as McNary served as the deputy coroner at that time. (Ern Weller.)

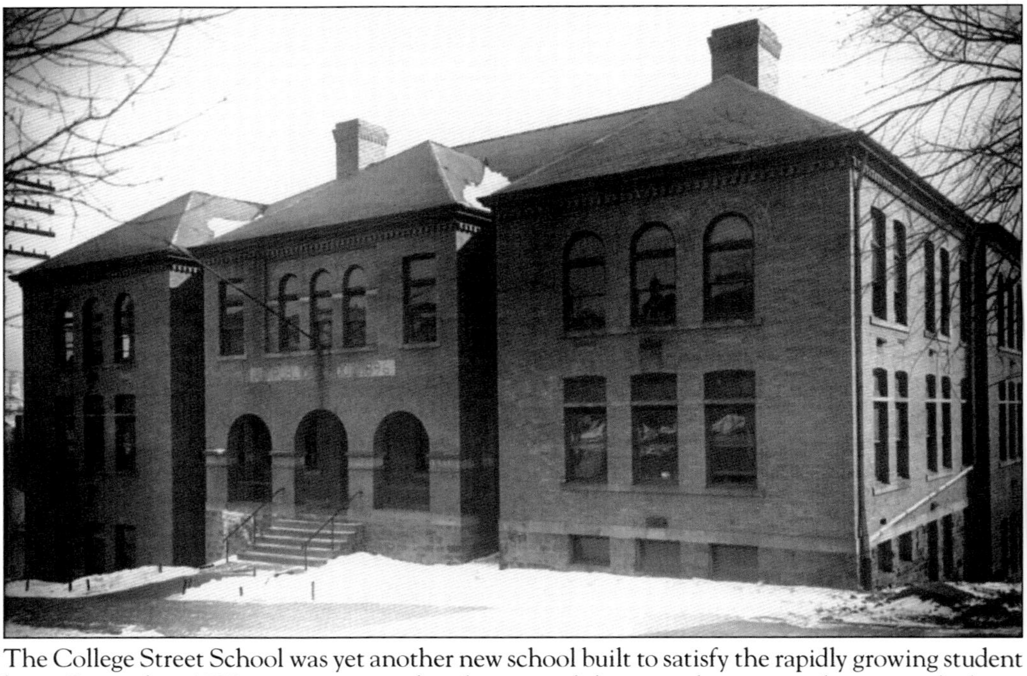

The College Street School was yet another new school built to satisfy the rapidly growing student base. Opened in 1897, it was equipped with many of the upgrades new to the era—telephone wiring, hot-water radiators, and the capacity for electricity, although regulations against daytime electricity use for lights maintained the need for gaslights until 1909. (Martin Estep.)

The Chartiers United Presbyterian Church also has its roots in Canonsburg dating from 1775, when Rev. Matthew Henderson visited in response to a petition sent to the Associate Presbytery of Pennsylvania at Philadelphia. Reverend Henderson later served as the church's first pastor from 1781 to 1795. This photograph of the present facilities, built in 1870, predates the lowering of Pike Street in 1903, which allowed for access to the church from the lower level.

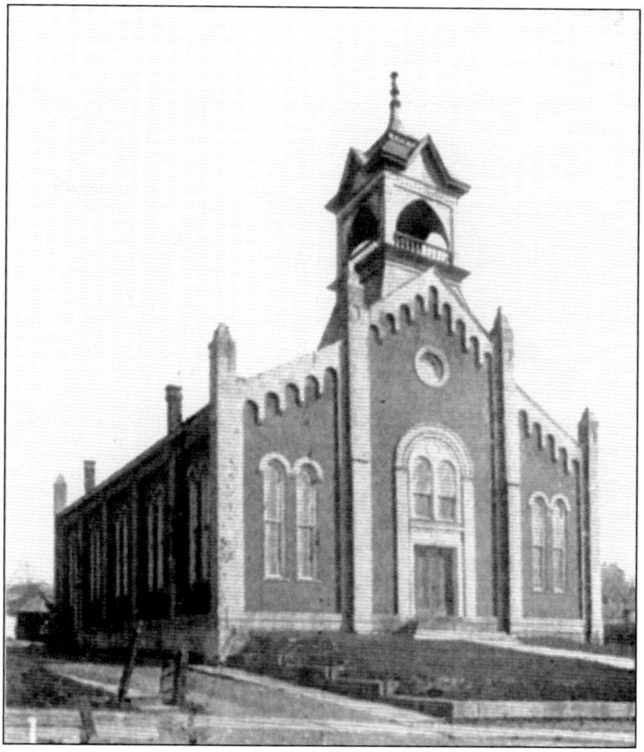

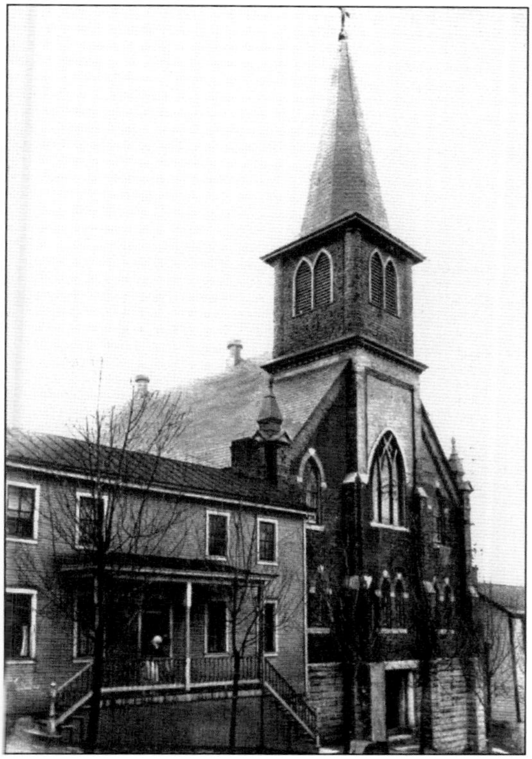

The St. Patrick Roman Catholic Church had humble beginnings, with just six Irish families residing in Canonsburg in 1880. The numbers soon swelled, and the community moved into a vacated Methodist church in 1891. A new church, seen here, was built for St. Patrick and served the congregation from 1907 until a modern, 1,000-seat church was constructed in the late 1950s.

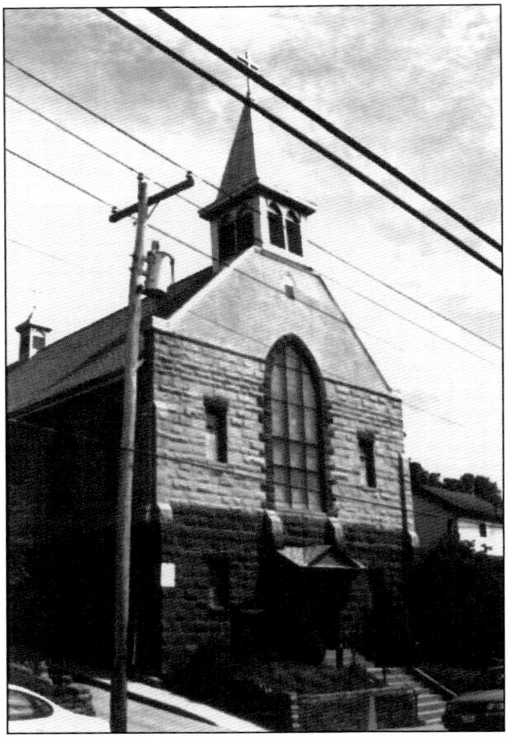

The Sacred Heart of Jesus Polish National Catholic Church began in Canonsburg in 1918 as the SS. Peter and Paul Parish. The church went through several financial crises from the 1920s through 1940s but always managed to survive, thanks to the efforts of the Very Reverend John C. Zieba, who served the church for 52 years. (Gina Nestor.)

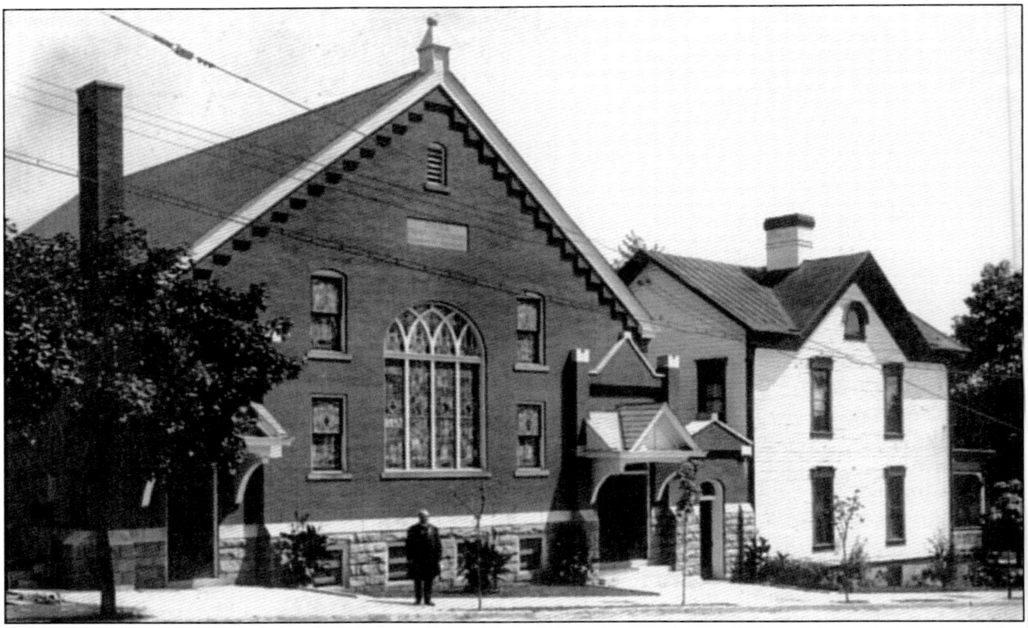

When most members of the College Church voted to leave the college campus and form the First Presbyterian Church, the remaining assembly reorganized as the Central Presbyterian Church in 1888. They remained on campus until 1922 when their own church was constructed on Belmont Avenue. Following the merger of the Presbyterian churches in 1967, the church was sold and became the Belmont Christian Church.

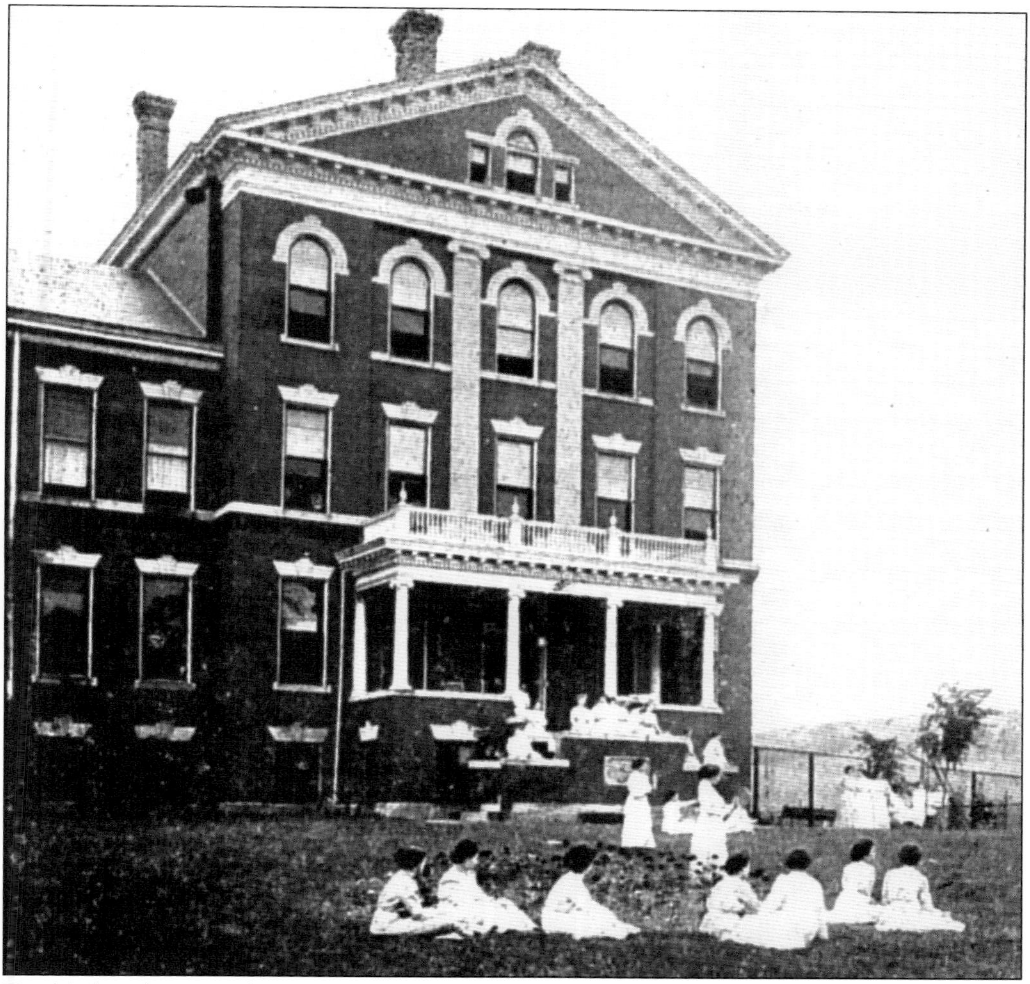

Troubled and wayward students of Washington County may have found themselves on the campus of the Pennsylvania Reform School, which moved from Pittsburgh in 1876. In 1912, the school was renamed the Pennsylvania Training School at Morganza. While sentenced to the school, male students would find themselves involved in a rigorous daily schedule of classes, farming, and parade drills. They would also learn vocational skills, such as carpentry, painting, tailoring, and bricklaying. Female students, seen here outside a girls' dormitory, would be taught domestic skills, such as cooking and laundry. During its peak in the 1950s, the campus stretched out to 1,200 acres, with more than 80 buildings. In the 1960s, the school was renamed the Youth Development Center. It was also decided that students should not be forced to work. After decades of self-sufficiency, the campus soon found itself full of empty farm buildings and wasted farmland. The school closed in 1967.

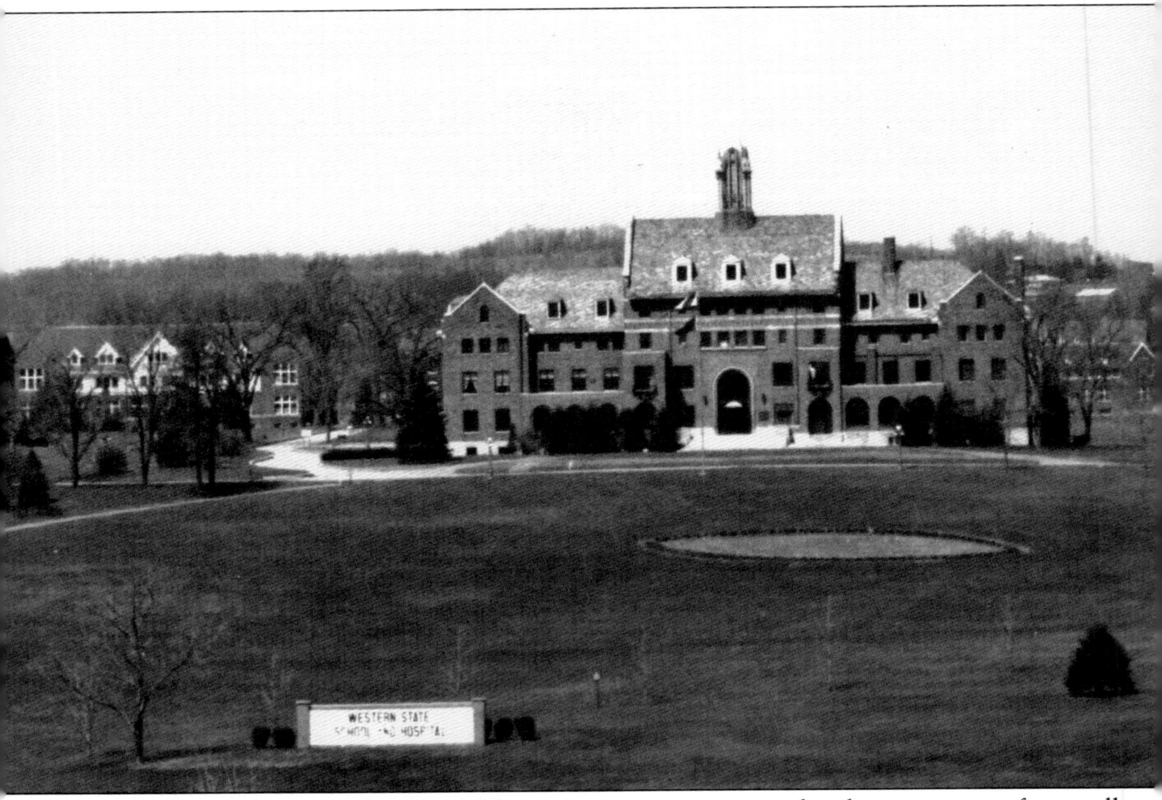

The Western State School and Hospital, a new institution for the treatment of mentally handicapped children, moved on to the Morganza campus and shared facilities with the Youth Development Center, beginning in 1962. In 1967, the Youth Development Center closed, leaving the Western State Hospital alone at the complex. After the reform school closed, much of the campus began to be developed for new neighborhoods of private housing to be known as Southpointe. During its peak in the early 1970s, the hospital housed more than 600 patients. In 1980, the facilities for skilled nursing were closed. This resulted in a name change for the complex to the Western Center, as it was technically no longer a school or hospital. The center closed its doors in May 2000. (Frank Mirisciotti.)

Six

Moving into the Present

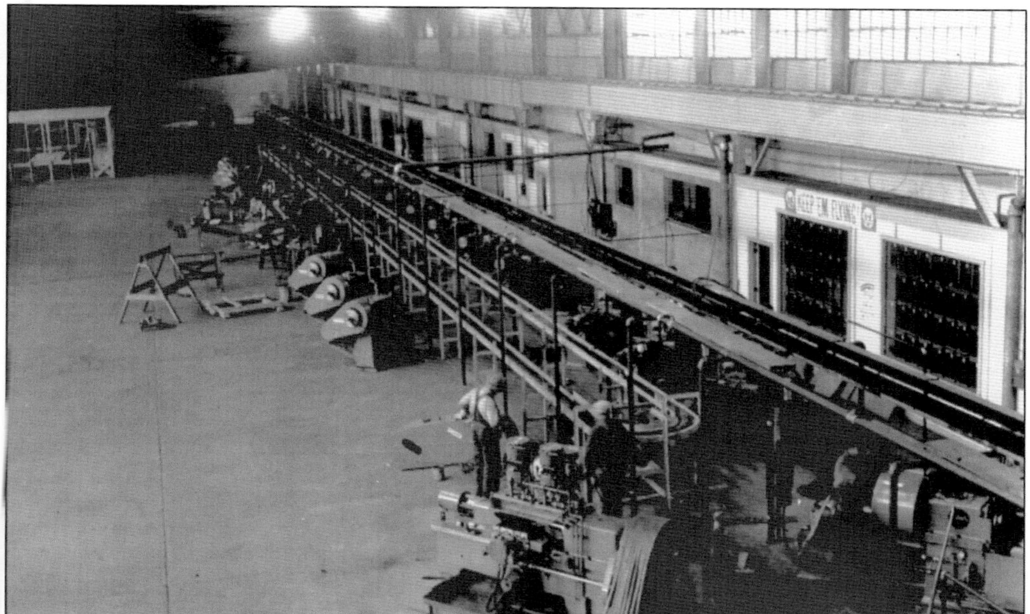

In 1902, the Canonsburg Steel and Iron Works replaced the recently closed American Tin Plate operations. It produced tons of sheet metal, which would find use in the rapidly growing automobile production factories, as well as materials used in housing, such as roofing and ceilings. A workers' strike in 1931 eventually led to the closing of the plant. But in 1941, the plant reopened when it entered a contract with the U.S. Navy to produce shells. The plant produced more than two and a half million shells through August 1945. (Herbert Wilson.)

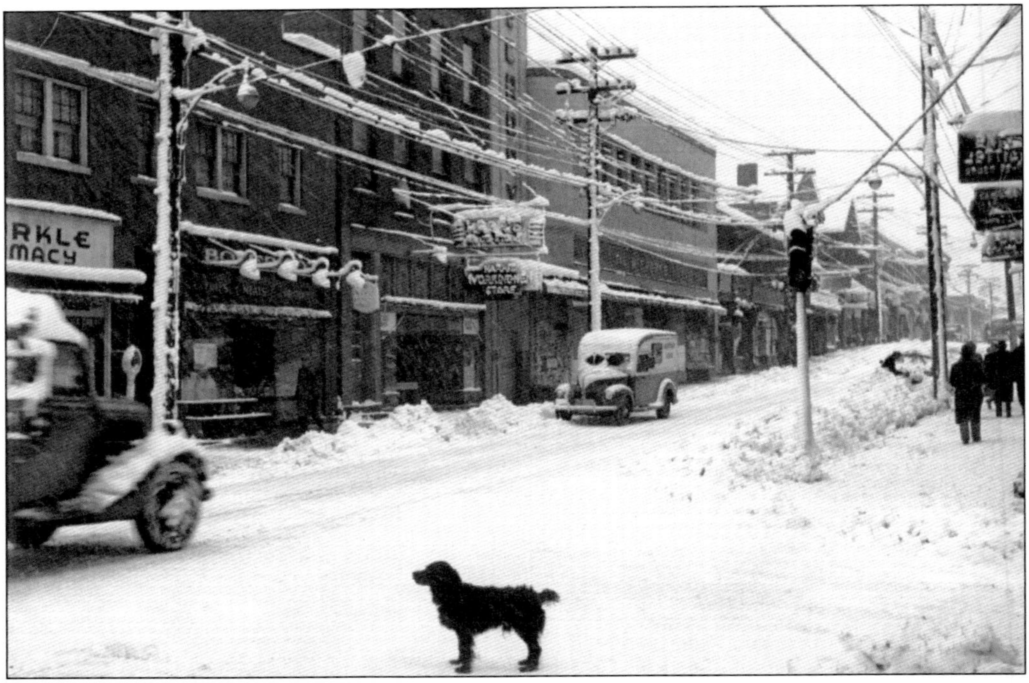

This 1940s-era snowstorm highlights the spiderweb of utility and trolley wires that covered West Pike Street and many other avenues in town. In time, all the overhead wiring for utilities were moved underground. Trolley wiring became obsolete in the 1950s. All the buildings shown here still stand. (Joseph A. Solobay collection.)

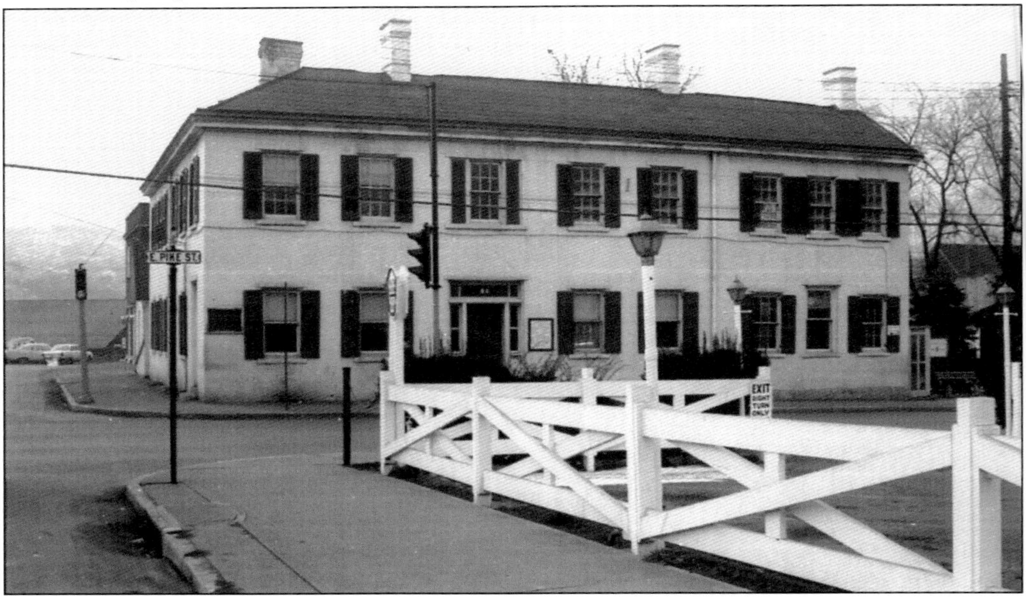

Canonsburg has had a number of borough buildings through the years. This white brick building on the corner of Pike Street and Greenside Avenue was built by Dr. Jonathan Letterman around 1830. It served as the borough building from 1925 through 1964. The current municipal building is located directly behind this location. (James T. Herron.)

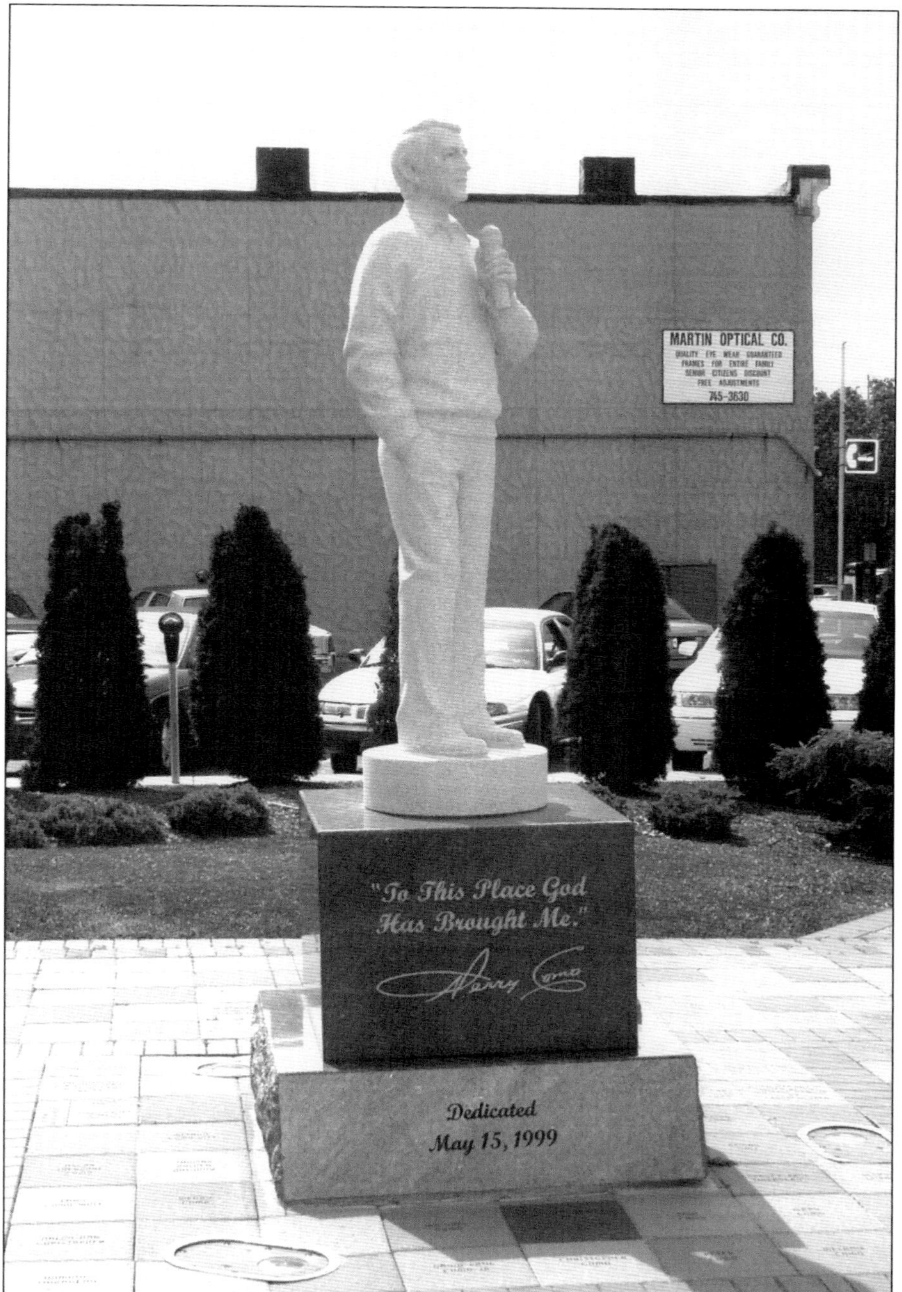

A statue was dedicated on May 15, 1999, to the honor of Canonsburg native Perry Como for his musical achievements. Members of the Como family were present for the dedication. Como was unable to attend due to his failing health. The statue was the first major project by the Greater Canonsburg Heritage Society, which formed in 1997 to preserve the legacy of people, events, and places important in the town's history. The life-size, granite statue was sculpted by artist Stanislaw Lutostanski in Barre, Vermont. The unveiling kicked off a weekend of special events, including performances and a banquet. (James T. Herron.)

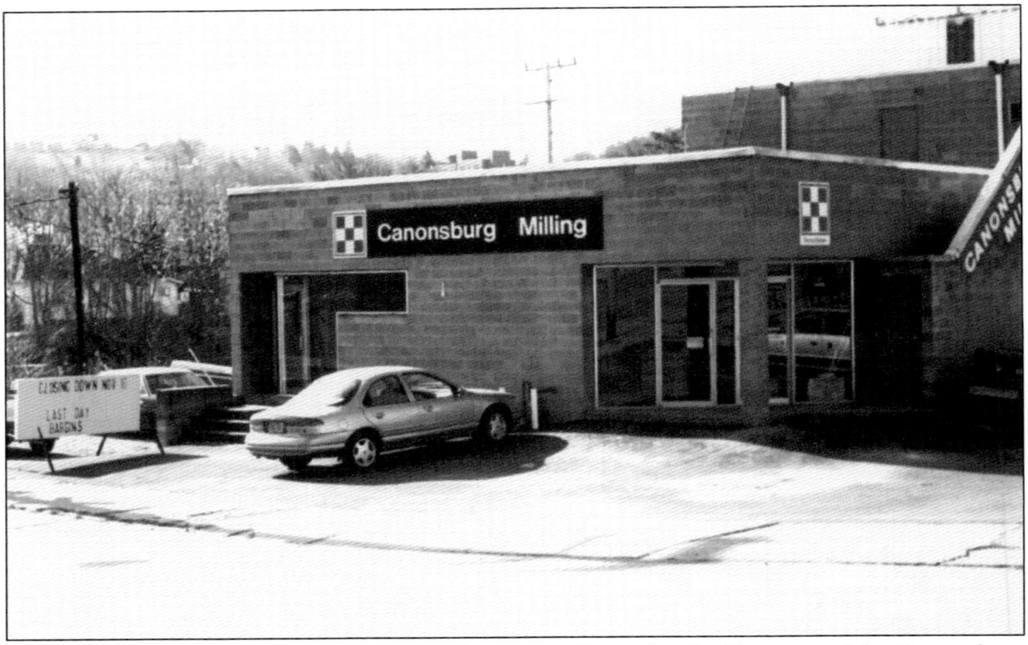

The last link in the lineage to John Canon's historic mill was this final location of the Canonsburg Milling Company, seen here on its last day of business in November 1996. Although it had many owners over the two centuries since Canon's original mill opened around 1780, it had survived as a single incorporated business since 1901. (James T. Herron.)

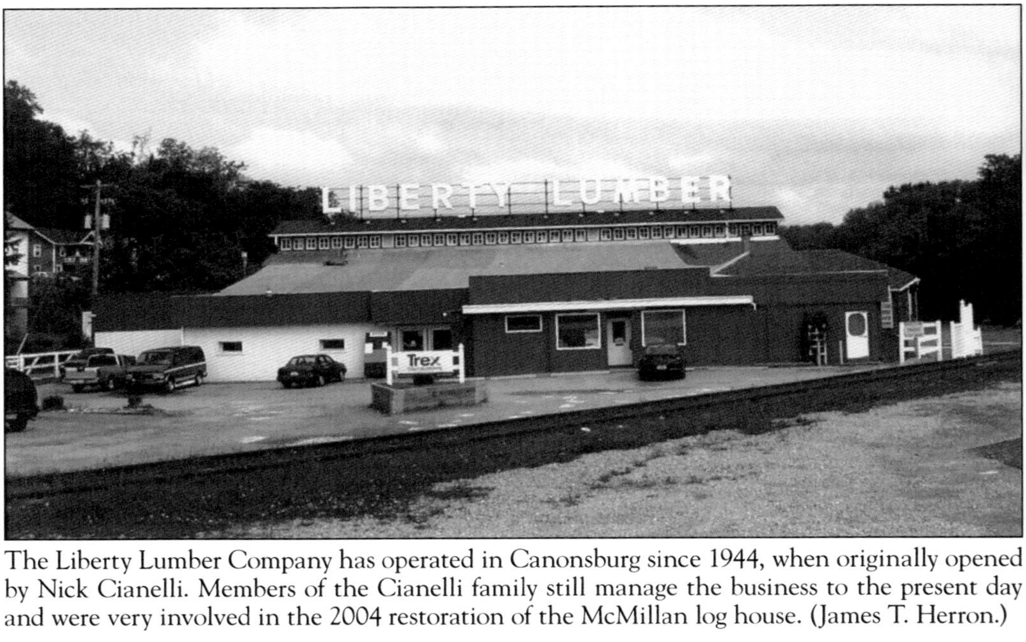

The Liberty Lumber Company has operated in Canonsburg since 1944, when originally opened by Nick Cianelli. Members of the Cianelli family still manage the business to the present day and were very involved in the 2004 restoration of the McMillan log house. (James T. Herron.)

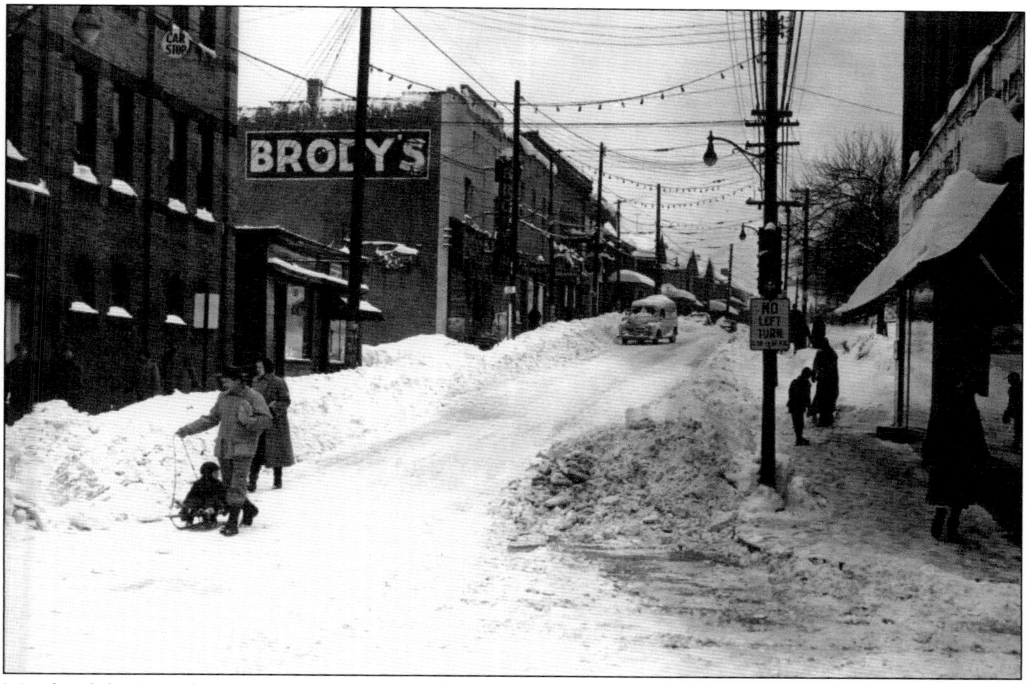

Much of the Northeast was blanketed with snow when a historic blizzard struck during a four-day span over the Thanksgiving weekend of 1950. More than three feet of snow covered much of Washington County. The blizzard left cars buried and unusable under snowdrifts. Most main streets were virtually devoid of all traffic, except for those lucky enough to travel by parent-guided sleds. (Ducky Swan.)

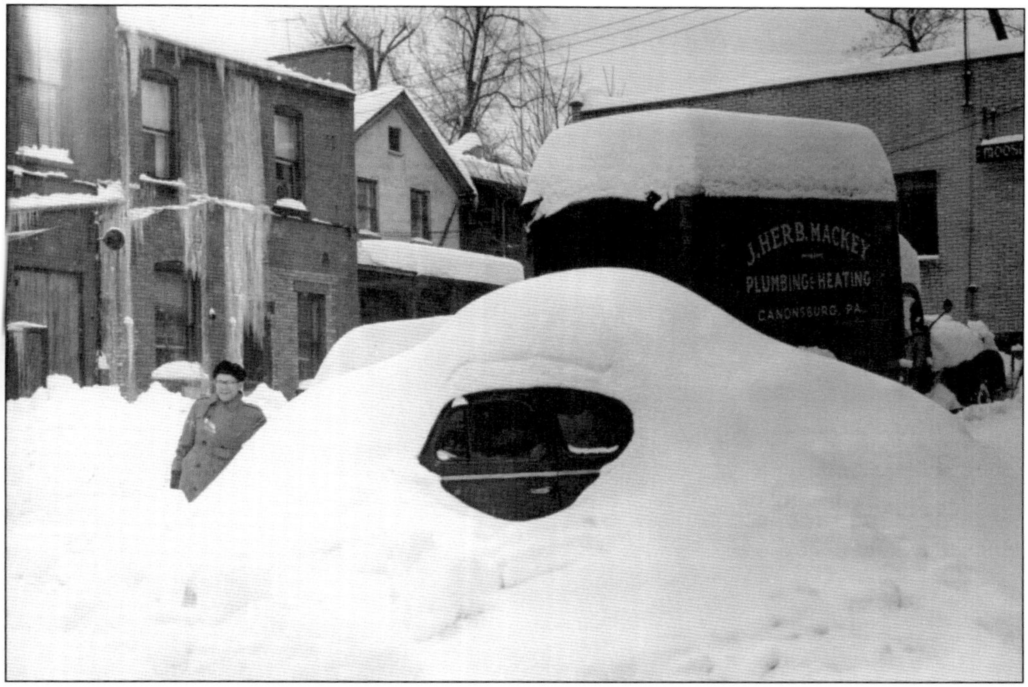

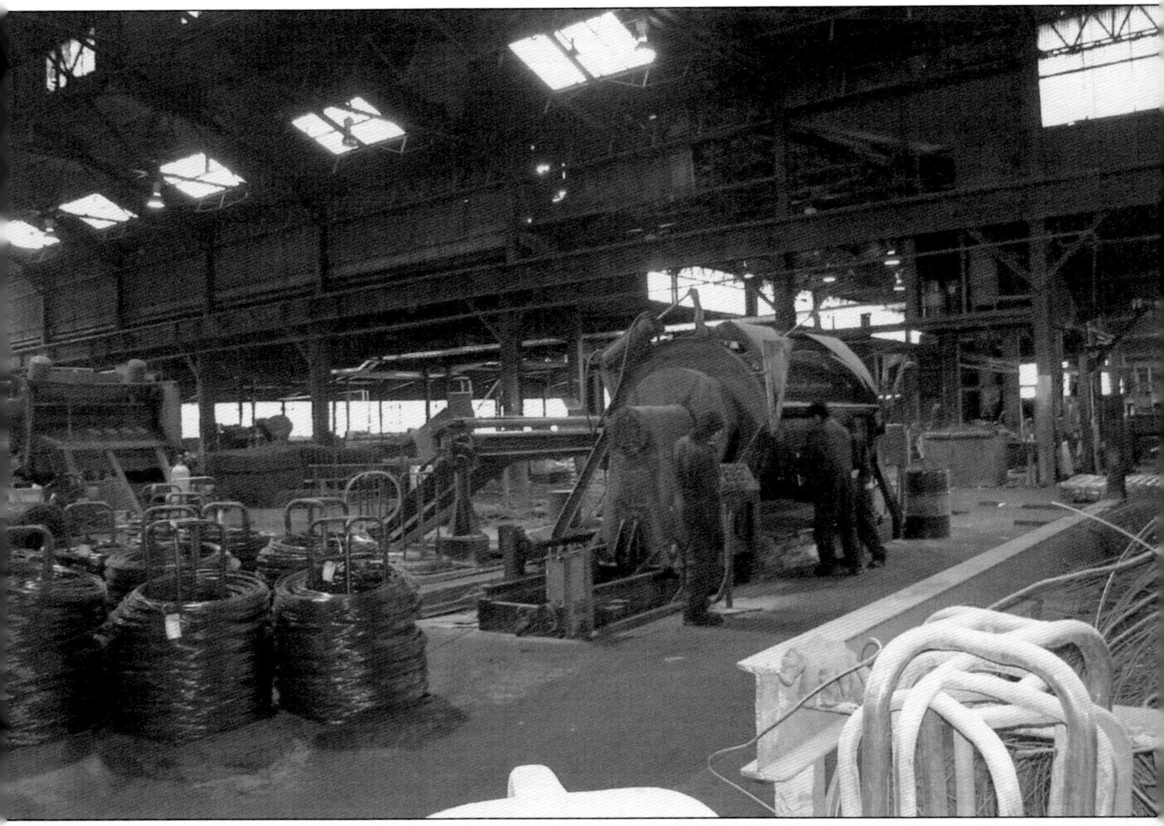

Following the end of its shell production during World War II, the former Canonsburg Steel and Iron Works plant became a new location for the Forbes Steel and Wire Corporation from 1947 to 1989. It produced wiring fence and mesh from raw materials milled at other plants in western Pennsylvania and New Jersey. Insteel purchased the business in 1989 and closed the plant the following year. In 1992, Charles A. Tatano, a former Forbes Steel employee, reopened the plant as the Tatano Wire and Steel, continuing with the production of mesh wiring. Production of the wire mesh is seen in this March 2003 photograph. (James T. Herron.)

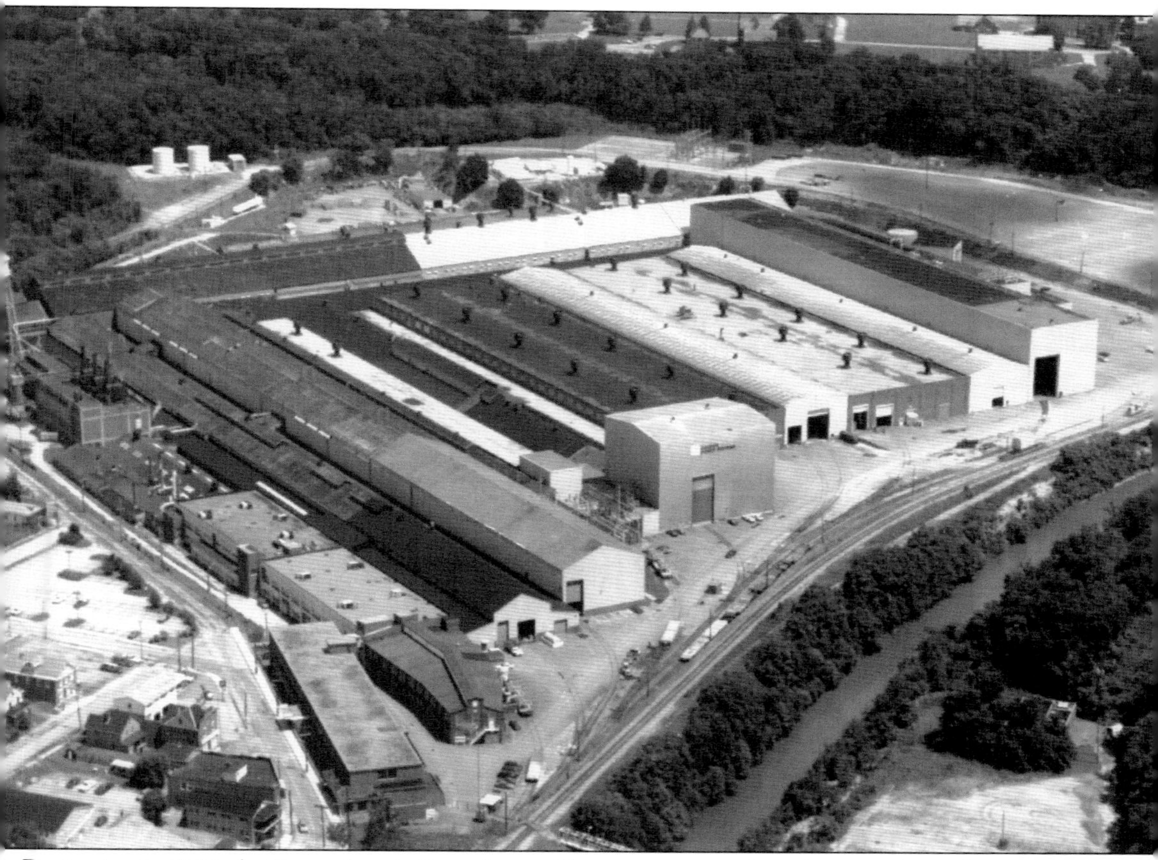

Beginning in 1946, the Pennsylvania Transformer Company initiated production of transformers in the former Alcoa plant, seen in a 1990 photograph. In the early years of operation, half the plant was also used by other companies, including the Radio Corporation of America (RCA), which produced vinyl records and record players. Other tenants included National Can Company, National Metal Products, and Canonsburg Metal Polishing Company. In 1949, the Pennsylvania Transformer Company purchased the entire plant from the government's war assets association, which had owned the facility since the end of World War II. The McGraw Electric Company, which later became McGraw-Edison, purchased the plant in 1952 and owned the property until selling it to Cooper Industries in 1985. The Fayetteville Transformer Company bought the transformer line from Cooper and presently operates Pennsylvania Transformer Technology from the location.

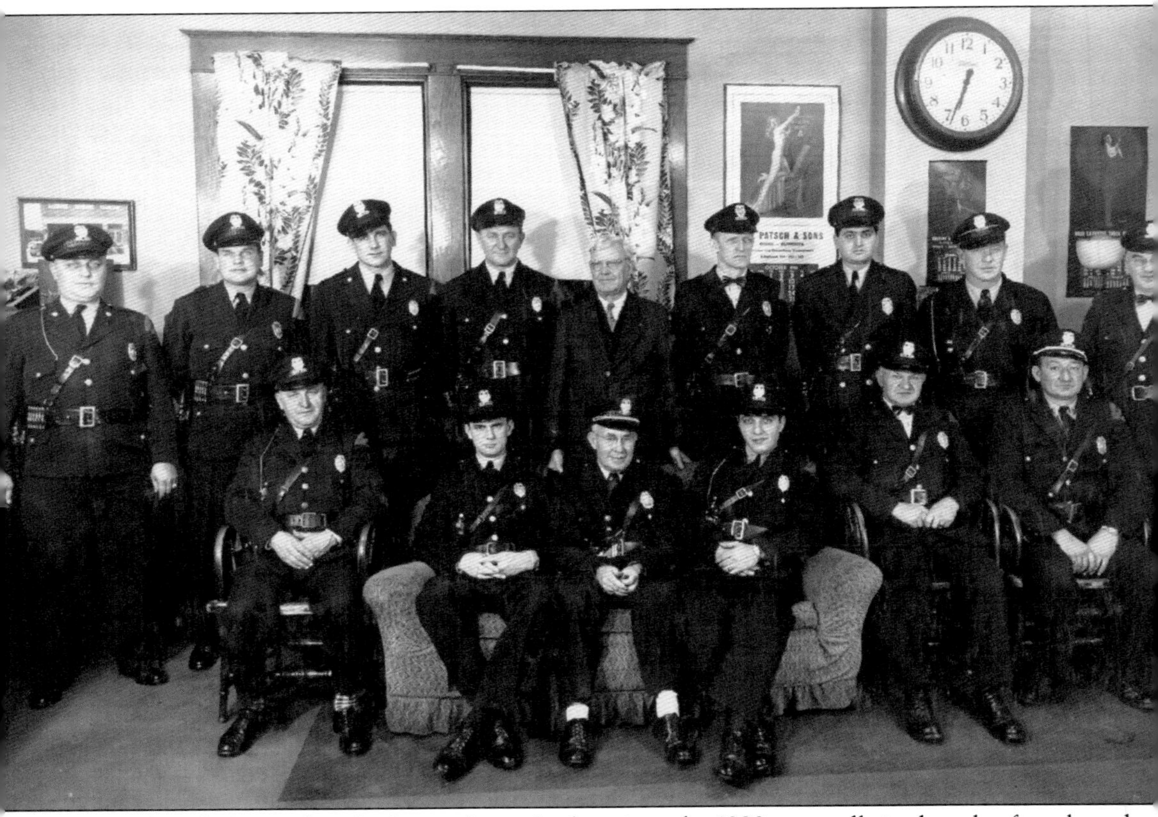

Although Canonsburg had some form of police since the 1880s—usually in the role of an elected high constable—a true force of police dates only back to the early 1900s when multiple officers were hired at a time. The first traffic control assignment was made in 1919, as the first electric traffic lights, on the corner of Pike Street and Central Avenue, would not arrive until 1925. The town's first motorized vehicle was a motorcycle in 1925, eight years before the purchase of its first squad car. Street traffic was assisted in 1948 by the debut of 120 parking meters, much to the chagrin of car owners. This 1946 gathering of the department includes, from left to right, (first row) Andy Graytok, Lt. Norbert Lesniakowski, Chief James Haney, Lt. Patrick Matrogram, Walter Olminski, and Michael J. Smith; (second row) Charles Susnak, Henry Smith, Michael Sapp, Steve Duscai, Burgess Harry Cook, Earl Smith, Joe Feconda, Michael Leson, and Orion Hoch. (Amon Studio.)

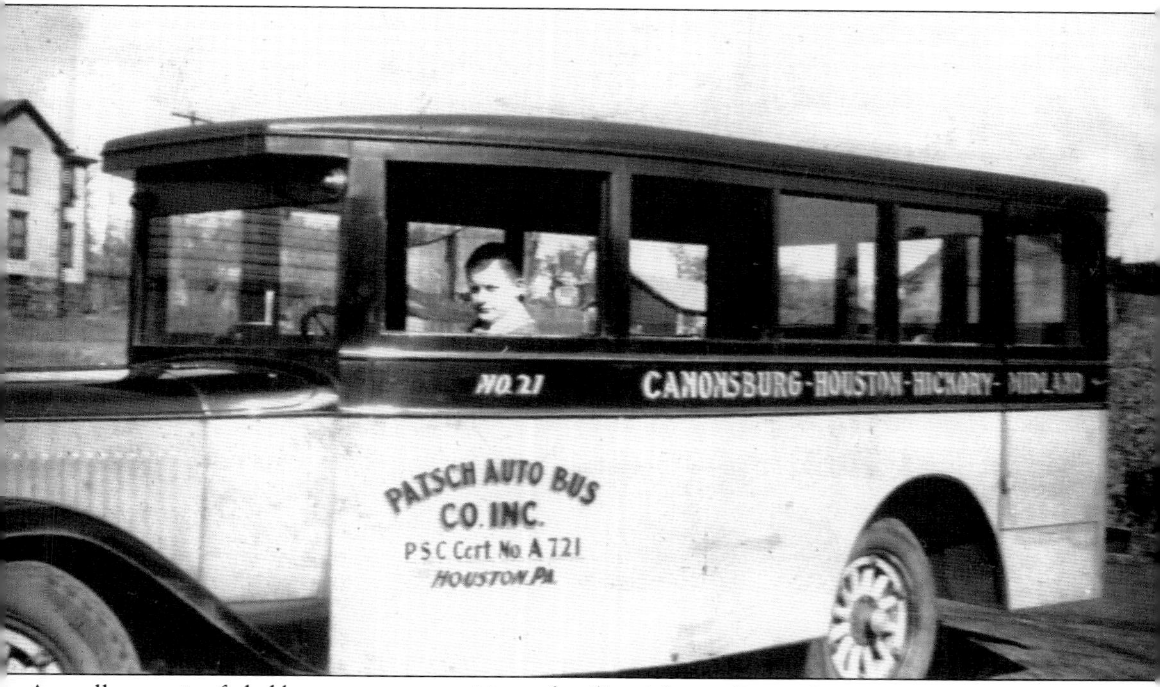

As trolley service faded between communities, a familiar sight on Canonsburg streets were taxis and minibuses operated by Isaac C. Patsch of Houston, which offered taxi service as far back as the second decade of the 20th century. Patsch ran the City Loop, a minibus that circled through Canonsburg streets and adjacent neighborhoods. Patsch also sold the first squad car to the Canonsburg Police Department in 1933. While Patsch certainly owned distinctive taxis, he had competition for business. Other popular means of public transportation in the early days of automotive traffic included the Blue Ridge Bus Company, Suburban Bus Lines, and Hoxworth Taxis. Driver Frank Ross is seen in this photograph in one of the distinctive Patsch autobuses. (Salandra Funeral Home.)

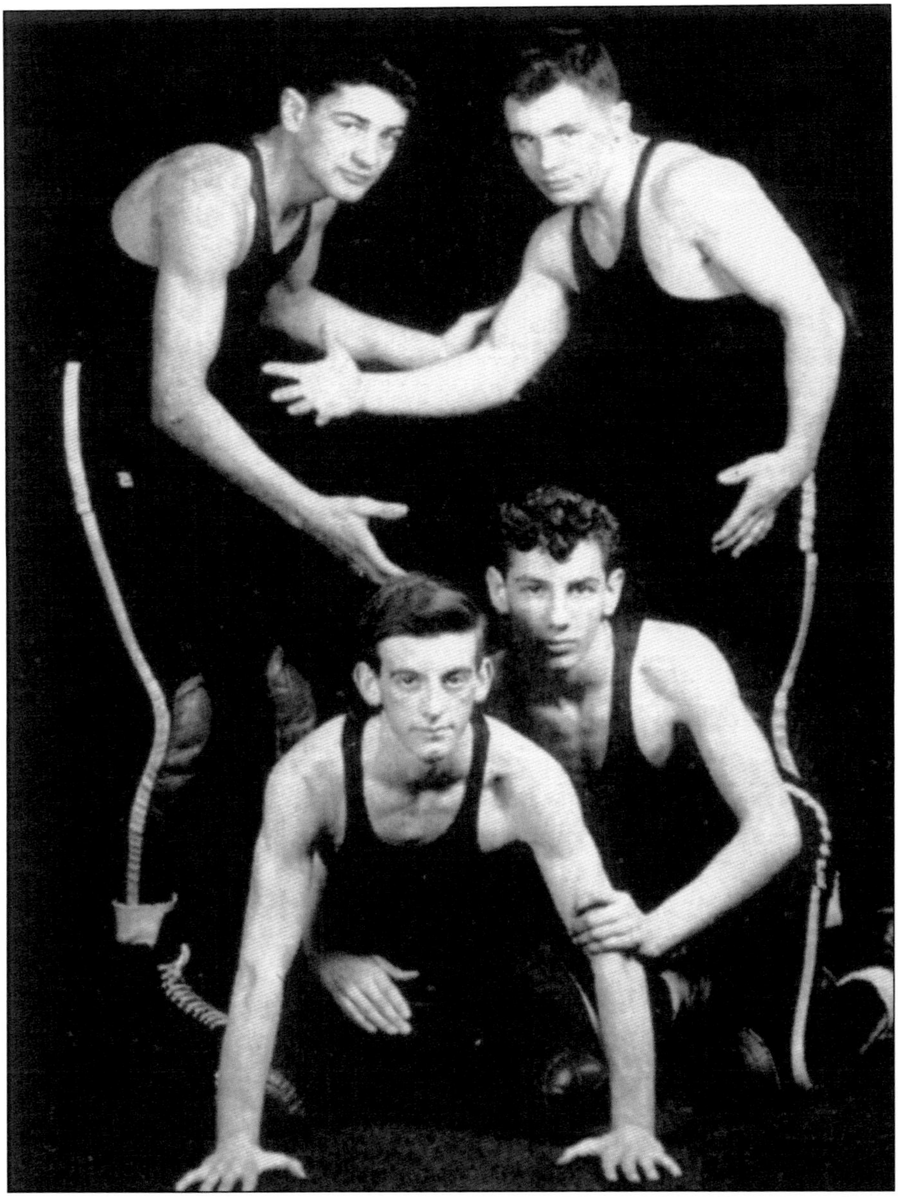

Student athletics in Canonsburg can be traced back to the days of the Jefferson Academy, when students were recruited for their athletic abilities. Unsanctioned athletics continued on the high school level until around 1906, when the Canonsburg High School Athletic Association was formed to schedule and monitor athletic events. School colors of brown and gold were officially chosen before an athletic contest in 1913. The use of the nickname "Gunners," associated with various sports teams throughout town, was also attached to the high school squads during this era. Canonsburg High School's athletic squads began competing with other Western Pennsylvania Interscholastic Athletic League schools in the 1920s, and championship trophies started to bear Canonsburg's name in the 1930s. Titles were won in baseball, track, and wrestling, among other sports. These wresting champions from 1950 are (clockwise, from top left) Joe Solomon, Don Haney, Manual Pihakis, and Ronald Roman. (Canon Log.)

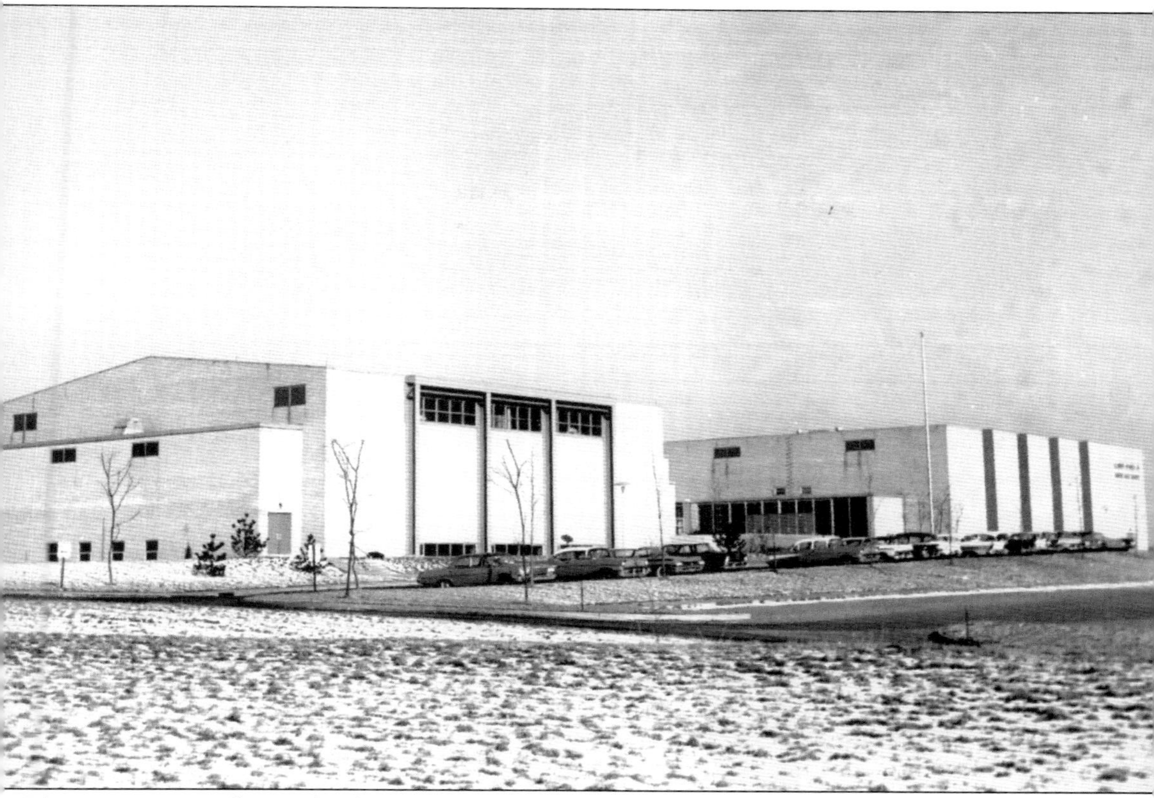

The Canon-McMillan School District was formed in 1954, with the completion of the Canon-McMillan Senior High School following in 1959 on the top of Elm Street, just outside the Canonsburg border in North Strabane. The merged district was formed to combine the Canonsburg, Cecil, and North Strabane school districts. The campus has gone through a number of renovations since this early-1960s photograph from the rear, including the removal of the foreground driveway and lawns for interstate roadway expansion. Another round of renovations was completed in the early part of the 2000s.

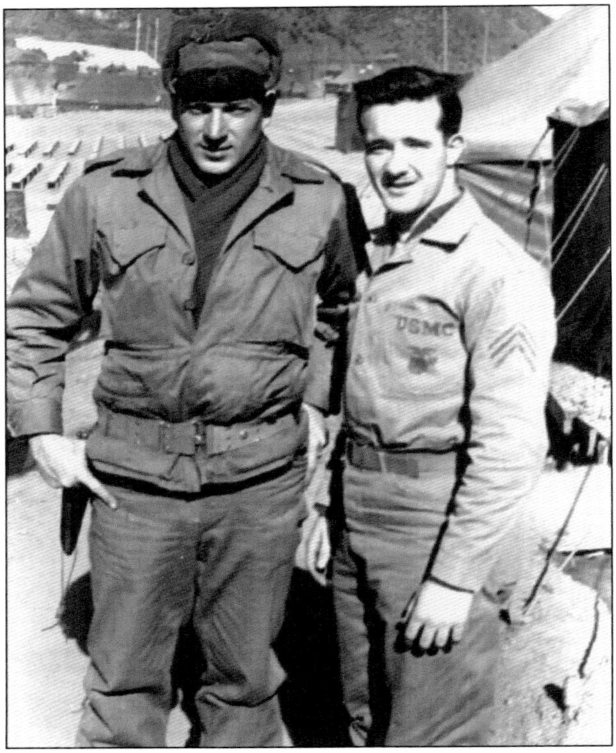

Two Canonsburg marines, Jim Banner (left) and Harold "Chick" Hampson, met up in Korea during service at the First Marine Division Headquarters. Banner, a high school track and cross-country coach when not in service, was honored with both the Silver Star (heroism) and the Purple Heart (wounded during combat). In the rear, benches can be seen prepared for USO shows and other official gatherings. In another incident of a Canonsburg military reunion, marine John Yanchak (left) and soldier Joseph Solobay are reacquainted in Korea. (Left, Lloyd Hampson; below, Joseph A. Solobay collection.)

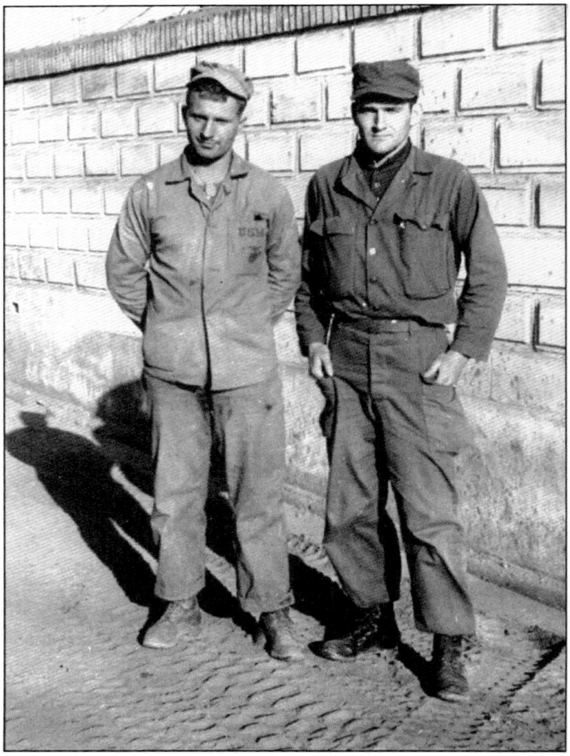

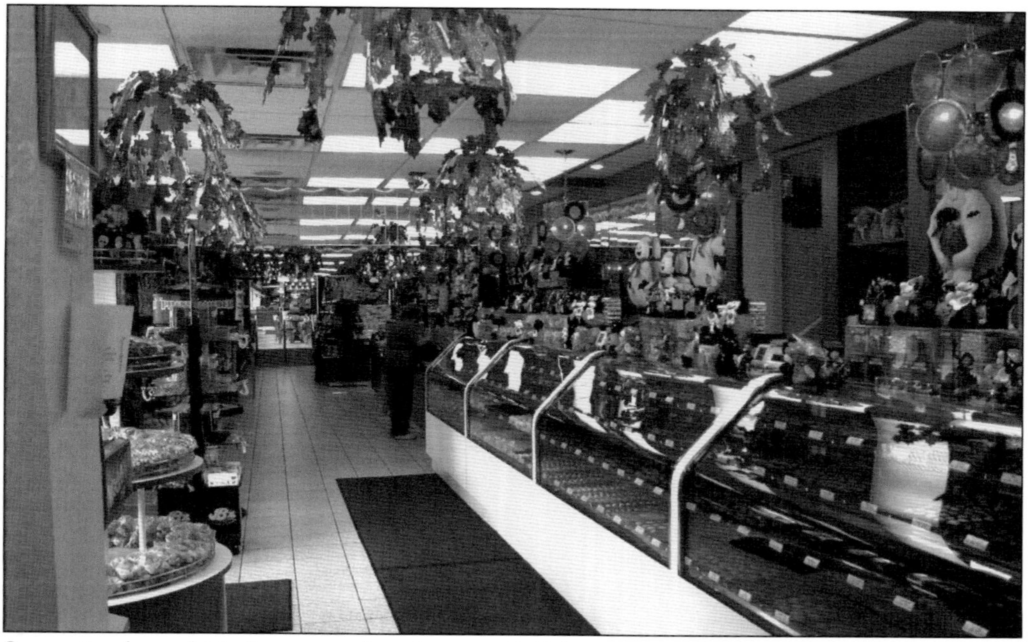

Sarris Candies, which first opened its doors in 1963, has grown from a small family operation to a factory with over 300 employees, with countless chocolate and candy products available over the counter or nationally through Hallmark card stores. Frank Sarris, who opened the store, learned about the business in a candy-making book. The Adams Avenue factory has grown and now also includes the Sarris Ice Cream Parlour, where Tammy Smoke is seen serving customer Renie Pihiou in the photograph below. (James T. Herron.)

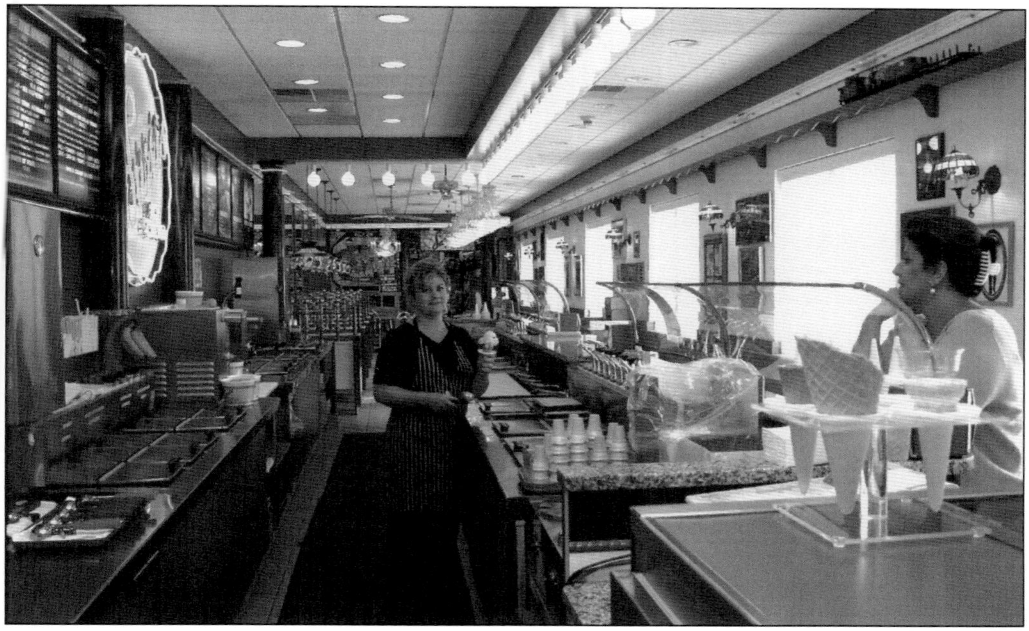

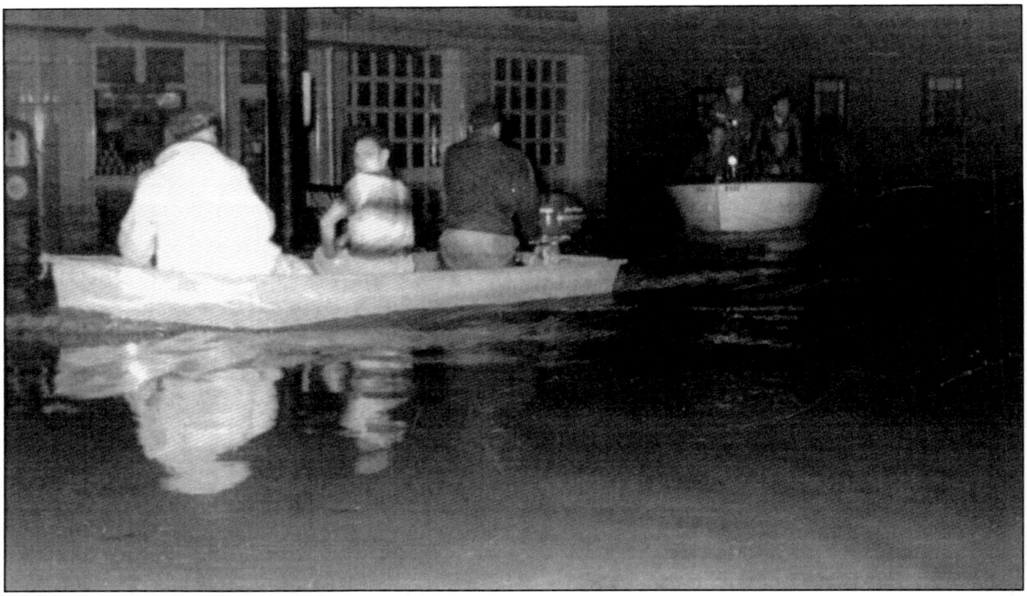

Another devastating flood hit the town in August 1956, with rescue crews seen making their way through streets in boats. The flooding issue was finally resolved with the establishment of the Curry Field Project, which in part served to relocate and expand Chartiers Creek in the early 1970s. (Joseph A. Solobay collection.)

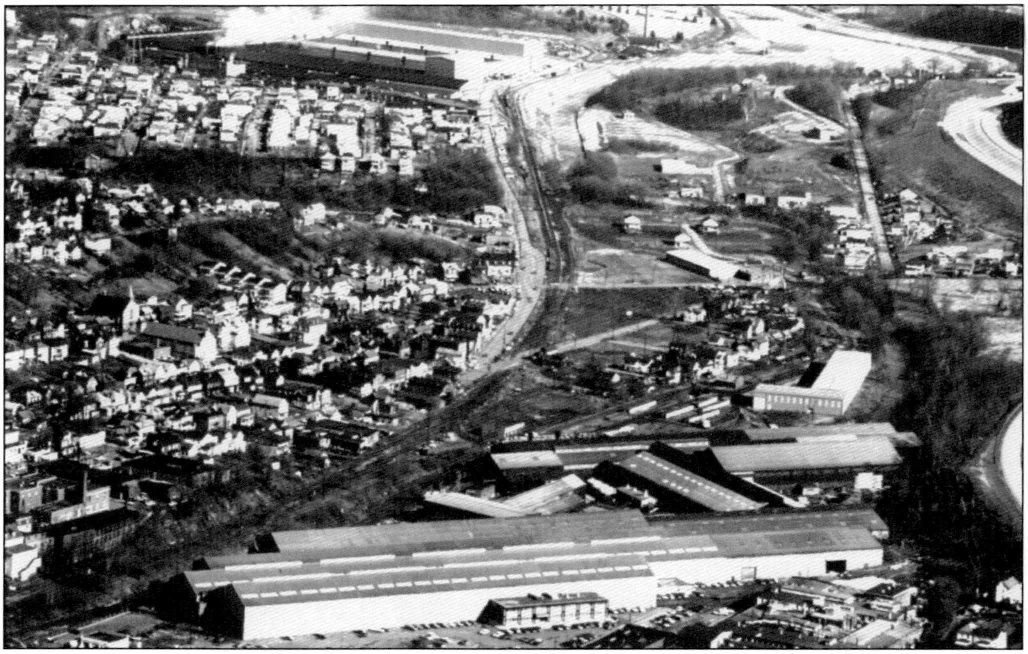

This aerial photograph from 1972 shows some of the redevelopment project in its early stages. The new channel for the relocated Chartiers Creek is still under construction at the top center of the photograph. The move allowed for the widened creek to run alongside Adams Avenue (up the center of the photograph) and away from its previous location behind the factories to the far right. (Bridge Works.)

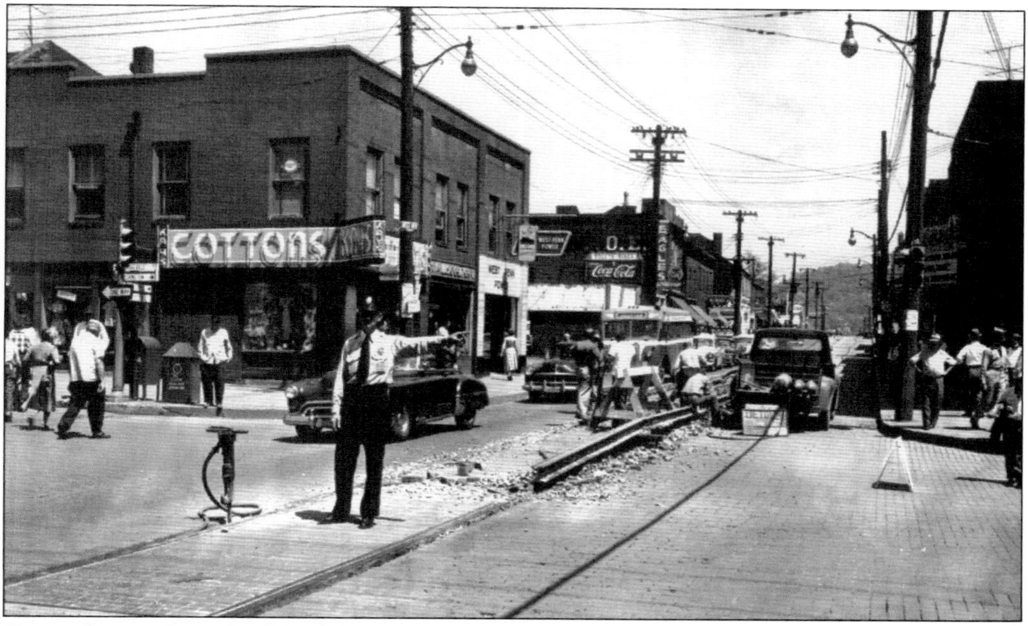

Canonsburg police chief (and future mayor, 1962–1969) Norbert Lesniakowski directs traffics around workmen removing the last of the town's trolley tracks in 1957. Trolley service had been discontinued in August 1953. (Joseph A. Solobay collection.)

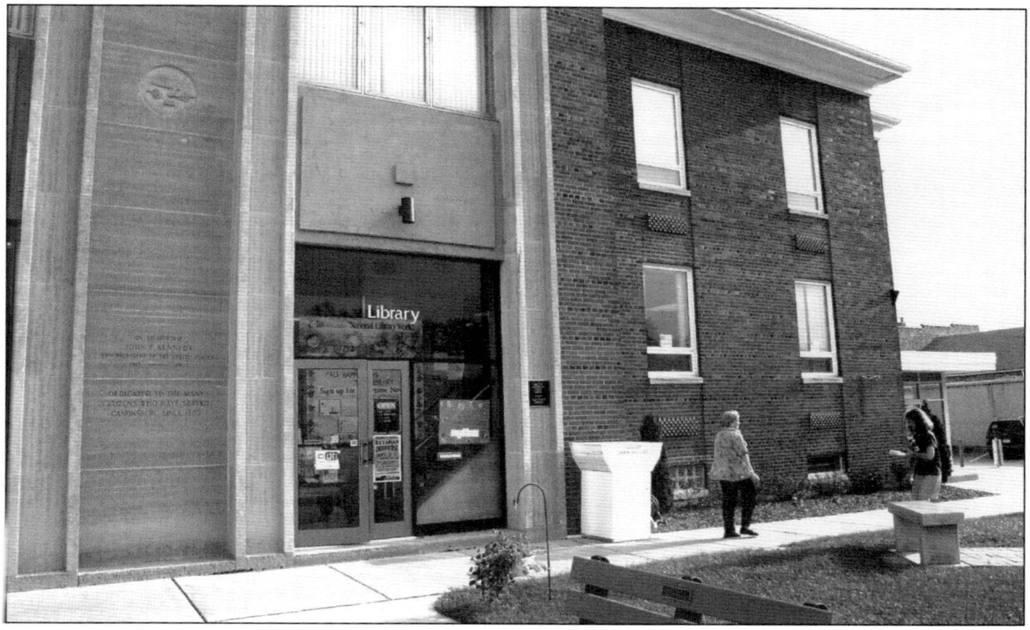

Libraries have a long history in Canonsburg, with roots going back to the Canonsburg Academy and Library Company in 1794. The current Canonsburg Public Library has origins in 1925, when the library was organized by the Women's Christian Temperance Union. That same year, the library moved into the new borough building, where it was housed until moving to a house on West Pike Street in 1959. Permanent yet small space was designated for use by the library in the present borough building when it opened in the mid-1960s. (James T. Herron.)

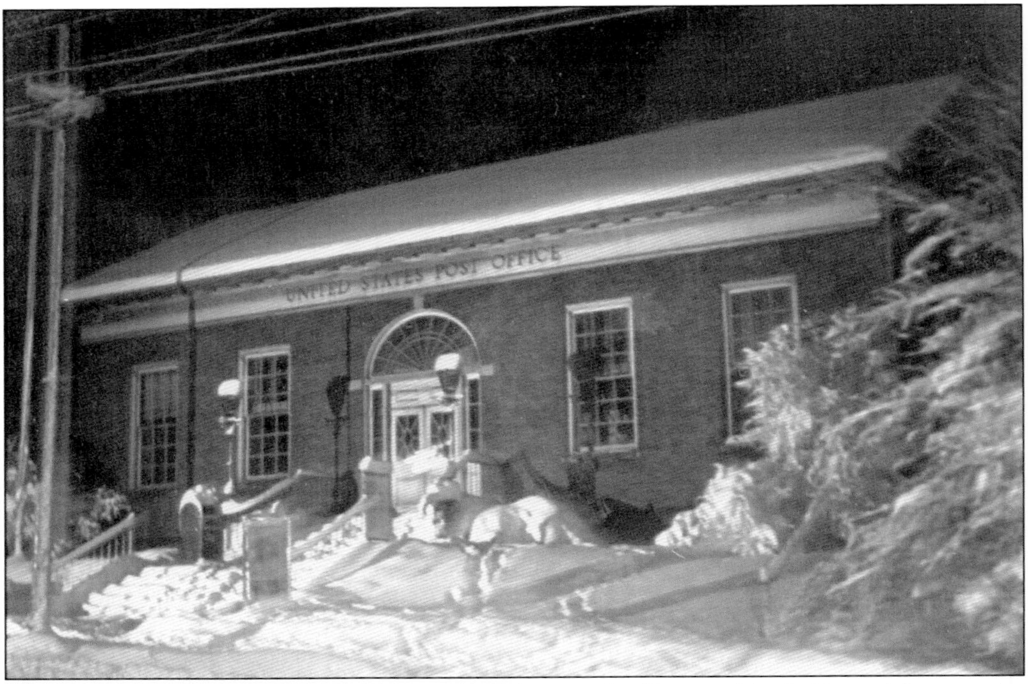

After the 1929 relocation from the Morgan Building to a building on North Central Avenue, the main branch of the Canonsburg Post Office opened this West Pike facility in June 1937, seen here in a 1944 winter storm. The steady increase in the volume of mail over the decades, however, has necessitated the building of the Canonsburg-McMurray Carrier in 2001. This annex now serves as the base for mail carrier pickup and distribution. The West Pike branch is presently limited to only over-the-counter postal transactions. (Above, Bill Kotyk; below, James T. Herron.)

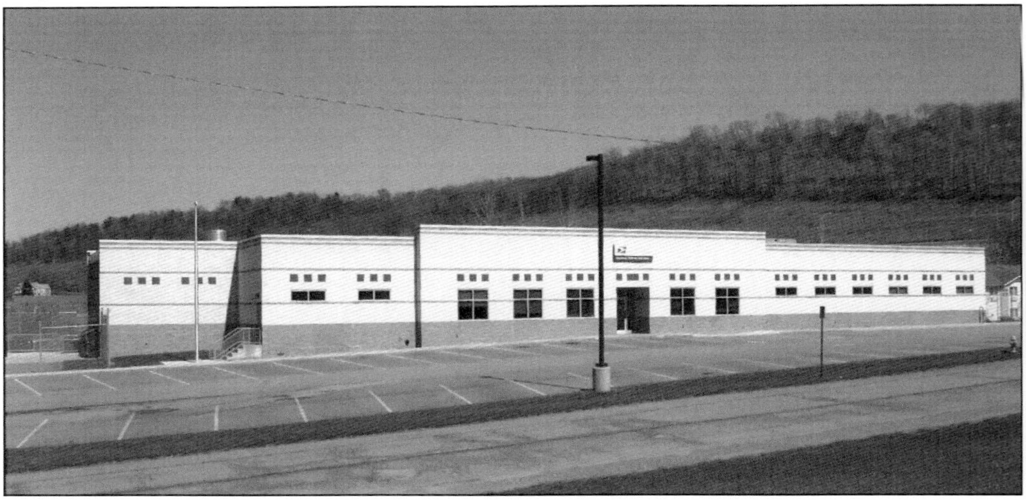

Seven

Notable Citizens

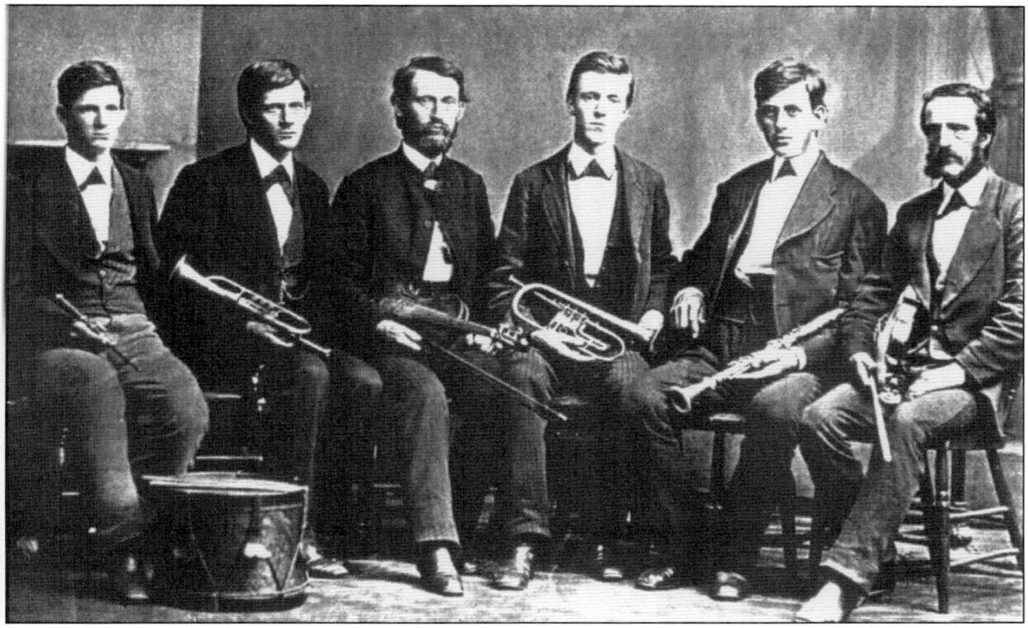

The Brown Brothers musical group was a popular attraction in Canonsburg during the 1860s and 1870s. Members of the band include, from left to right, Matthew B. Brown, D. Finley Brown, Henry H. Brown, Alexander B. Brown, William F. Brown, and J. Nevin Brown.

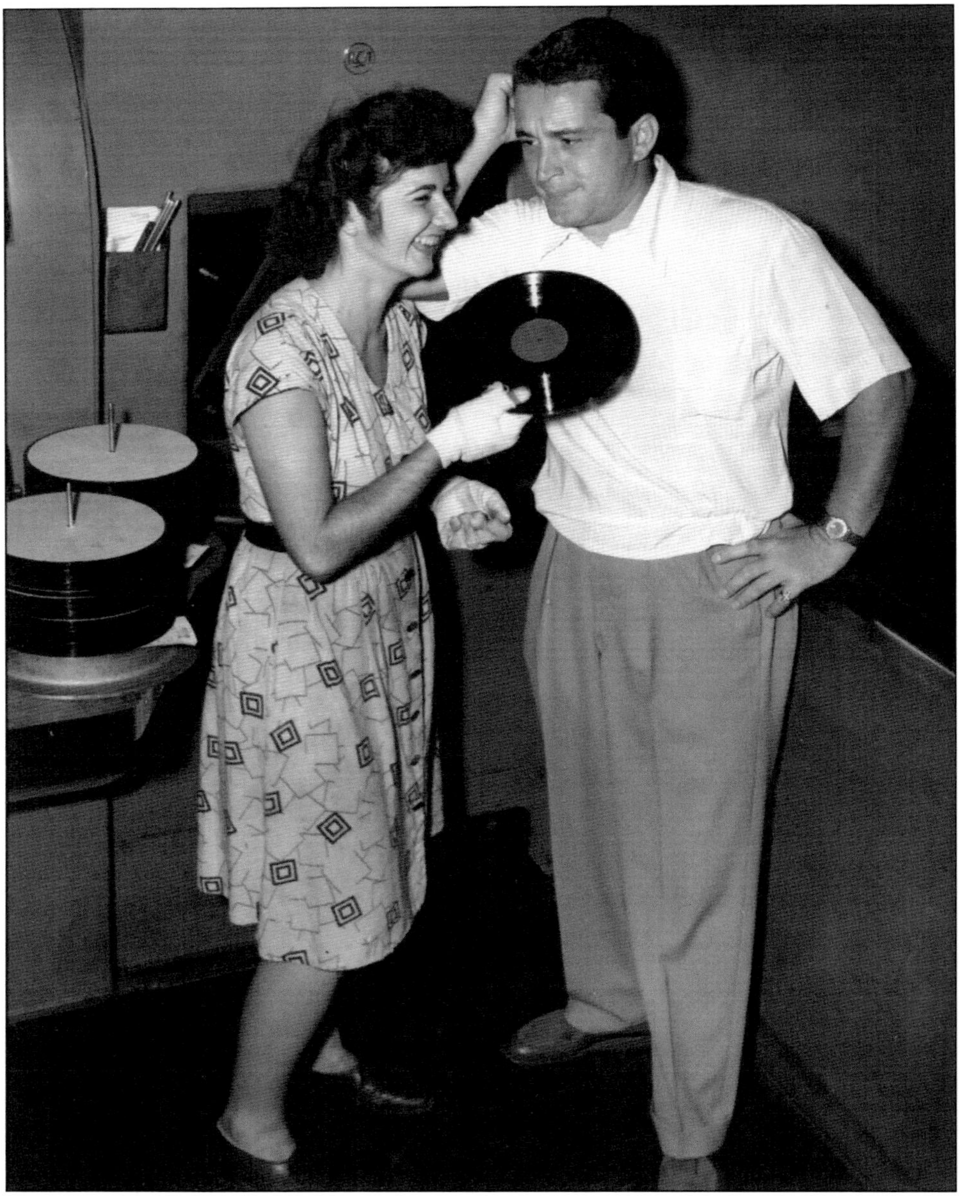

Perry Como (1912–2001) grew from his humble beginnings in Canonsburg to become one of America's biggest-selling vocal recording artists, scoring more than a dozen No. 1 singles from the 1940s through the 1960s. Como actually performed some of his early musical magic on customers in his own barbershop in the late 1920s. Beginning in 1933, Como began regularly appearing in bands as the featured vocalist, including stints with Freddy Carlone and Ted Weems. He almost considered retiring from music and returning to barbershops but was persuaded to continue in show business. His first hit records came in the 1940s, followed by appearances in several motion pictures. After a successful run on radio in the late 1940s in his own variety series, he starred in his own weekly musical variety series on television from 1950 to 1963, followed by seasonal holiday specials in the late 1980s. Como is pictured here at the Canonsburg RCA plant with Marge Gomber Zubenko. (Frank Mirisciotti.)

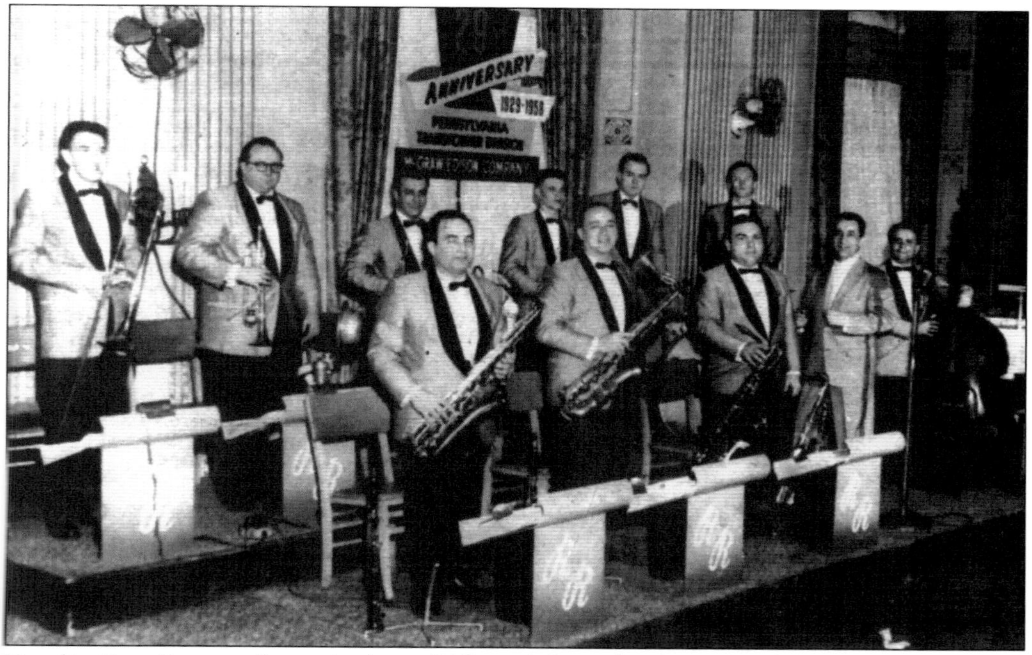

Vocalist Russ Romero (born Anthony D'Orazio) fronted a dance band for several decades in Canonsburg, beginning around 1946. Band members in this 1956 version include, from left to right, (first row) Phil Arnone, Tony DeFife, Raldo Parascenzo, Russ Romero, and Joe Chimento; (second row) Tom Ebert, Henry Crampe, Walt Kern, Jack Blackhurst, Alan Parker, and Lou Popiolkowski. (The Canon.)

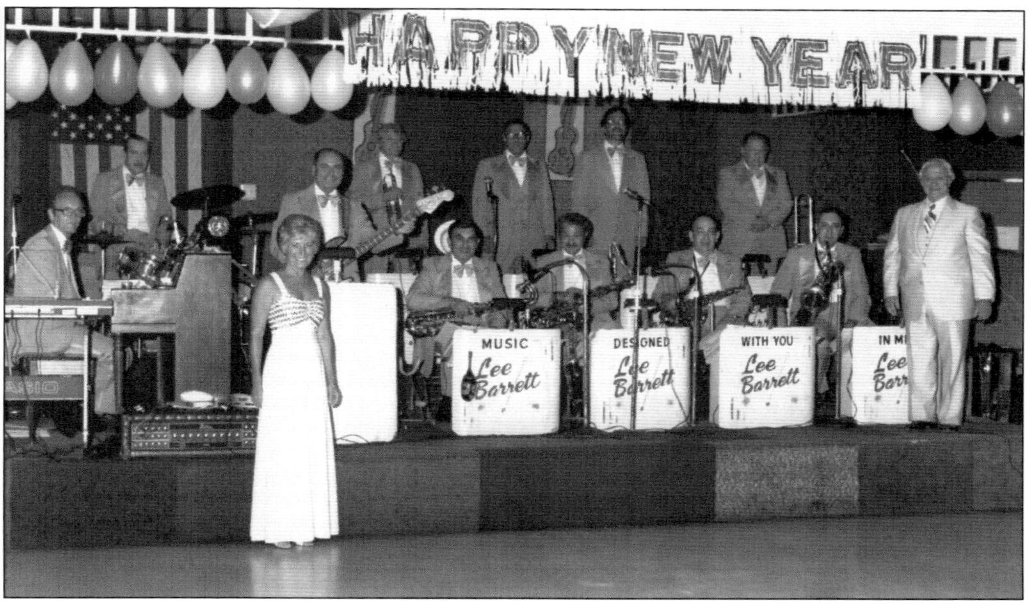

The Lee Barrett Orchestra was a popular attraction at many Canonsburg dances, parties, and functions beginning in 1936. Fronted by Barrett (real name Leon Imperatore), the band also featured brothers Goody, Albert, and Erman Imperatore, Santo Chimento, Lou Holder, Russ Romero, and June Ward DiSibio, among other players.

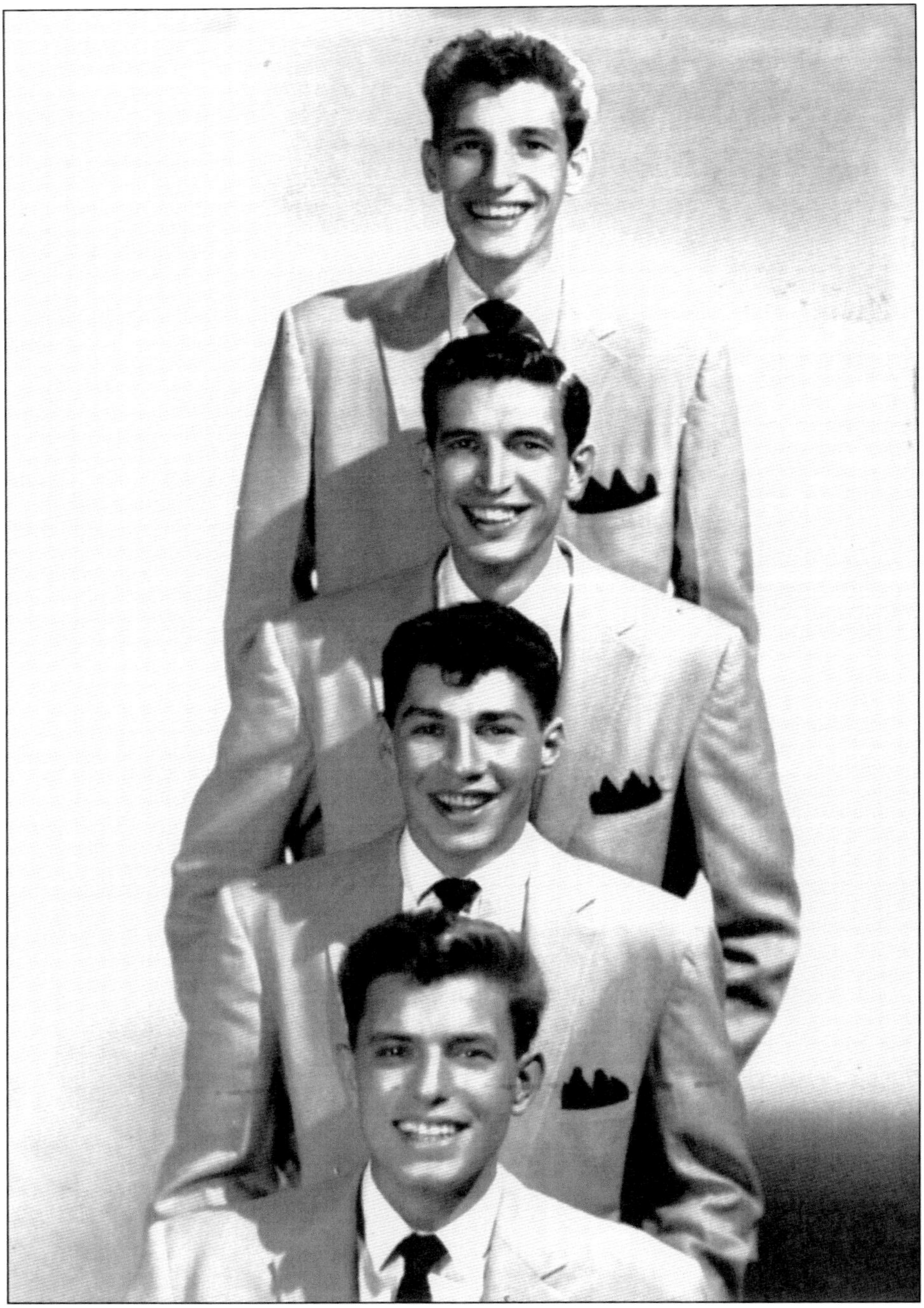

The Four Coins was a successful vocal group in the 1950s and 1960s and included graduates of Canonsburg High School. Members in this version include, from top to bottom, George Mahramus, Michael Mahramus, James Gregorakis, and George Mantalis. The band scored five top 40 hits on the *Billboard* charts, including its biggest hit, "Shangri La," which peaked at No. 11 in 1957. The band's career included appearances on *The Ed Sullivan Show, The Perry Como Show, The Steve Allen Show,* and *The Tonight Show.* After an absence of more than 30 years, the band began reuniting for occasional performances, beginning in 2003. (The Four Coins.)

Arthur J. Hopper, along with his brothers James G. and Wesley, purchased the undertaking business from Alex Speer and began a successful operation as the Hopper Brothers. James and Wesley were among the first licensed undertakers in Canonsburg, as required by a new 1905 law. Arthur later operated the town's first motorized hearse in 1916.

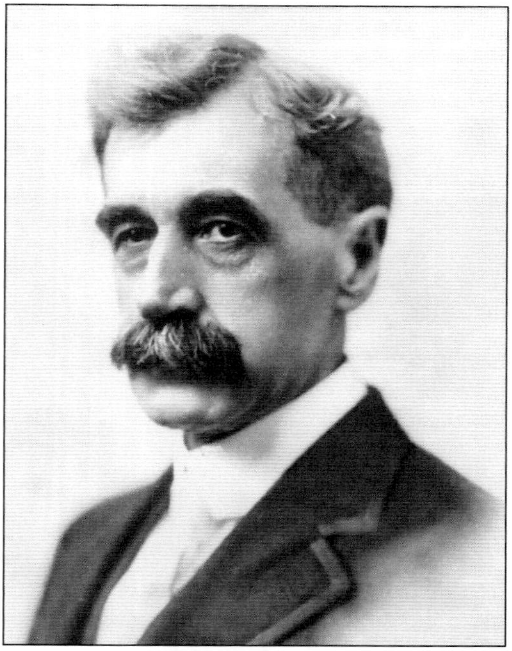

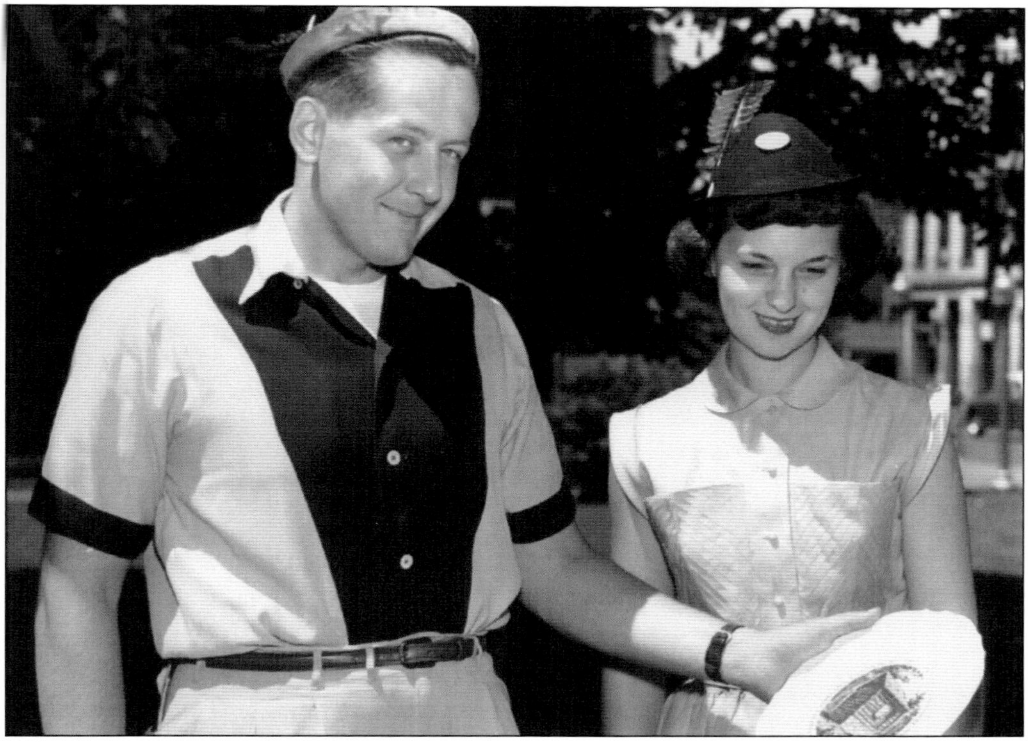

Jack George is seen displaying a commemorative plate manufactured by his Canonsburg Pottery factory for the town's sesquicentennial celebrations in 1952. The George family had been involved with the Canonsburg Pottery Company since it began in 1901. Joining him is parade queen Mildred Ross.

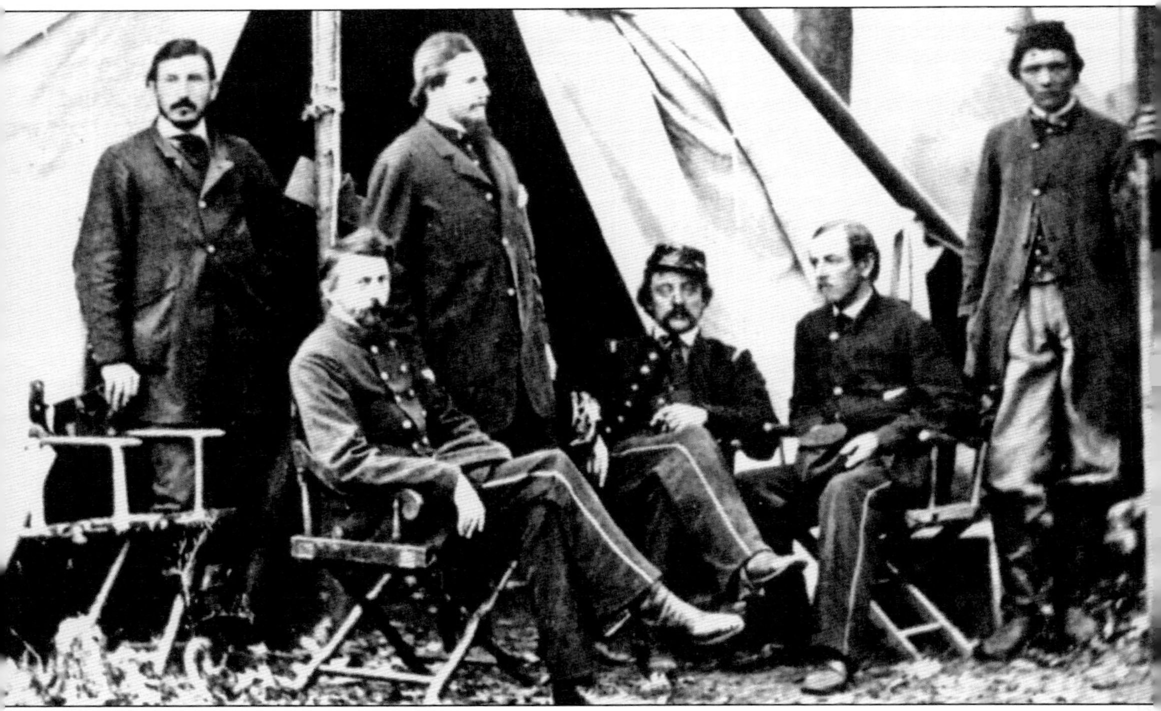

Canonsburg native Dr. Jonathan Letterman (1824–1872), seated at left, helped to change the face of battlefield medicine during the Civil War. He was a Jefferson College graduate in 1845, followed by a degree from Jefferson College Medical School in 1849. In his effort to improve battlefield medical treatment, Letterman pioneered the still-used concept of treating wounded soldiers in tents located near the battlegrounds, as opposed to the previously established method of transporting patients back to hospitals near the rear. To this end, Letterman created the ambulance corps, using separate men and equipment for these services. Letterman also believed that the use of tents as mobile treatment facilities provided the necessary fresh air to make treatment more efficient, another practice that continues to the present. Following the Civil War, Letterman moved to California to practice medicine, where he later died in 1872 at only 48 years of age.

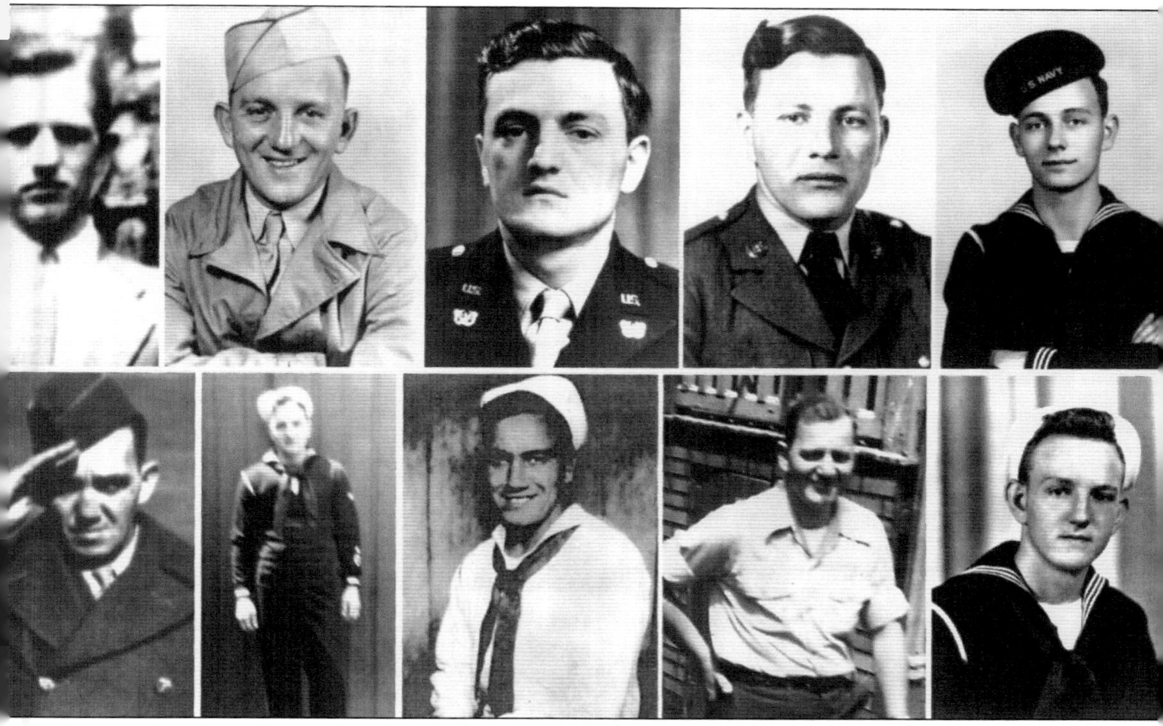

Perhaps no family in Canonsburg has had a stronger link to service than the Barsody family. Ten brothers served in the military, including nine in World War II. In the top row from left to right are Albert Barsody (the only brother to die in service), Anthony Barsody, Elmer Barsody, Frank Barsody, and James Barsody; in the bottom row are John Barsody, Joseph Barsody, Leonard Barsody, Steve Barsody, and Thomas Barsody, who served in the Korean War.

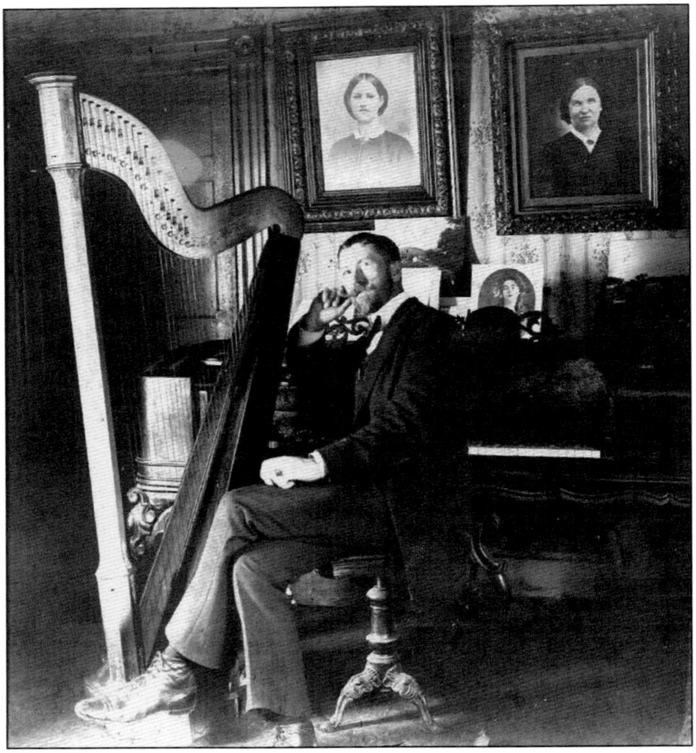

Canonsburg has enjoyed a rich tradition of photographers who have successfully captured the story of the town. Noted photographers over the years have included the likes of Lon Porter, T. W. Cowey, Ern K. Weller, Sue Cowan, Ignatius Nagy, Force C. Dunlevy (seen at left in a self-portrait), Martin Estep, Allen "Ducky" Swan, and Frank Mirisciotti (seen below). These talented professional and amateur photographers, along with many others, are responsible for many of the photographs seen in this collection. (Left, Force C. Dunlevy; below, Frank Mirisciotti.)

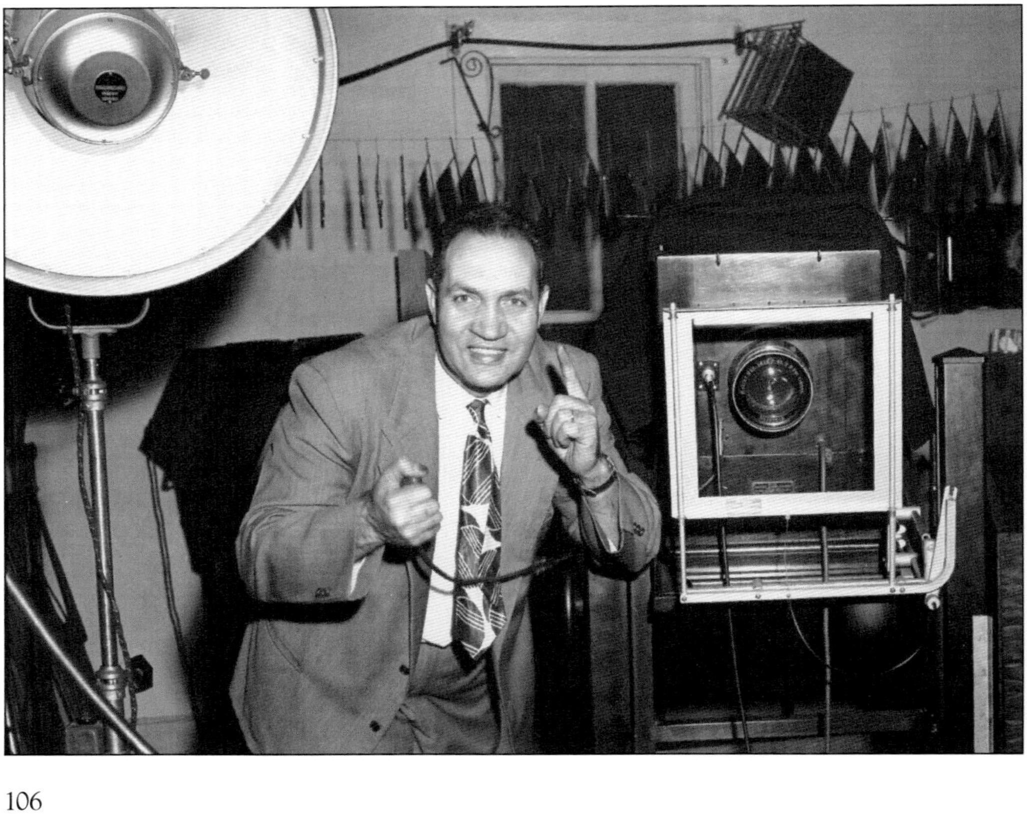

The Vella Dance Studio has been an institution in Canonsburg since the 1930s and continues to the present. Louise Vella, seen here, joined her older sisters Jane and Angela in running the school. At its peak, the family had approximately one dozen dance schools in operation across the region. (The Canon.)

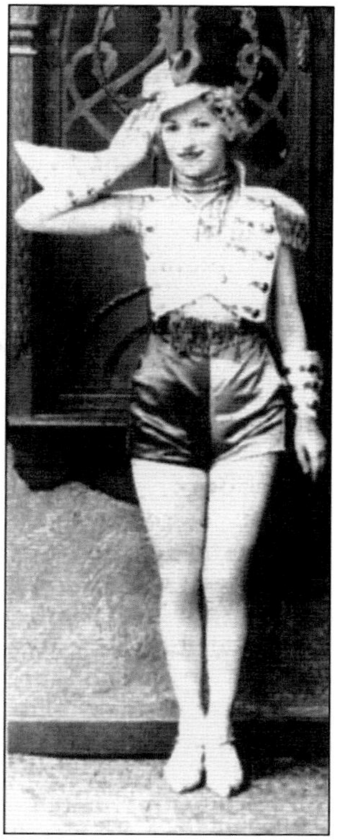

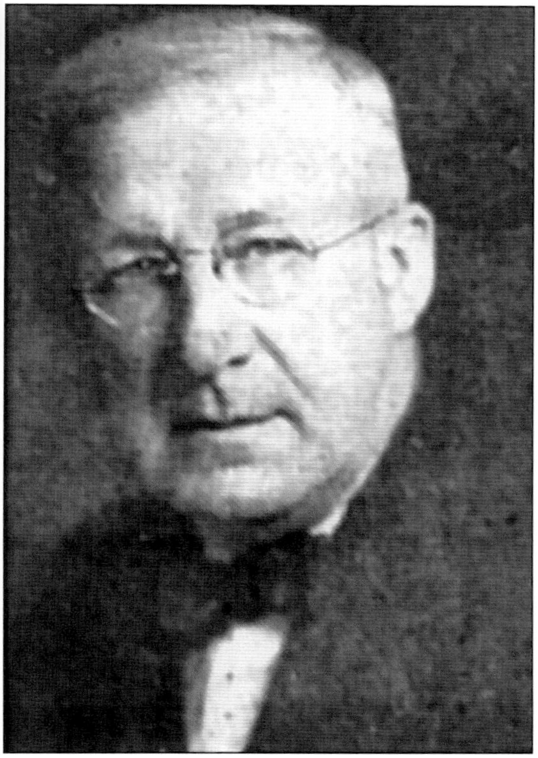

William H. McNary was one of Canonsburg's earliest entrepreneurs, as his holdings took many shapes. McNary started in the furniture and undertaking business, which remained his main focus. He later bought out the Vance Brothers livery stables, before moving on to motorized equipment sales following the arrival of the automobile.

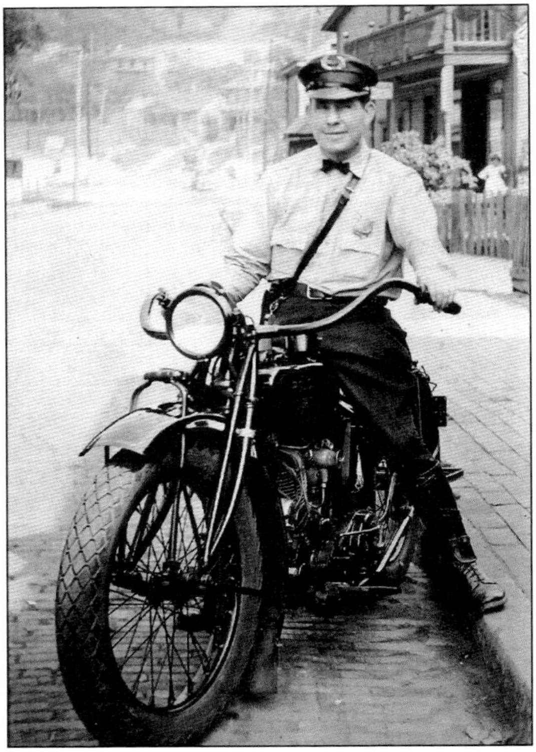

Police chief James T. Haney patrolled the streets of Canonsburg on one of several motorcycles owned by the force in this era and served in the position of chief from 1941 to 1950. (Haney family.)

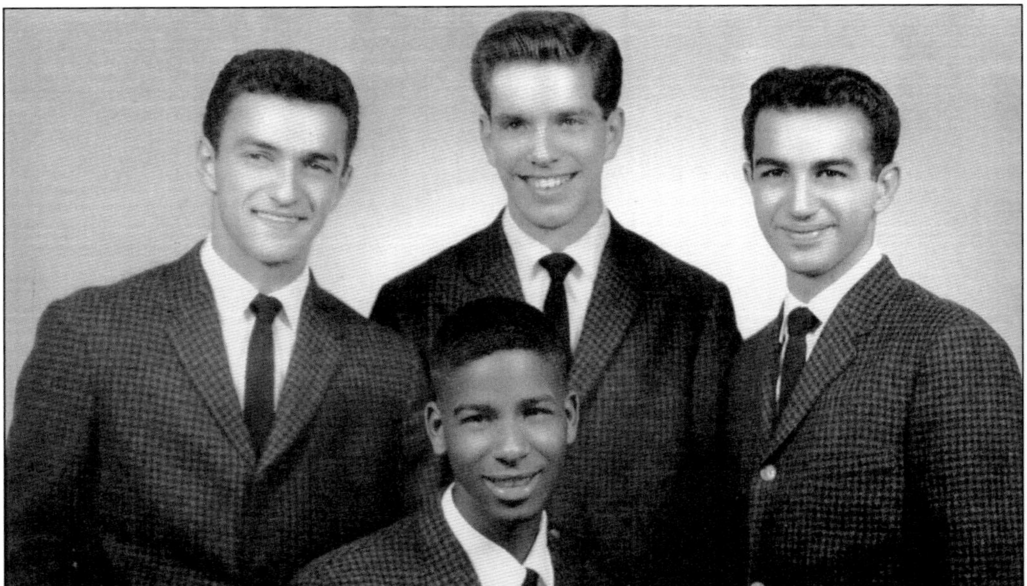

The Donnybrooks was a local quartet of singers that first formed in elementary school under the name the Phaetons. They later went on to local fame after performances on KDKA's *Art Pallan's Talent Search*. They were later awarded a contract with Calico Records under the name the Four Pals. Their recording of "Everytime We Kiss" achieved limited radio success. The band soon disbanded but has reunited for special events. (The Donnybrooks.)

Standing behind Canonsburg in the state government is locally born Timothy J. Solobay, who serves as state representative for Washington County's 48th legislative district. Solobay was elected in 1998, following a 16-year service as state constable in Canonsburg. (Joseph A. Solobay collection.)

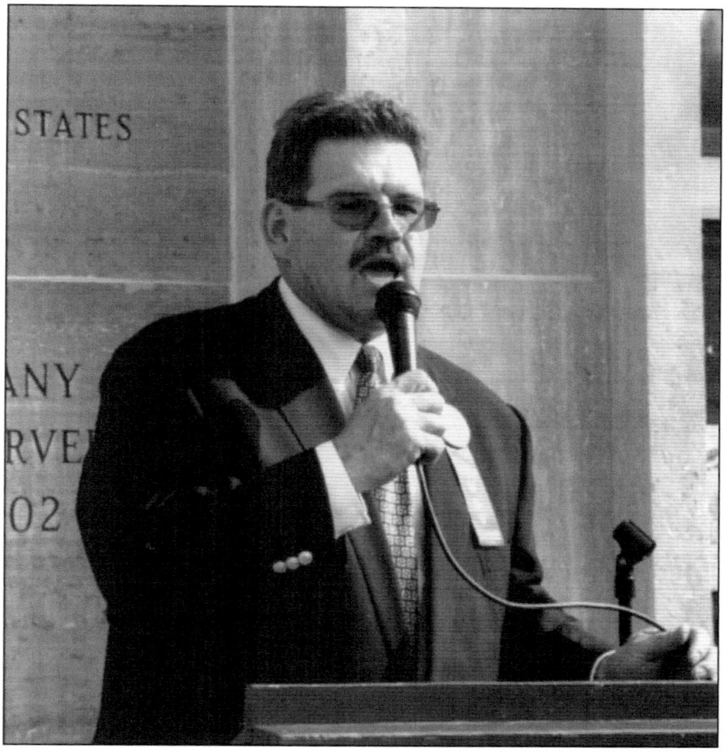

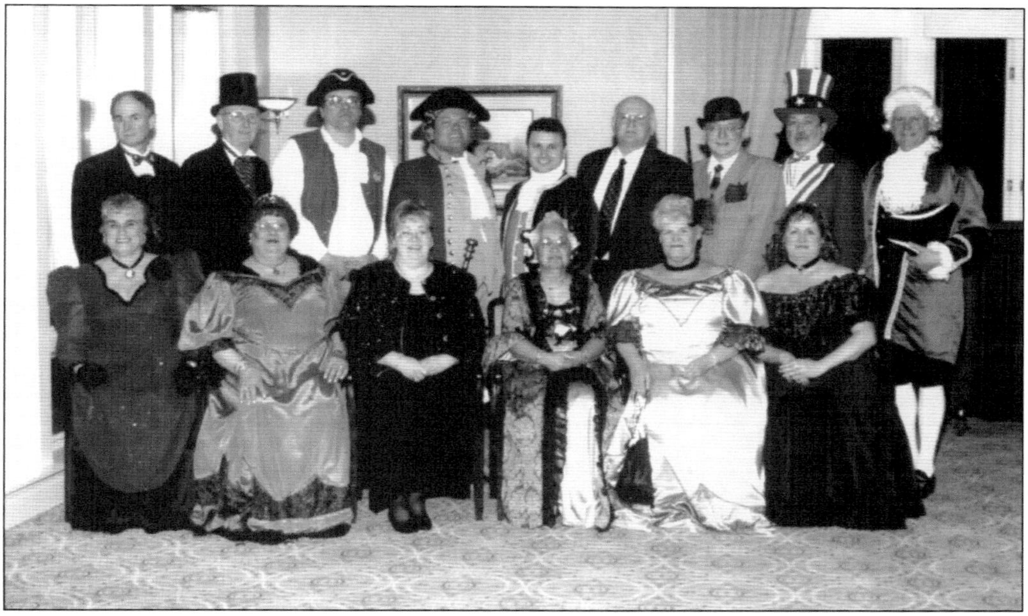

Members of the Canonsburg 2002 Centennial Committee pose in festive garb. From left to right are (first row) Jean Popp, Carmina V. Vitullo, Joanne M. Church, Betty Robinson, Linda L. Kacvinsky, and Sheryl Gadani; (second row) Donald Austin, Joseph F. Gowern, Thomas Shinshasky, Joseph P. Salandra, Robert A. Maceiko, Joseph A. Solobay, James T. Herron, Steve F. Zemencik, and Anthony L. Colaizzo. (Mirisciotti Studio.)

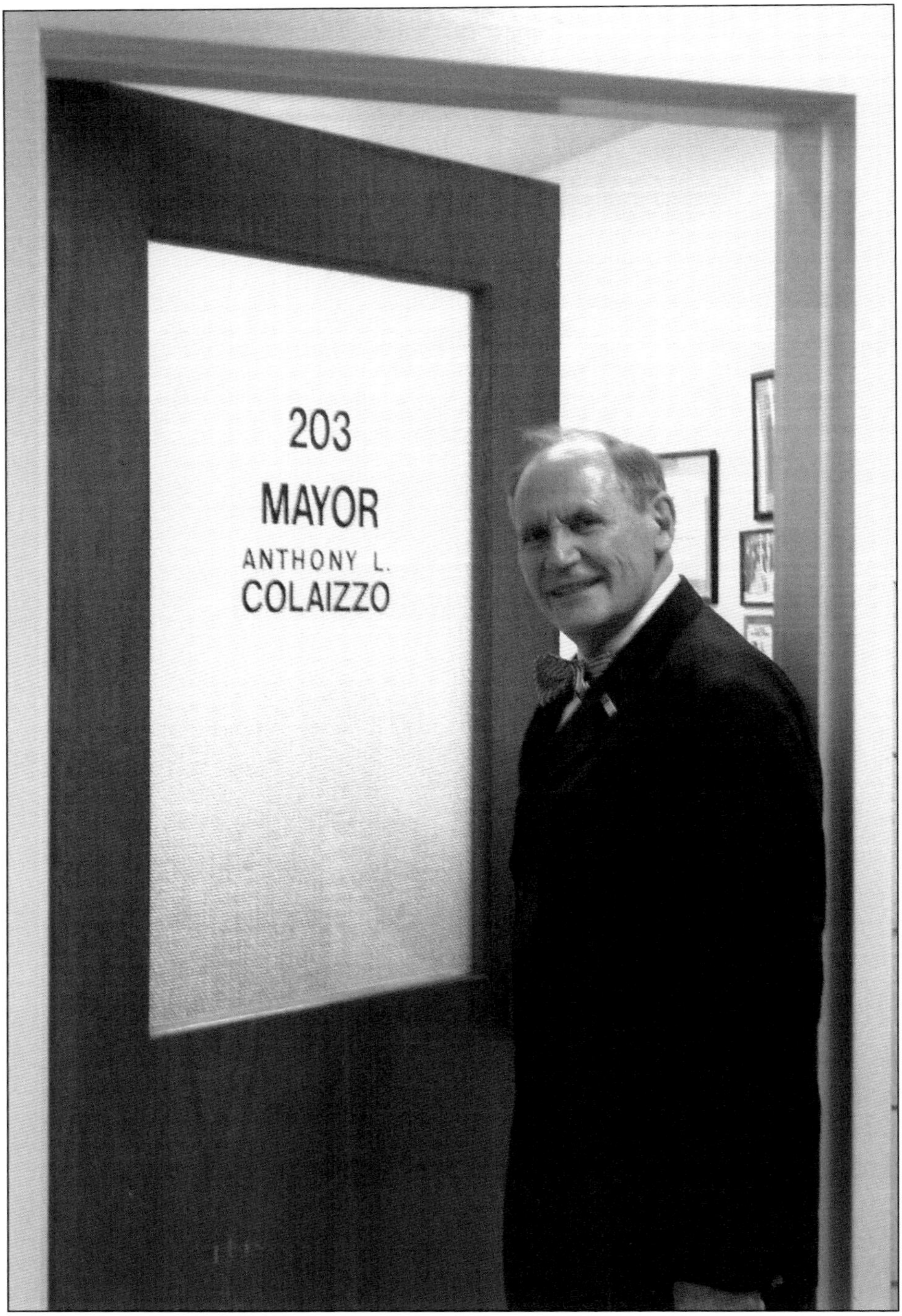

Beginning with the town's incorporation in 1802, Canonsburg has had a rich succession of burgesses and mayors. (The title officially changed in 1961.) Samuel Murdoch served as the first burgess from 1802 until 1816. Harry Cook served the longest stretch in office, running the town from 1929 to 1949. Veteran Anthony J. Colaizzo, with his ever-present bow tie, has held the post of mayor since May 2000. (James T. Herron.)

Eight

Parades and Other Recreations

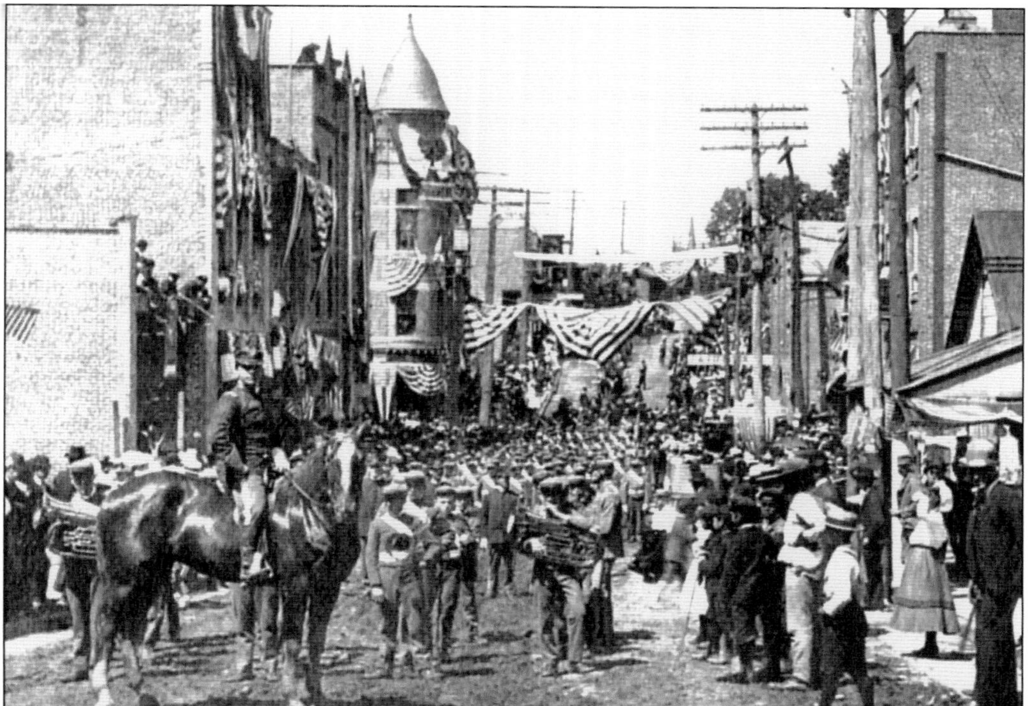

This huge parade down Pike Street was in honor of Canonsburg's centennial celebration in 1902. Professional decorators were hired for the huge banners for the event. Parade attendees had to battle thick mud on the still-unpaved streets, thanks to a heavy rainstorm on the previous evening. (Ern Weller.)

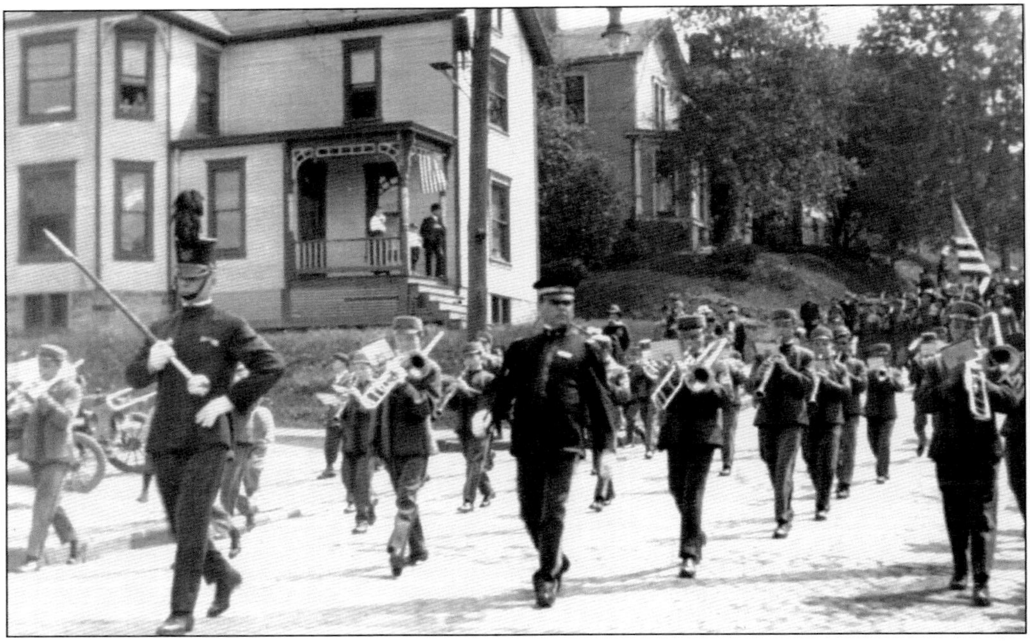

The Morganza Band marches on College Street during a Memorial Day parade in May 1917. The Morganza Band became the featured band following the demise of the Canonsburg Brass Band in the 1880s. (Star Theater.)

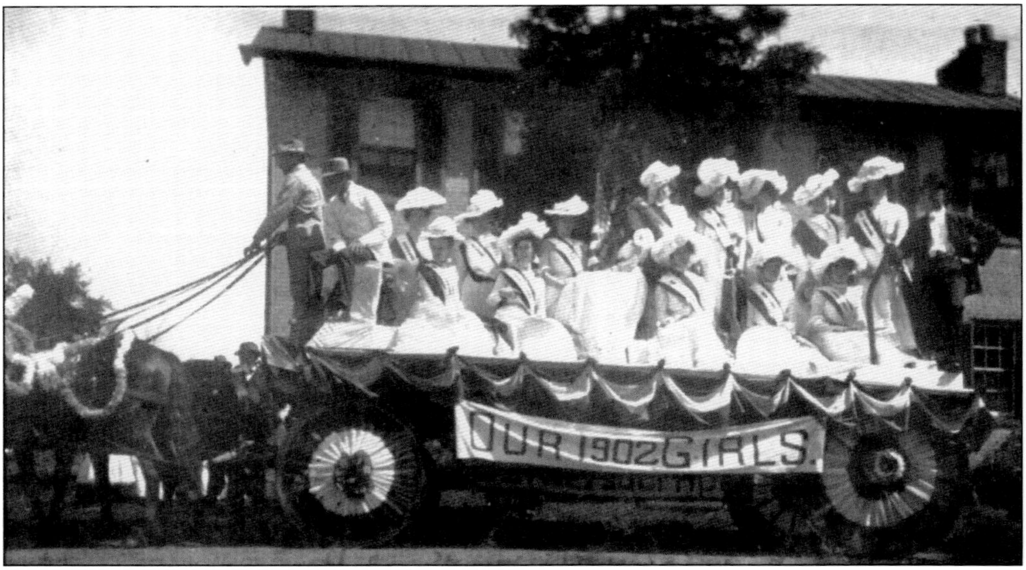

This float of well-dressed Canonsburg women of the day took part in the town's centennial parade in 1902, with each one representing one of the country's original 13 colonies.

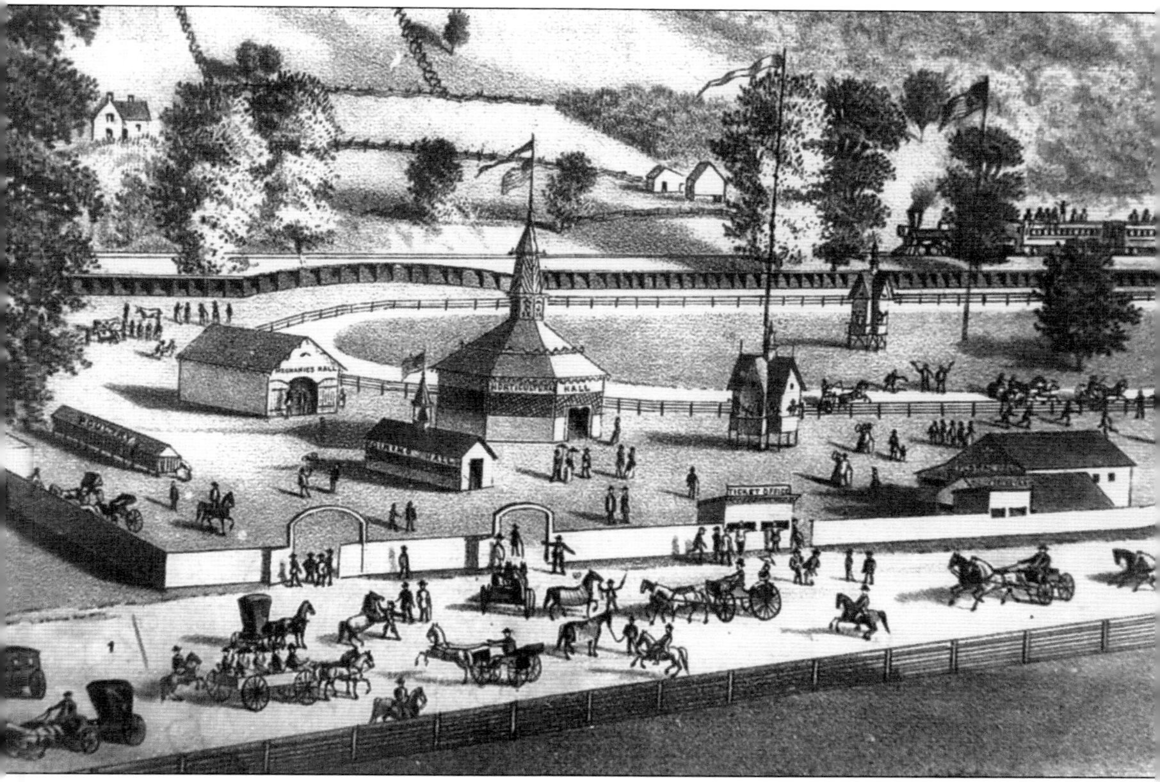

Residents in the 1870s and 1880s may have found a day of entertainment at the Canonsburg Fairgrounds on Cherry Hill Road, where music, contests, and racetrack betting were available to attendees. Most of the fairground buildings were sold off in 1884, although racing remained. Property being offered in the 1884 auction included a domestics hall, a mechanics hall, a floral hall, a poultry hall, two bandstands, and a judges booth. Curry Field later resided on the property. (Washington County atlas 1876.)

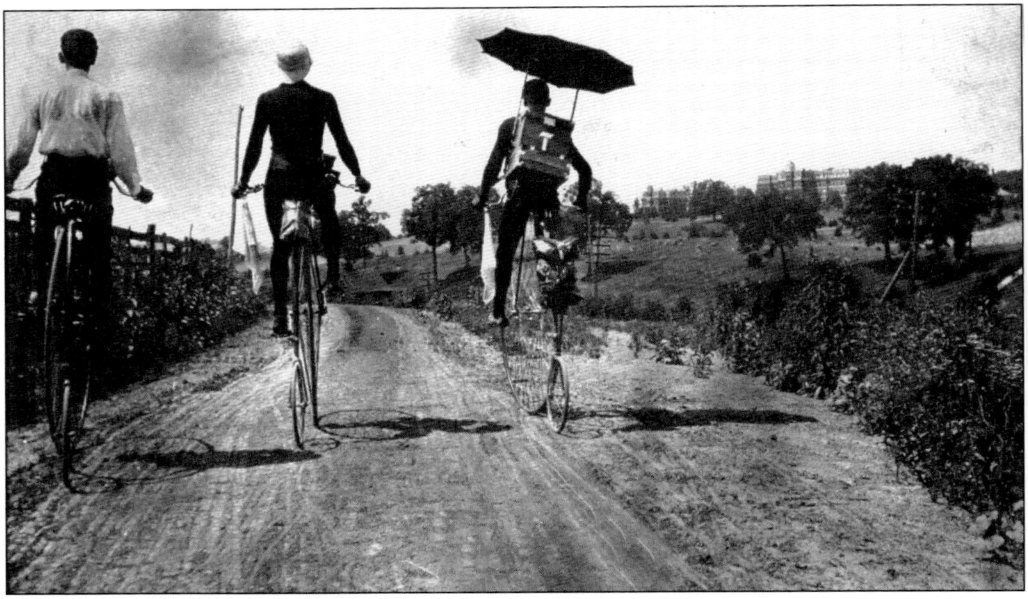

Bicycling was very popular in the 1890s, as noted by one newspaper article citing as many as 60 members in the Canonsburg Cycle Club. Races and prizes would attract riders from all over the country. This photograph shows three likely club members riding into town on penny-farthing bicycles. The rider wearing the umbrella is Frank Lenz, a noted Pittsburgh bicyclist.

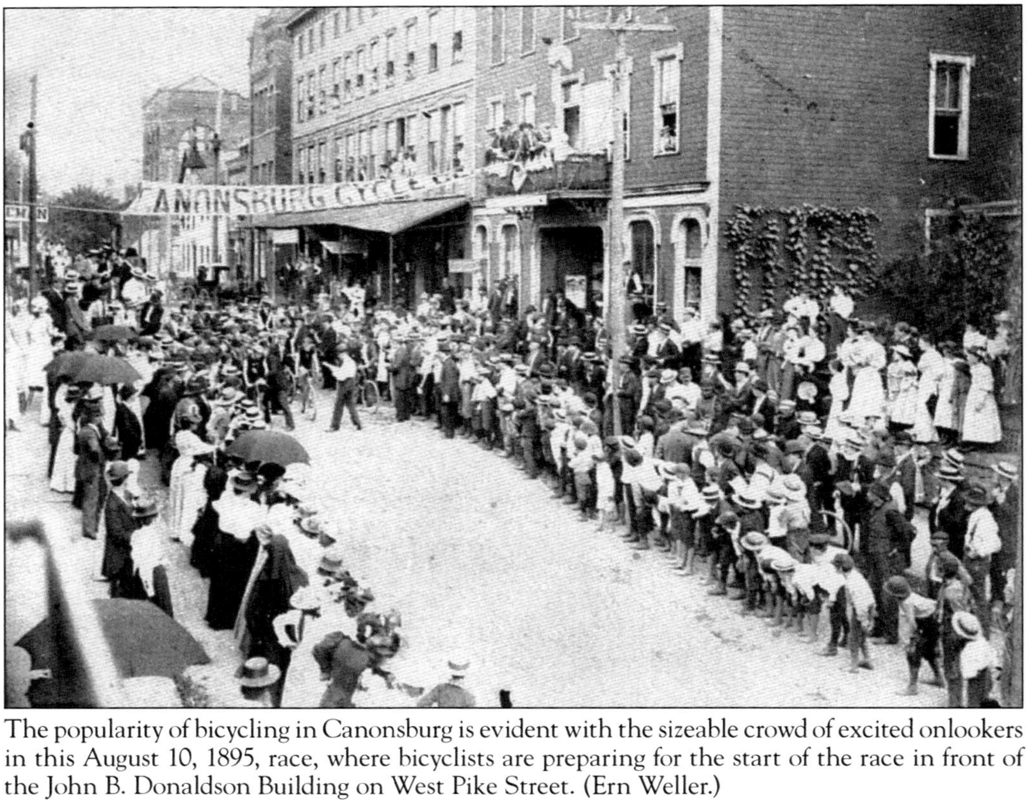

The popularity of bicycling in Canonsburg is evident with the sizeable crowd of excited onlookers in this August 10, 1895, race, where bicyclists are preparing for the start of the race in front of the John B. Donaldson Building on West Pike Street. (Ern Weller.)

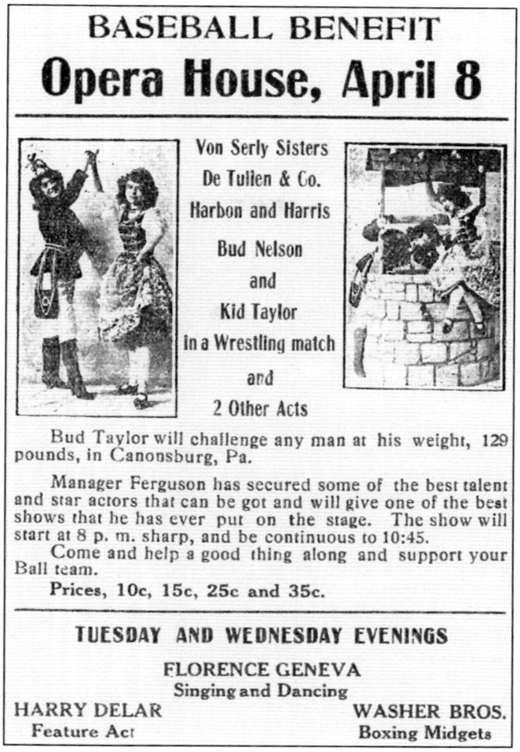

BASEBALL BENEFIT

Opera House, April 8

Von Serly Sisters
De Tulien & Co.
Harbon and Harris
Bud Nelson
and
Kid Taylor
in a Wrestling match
and
2 Other Acts

Bud Taylor will challenge any man at his weight, 129 pounds, in Canonsburg, Pa.

Manager Ferguson has secured some of the best talent and star actors that can be got and will give one of the best shows that he has ever put on the stage. The show will start at 8 p. m. sharp, and be continuous to 10:45.

Come and help a good thing along and support your Ball team.

Prices, 10c, 15c, 25c and 35c.

TUESDAY AND WEDNESDAY EVENINGS

FLORENCE GENEVA
Singing and Dancing

HARRY DELAR — Feature Act

WASHER BROS. — Boxing Midgets

In addition to standard live opera performances, the Morgan Building was also the site for a diverse range of live acts. Two advertisements promoting sports appeared in the *Daily Notes* during April 1909. The first advertised a wrestling match, with both males and female performers, that included audience challenges. A trained horse act appeared live onstage just a few weeks later. (Daily Notes.)

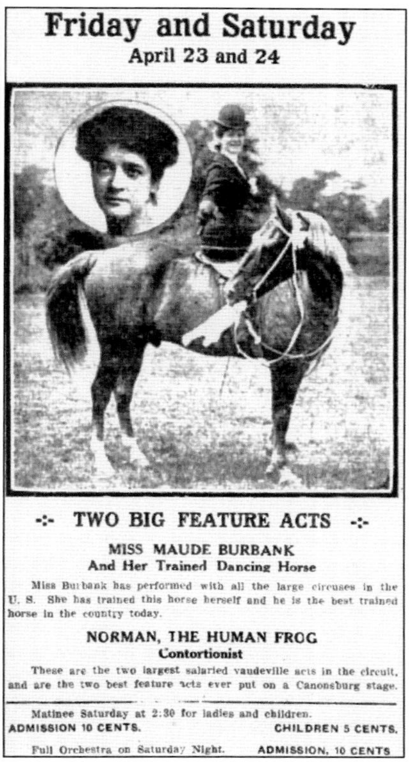

Friday and Saturday
April 23 and 24

TWO BIG FEATURE ACTS

MISS MAUDE BURBANK
And Her Trained Dancing Horse

Miss Burbank has performed with all the large circuses in the U. S. She has trained this horse herself and he is the best trained horse in the country today.

NORMAN, THE HUMAN FROG
Contortionist

These are the two largest salaried vaudeville acts in the circuit, and are the two best feature acts ever put on a Canonsburg stage.

Matinee Saturday at 2:30 for ladies and children.

ADMISSION 10 CENTS. CHILDREN 5 CENTS.

Full Orchestra on Saturday Night. ADMISSION, 10 CENTS

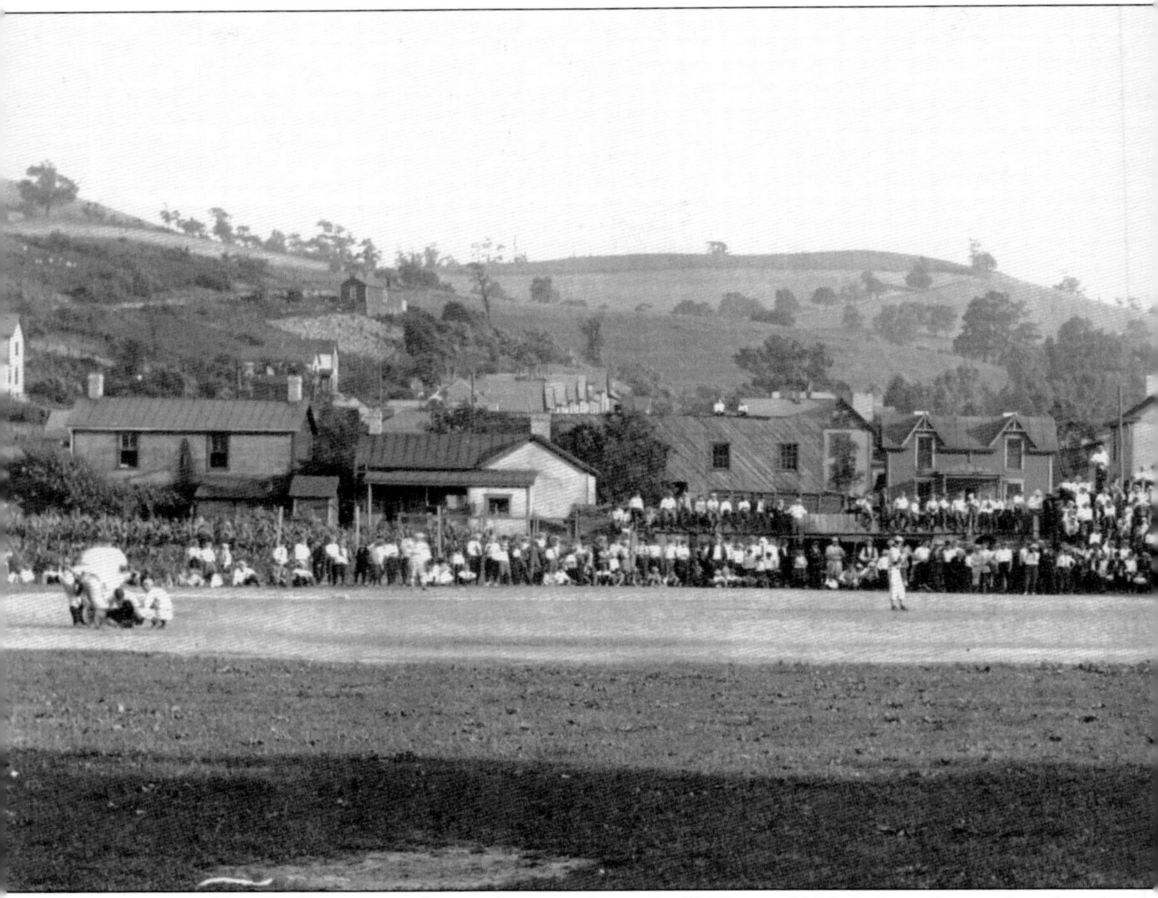

Organized baseball games in Canonsburg in the early 1900s would likely have been played at the South Side Ball Park, replacing the previously popular Smith Park. Teams represented the local schools, as well as the many teams comprised of factory and mill employees. The South Side

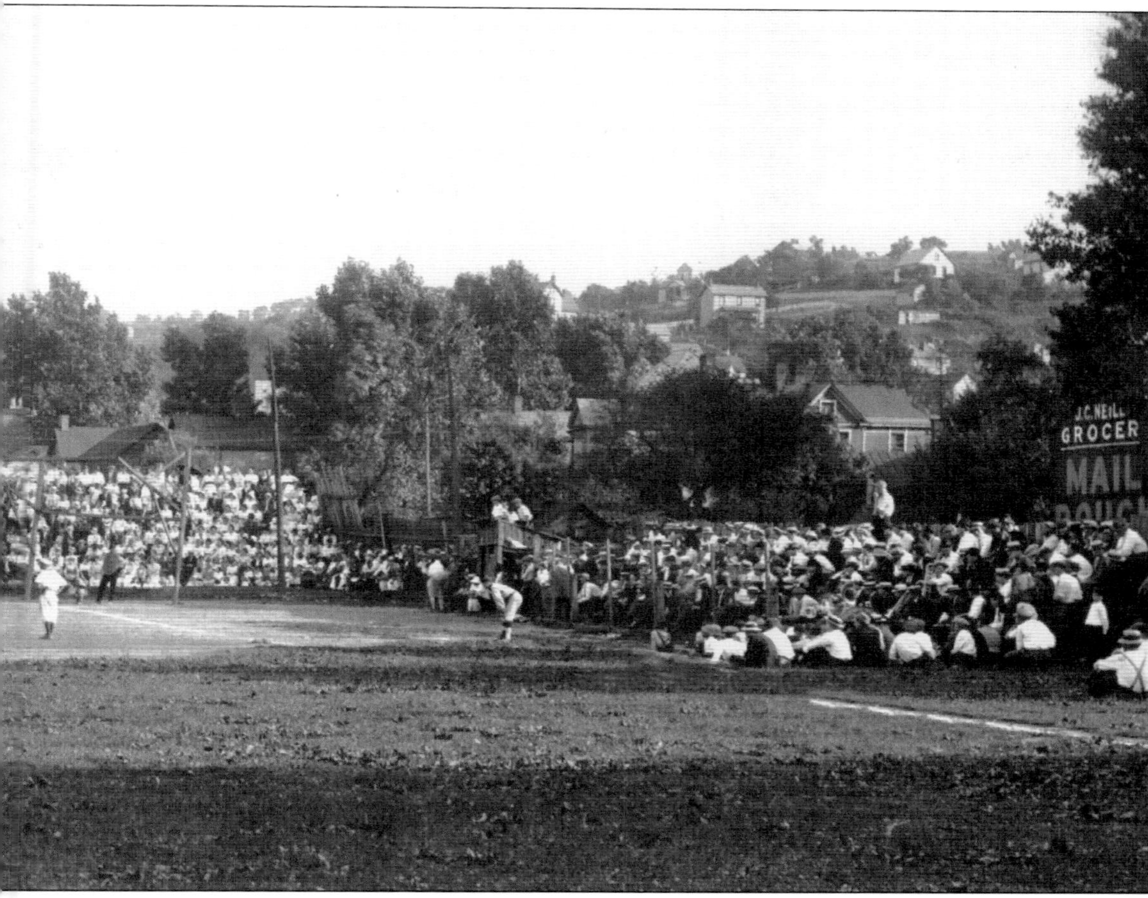

Park would later be replaced by Beck's Field and Curry Field, the site of the 1880s fairgrounds. (Weller Studio.)

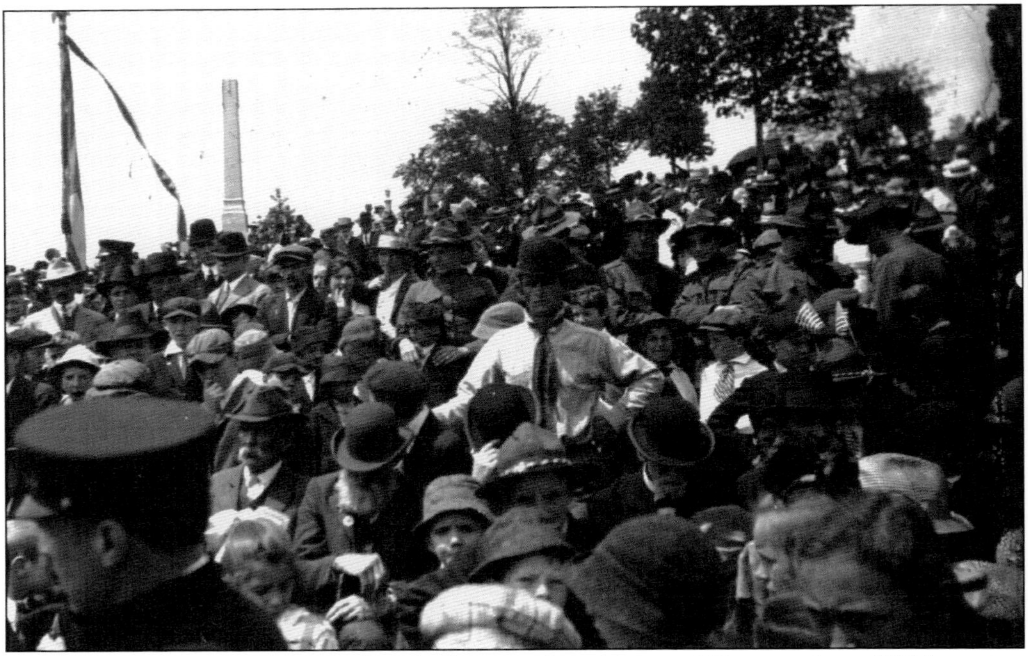

The Oak Spring Cemetery served as the location for a Memorial Day parade in 1917 honoring Civil War veterans. More than three dozen Civil War veterans were still living in the Canonsburg area. (Star Theater.)

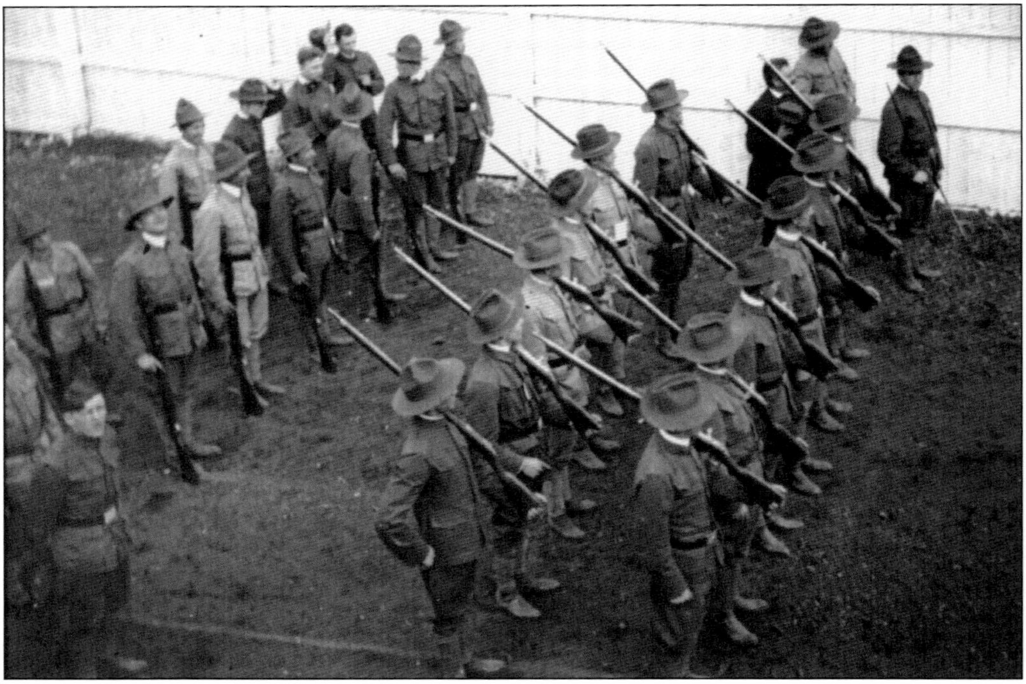

The Memorial Day parade of 1917 also featured a presentation by Company H, 10th Regiment of the Pennsylvania National Guard. The company would eventually be called into battle service in France during World War I. Five soldiers from Canonsburg died in battle. (Star Theater.)

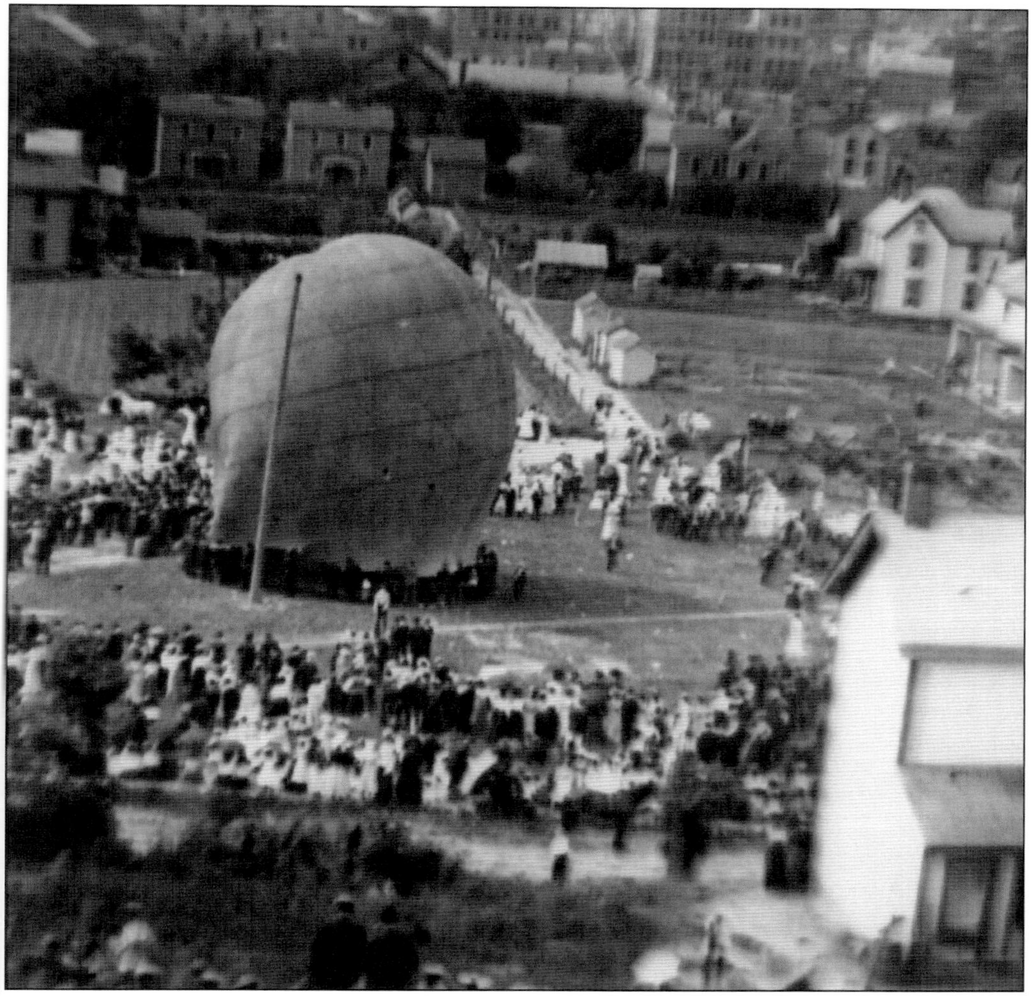

A special air show was planned for the centennial celebrations in June 1902. Aeronaut Alice Zeno, who shocked the crowd by performing in tights, was scheduled to make two ascensions across the town in a huge hot-air balloon. The first afternoon attempt failed, but a second nighttime flight was successful, although only for a short distance. Zeno safely jumped from the balloon via parachute.

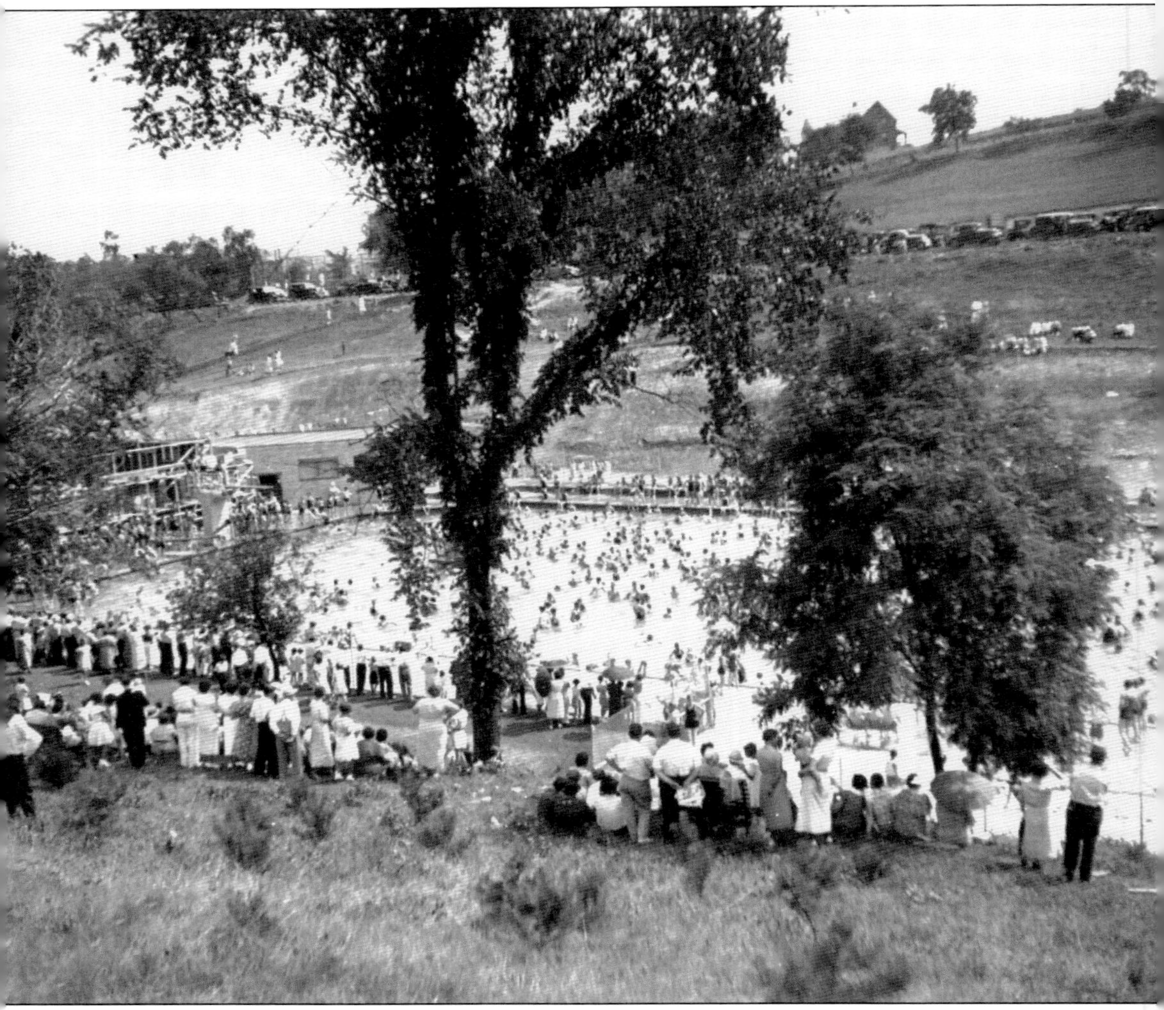

In the second decade of the 20th century, a citizens' group began a movement for creating an official town park. Even though the town council conceded and purchased land from the group in 1919, the land went unused for years. Construction on the property did not begin until 1923, and it was not until 1931 that the park's limited facilities finally opened for use. By the time the swimming pool officially opened on July 4, 1935, residents could entertainment themselves with park swings, seesaws, slides, tennis courts, and wading pools. (Sue Cowan.)

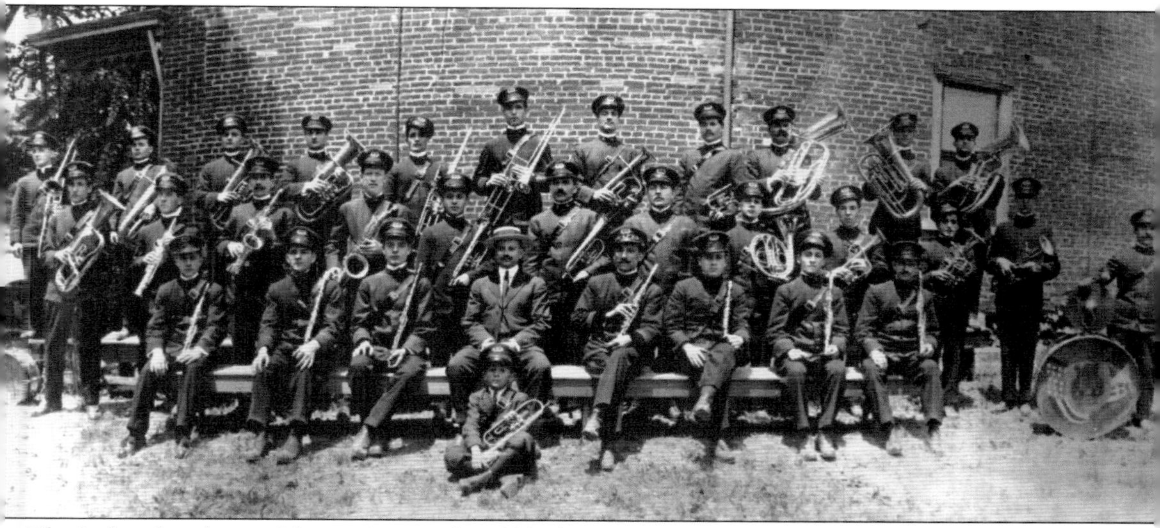

The Italian band, noted for its sharp red and black-trimmed uniforms, entertained at numerous parades and events from 1912 to 1929. The band was organized by Dionino Chiaverini, who is seen in this photograph seated in the center of the front bleacher. In 1936, Chiaverini reformed the band, which performed at the town's new pool in 1937. A name change to the International Italian Musical Association came in 1938, but the band apparently ceased performances a few years later.

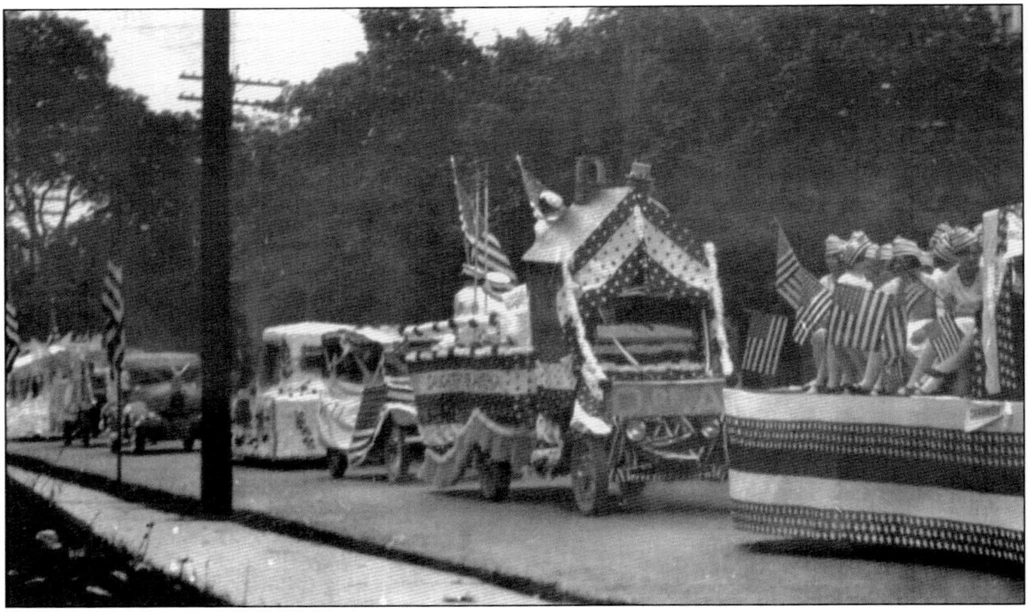

This parade shot captures the action of two days of festivities celebrating the town's 125th anniversary on June 23–24, 1927. The "Spirit of the Wilderness" was the theme of the celebrations. (Nancy Lanzy.)

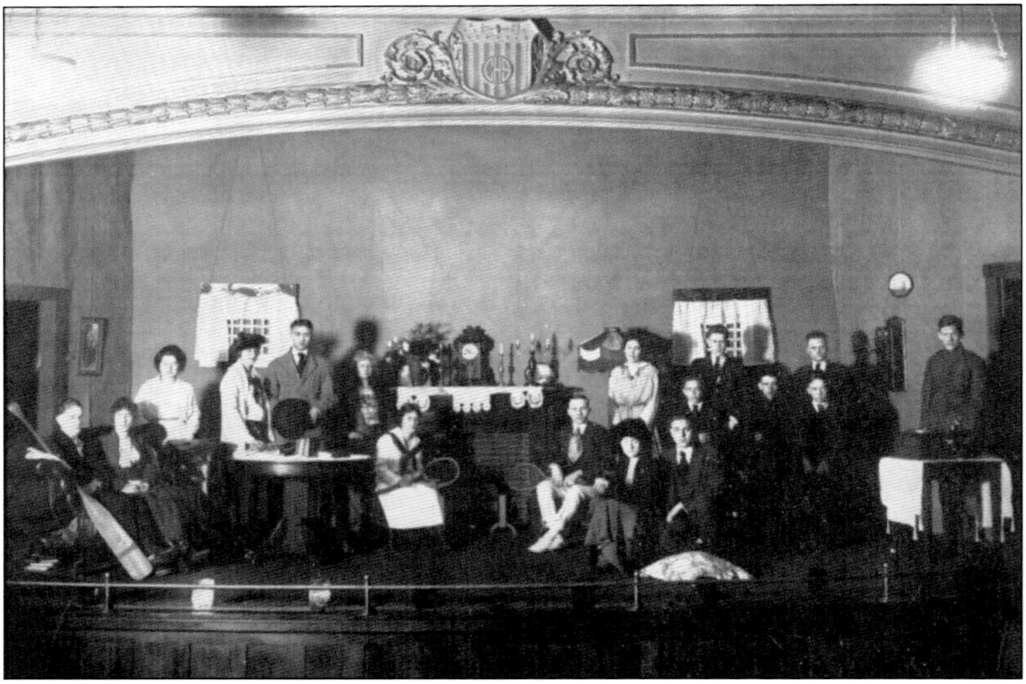

Amateur dramatics have long been a staple of high schools and dramatic groups. This photograph from 1920 shows members of the Canonsburg High School senior class performing the play *Teamwork*, presented on the stage of the Canonsburg High School building. The largest theater in Canonsburg was the Alhambra, owned by Fred and E. T. Beedle. (Pleiad.)

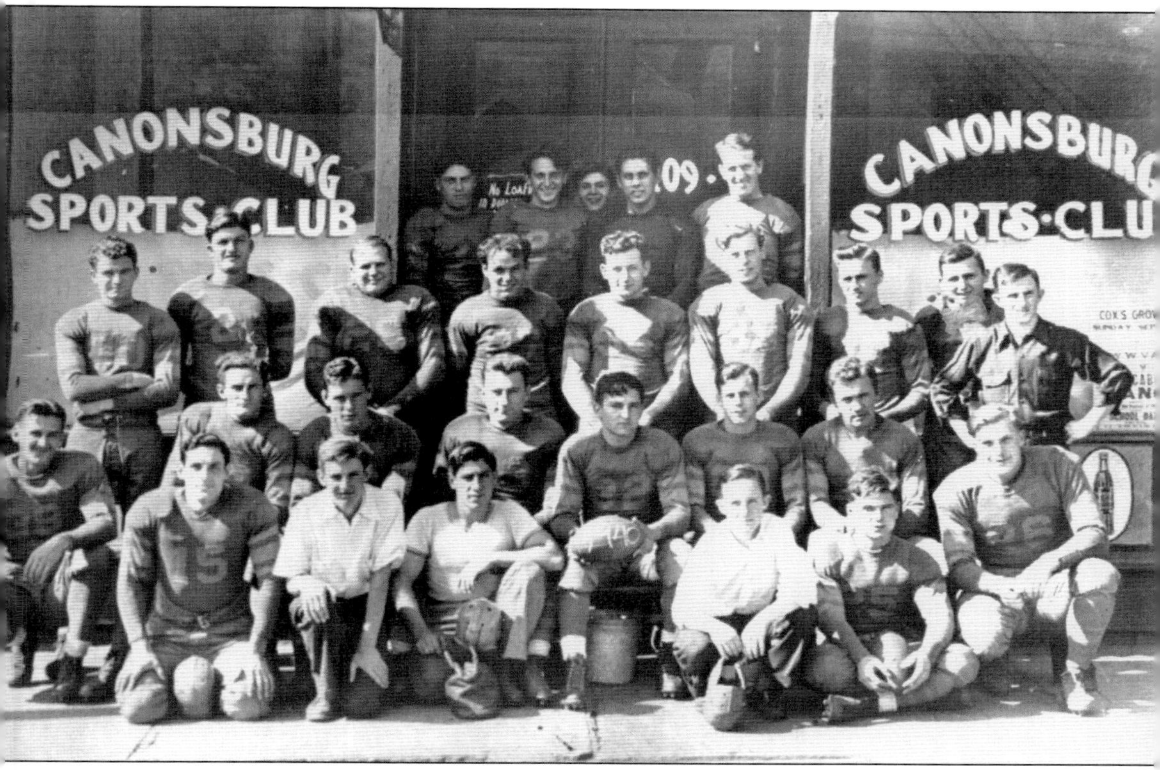

This 1940 Canonsburg Sports Club football team competed on a semiprofessional basis against other regional teams. With the United States' entry in World War II just around the corner, many such extracurricular activities disappeared within a few years. Players on this squad are, from left to right, (first row) L. Ciehanoski, J. Damico, J. Wincek, M. Damico, J. Foley, P. Ambrose, and W. Rybacki; (second row), B. Smith, F. Ambrose, K. Stypert, J. Imperatore, T. Totterdale, and J. Ridosh; (third row) O. Guadagni, F. Grohal, L. Sollon, J. Maggi, T. Snovak, T. DeLucia, B. Fecyhe, B. Fritz, and S. Foley; (fourth row) F. Ptak, B. Sollon, D. Golik, D. Abraham, and F. Scott. Their sports club was likely located at 207–209 Adams Avenue. (Joseph A. Solobay collection.)

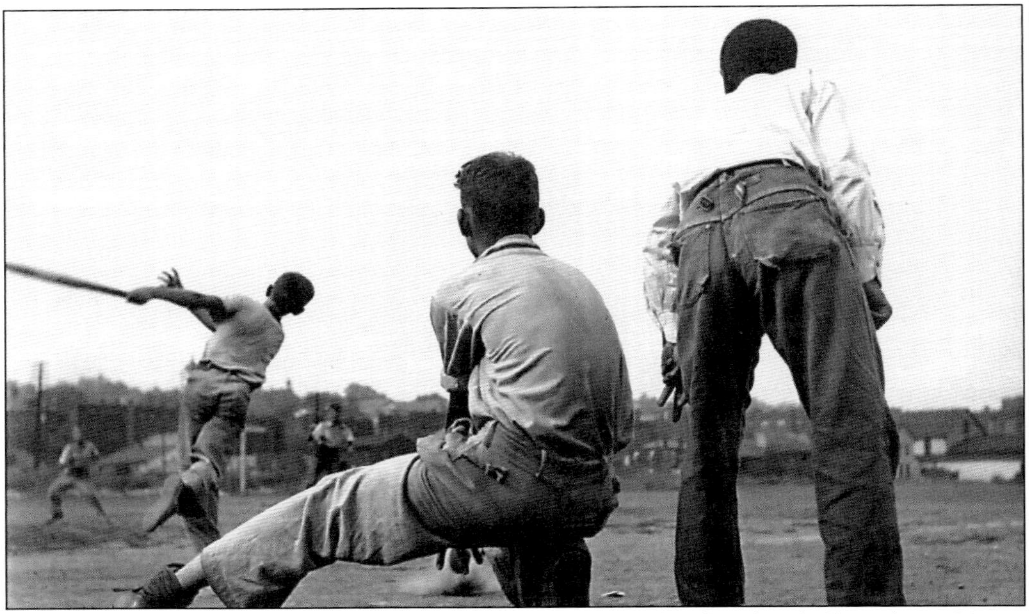

A group of young boys participates in an informal game of pickup baseball in the 1930s on Beck's Field. Many of the local teams used this baseball field. Famous players to play on the field included Pittsburgh Pirate and Carnegie native Honus Wagner, as well as the Homestead Grays. The field was purchased by Canonsburg High School as a site for new athletic facilities in 1941, although World War II delayed its completion until 1947. (Joseph A. Solobay collection.)

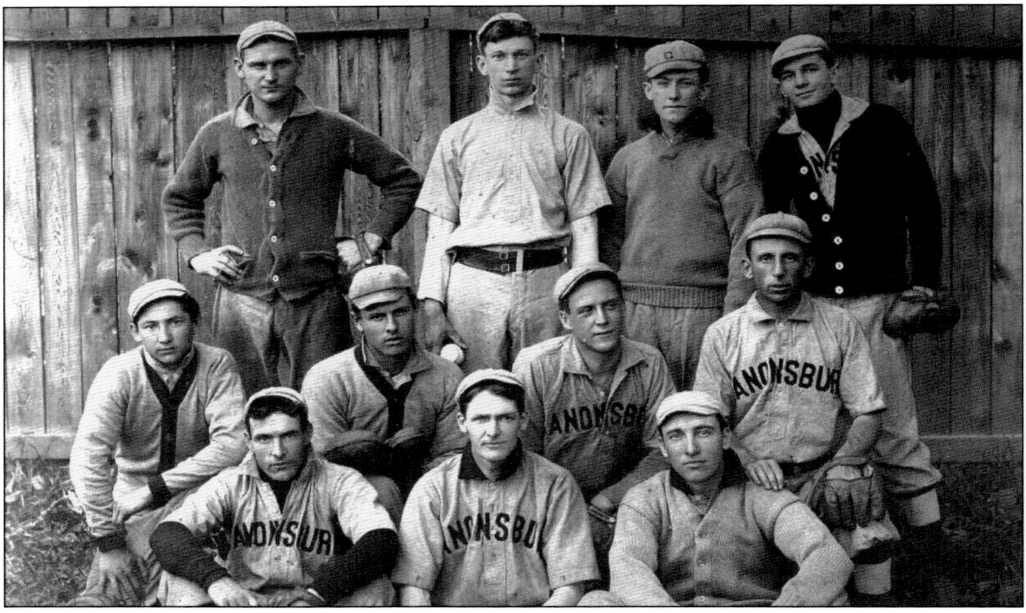

Semiprofessional baseball leagues were very popular in the early 20th century. Players would even be recruited from other cities and offered jobs as part of their compensation. This c. 1910 team features, from left to right, (first row) Benny Welch, Clark Sutherin, and Penrose Hall; (second row) Henry Schussler, William Byland, Thomas Sprowls, and John Speer; (third row) Barney Fritz, John Ewing, Walter McPeake, and Howard Hanson. (Force C. Dunlevy.)

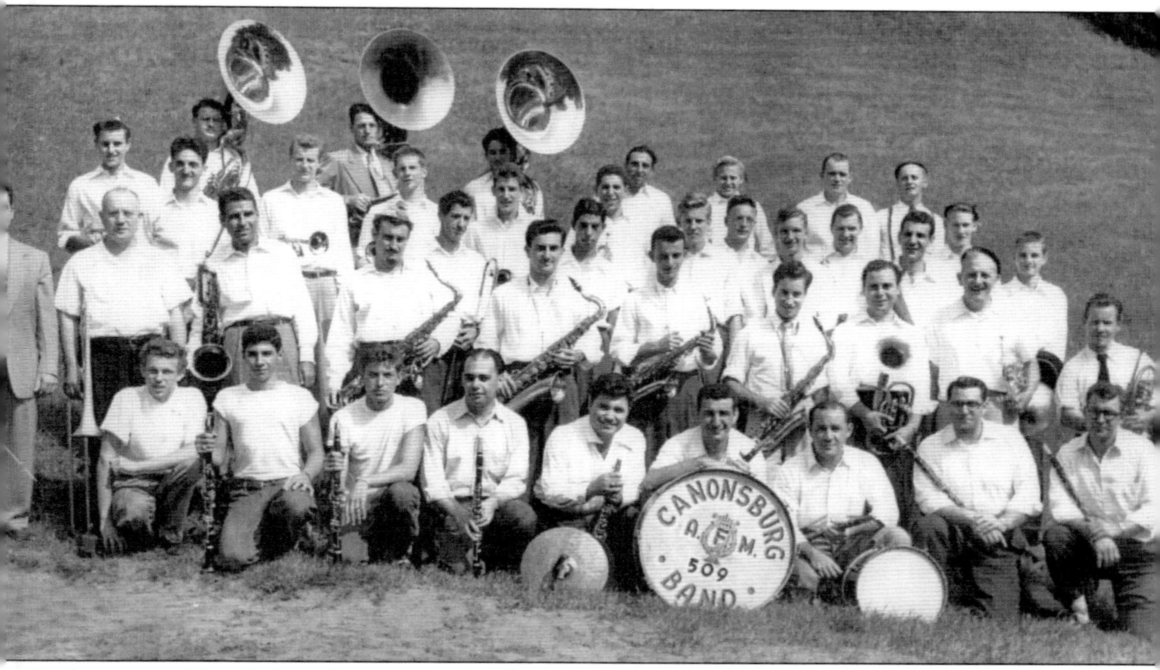

Orchestras and bands have been a popular fixture at events in the Canonsburg area for more than a century. This photograph captures the Musicians' Union Band of 1952, led by director Phil Arnone. In addition to future polka star Bobby Vinton, the band also featured players who would find success with the Four Coins and the Lee Barrett Orchestra. The band members are, from left to right, (first row) Bob Vinton, James Gregorakis, George Mantalis, Sam Campagna, Jim Colaizzo, Perry Vincent, John Jacoby, Paul DiSalle, and Joe Galanda; (second row) Phil Arnone (director), Art Daley, Pete Petros, Frank Spina, Ed Pounds, Bill Gall, unidentified, Tony Lucchetti, Idol Jordan, Santo Chimento, Dave Campbell, and Art McCormick; (third row) unidentified, Jim Bell, George Modrak, Bob Campbell, George Mahramus, Phil Tardio, Joe Dybell, Vince Sapporito, unidentified, Louis Chappo, John Vincent, Don Hutchinson, and Richard Kloska; (fourth row) Dave Adamson, Ray Battaglini, Frank Matz, Sam Lucciola, Paul Moscovic, Dave Bert, and John Mamrack. (John Mamrack.)

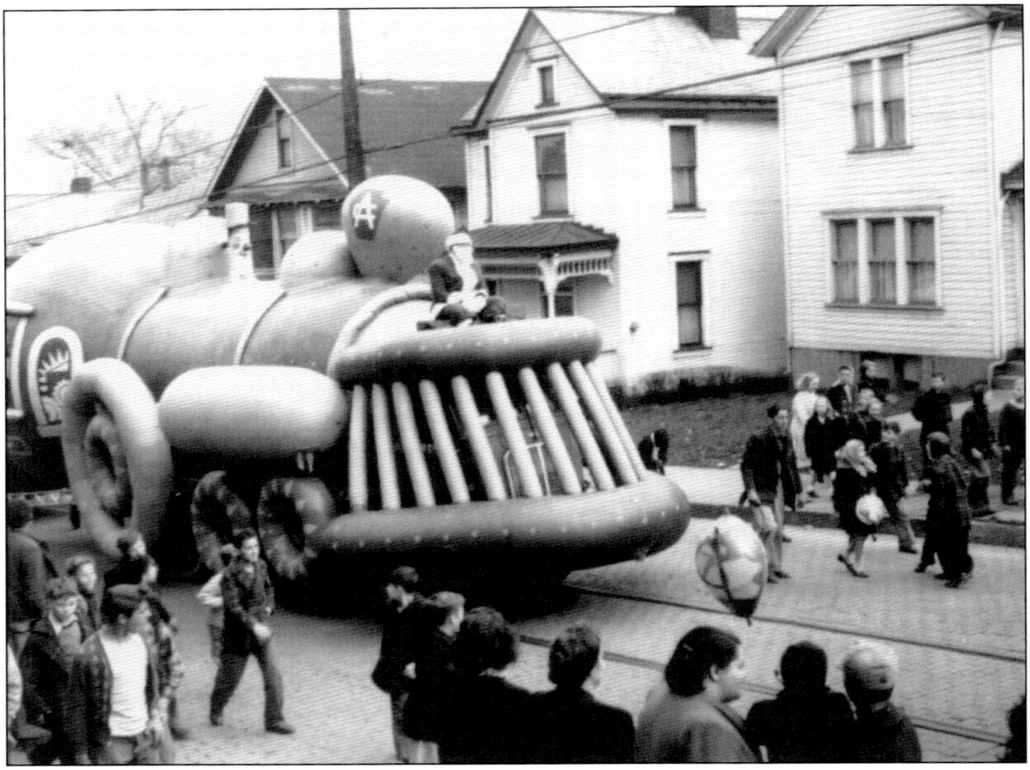

Balloons were a big part of the Christmas parade of 1948, which featured the much-anticipated annual arrival of Santa Claus, this time riding atop a locomotive train engine.

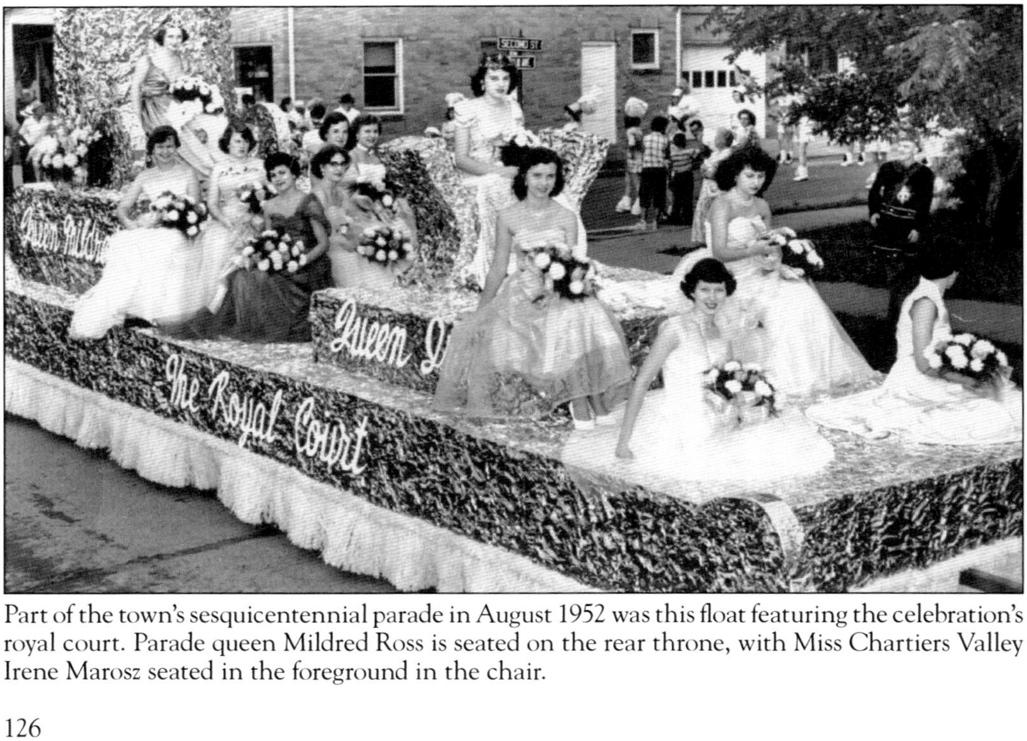

Part of the town's sesquicentennial parade in August 1952 was this float featuring the celebration's royal court. Parade queen Mildred Ross is seated on the rear throne, with Miss Chartiers Valley Irene Marosz seated in the foreground in the chair.

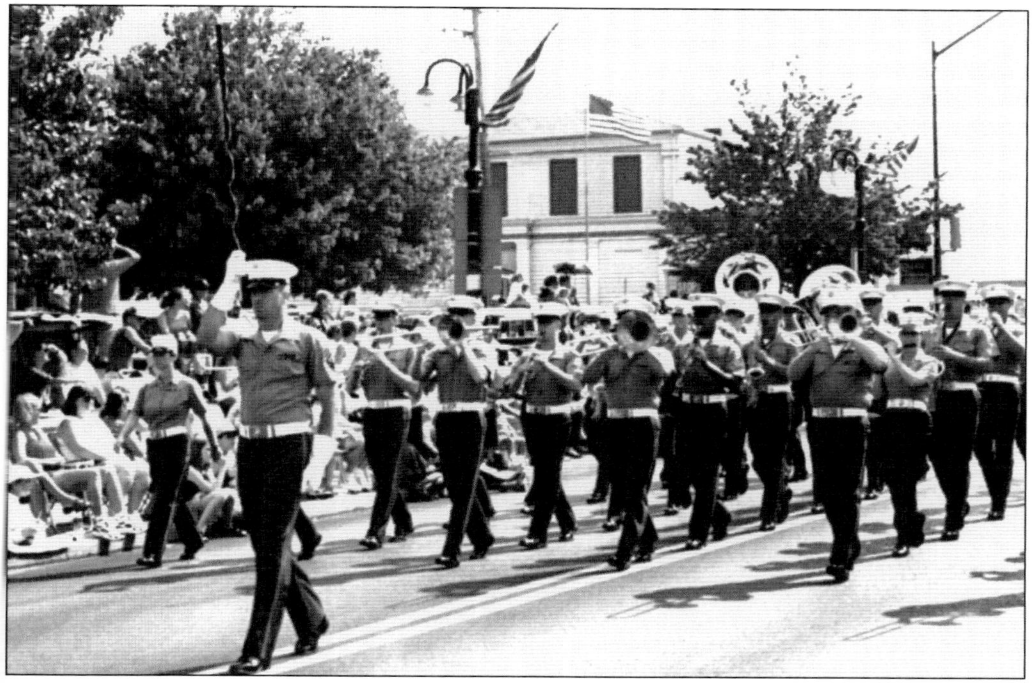

The Fourth of July parade in 1999 featured a special appearance by the marine band from Quantico, Virginia. It performed during the daytime parade and returned for a nighttime performance at the stadium. (James T. Herron.)

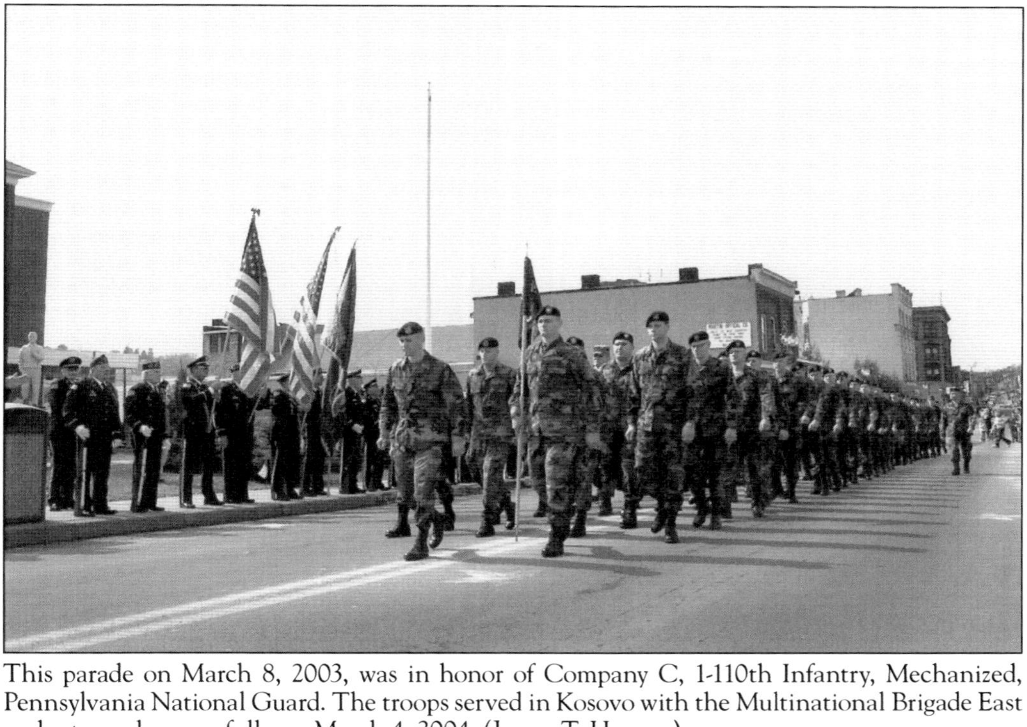

This parade on March 8, 2003, was in honor of Company C, 1-110th Infantry, Mechanized, Pennsylvania National Guard. The troops served in Kosovo with the Multinational Brigade East and returned successfully on March 4, 2004. (James T. Herron.)